Fascist Voices

Essays From The 'Fascist Quarterly' 1936-1940

Volume One

Fascist Voices
Essays From The 'Fascist Quarterly' 1936-1940
Volume One

Copyright © 2019 Sanctuary Press Ltd

All rights reserved. No part of this book may be reproduced in any form by any electronic or mechanical means including photocopying, recording, or information storage and retrieval without permission in writing from the publisher.

ISBN-13: 978-1-913176-07-5

Sanctuary Press Ltd
71-75 Shelton Street
Covent Garden
London
WC2H 9JQ

www.sanctuarypress.com
Email: info@sanctuarypress.com

Fascist Voices - Volume One

This edition contains essays by:

- John Beckett
- James Drennan
- Norah Elam
- General Franco
- Major-General J. F: C. Fuller
- Joseph Goebbels
- J. K. Heydon
- Max Hunger
- Jorian Jenks
- William Joyce
- Dr. Robert Ley
- Francis Mcevoy
- Sir Oswald Mosley
- Ezra Pound
- Vidkun Quisling
- Alfred Rosenberg
- Arthur Reade
- Anne Seelig-Thomann
- Claud Sutton
- Alexander Raven Thomson
- A. Yusuf Ali

Contents

The Philosophy of Fascism by Sir Oswald Mosley

Being a lecture delivered by Sir Oswald Mosley at the English Speaking Union on Wednesday, 22nd March 1933.

Our opponents allege that Fascism has no historic background or philosophy, and it is my task this afternoon to suggest that Fascism has roots deep in history and has been sustained by some of the finest flights of the speculative mind. I am, of course, aware that not much philosophy attaches to our activities in the columns of the daily press, and when you read that I was to lecture on "The Philosophy of Fascism," probably many of you said: " What has this gangster to do with philosophy?" However, I trust you will believe that those great mirrors of the public mind do not always give a very accurate reflection, and while you only read of the more stirring moments of our progress, yet there are other moments, which have some depth in thought and constructive conception. So far it is to some extent true that the Fascist philosophy has not assumed a very concrete and definite form, but you must remember that the Fascist faith has only been in existence little more than ten years: it is a growth of the last decade. Already, however, its philosophic background is capable of some formulation, and that has happened in a far shorter space of time than a corresponding development in any other great political faith of history. Just as the Fascist movement itself, in several great countries, has advanced towards power at a phenomenal speed, so the Fascist faith and philosophy as a permanent conception, an attitude to life, has advanced far more quickly than did the philosophies of the older faiths. Take Liberalism: A very long interval elapsed between the writings of such men as Voltaire and Rousseau, and the final formation of the Liberal creed in the hands of English statesmen at the end of the eighteenth and the beginning of the nineteenth century.

In fact these great political movements and psychological upheavals only very slowly crystallised into a definite system of thought, as well as a system of action; and in the Fascist case it is probably rather soon to expect at the end of ten years, that it should have assumed a concrete crystallised form. Nevertheless I believe that Fascist philosophy can be expressed in intelligible terms, and while it makes an entirely novel contribution to the thought of this age, it can yet be shown to derive both its origin and its historic support from the established thought of the past.

In the first instance, I suggest that most philosophies of action are derived from a synthesis of cultural conflicts in a previous period. Where, in an age of culture, of thought, of abstract speculation, you find two great cultures in sharp antithesis, you usually find, in the following age of action, some synthesis in practice between those two sharp antitheses which leads to a practical creed of action. This conception may seem to you to suggest, to some extent, a Spenglerian approach; and it is quite true that the great German philosopher has probably done more than any other to paint in the broad background of Fascist thought. But it is a very broad background. It is a great background of world history from which a Fascist suggestion emerges. Not very much more than that. And possibly he is inhibited from coming nearer to the subject by his innate pessimism, which, in its turn, I would humbly suggest to you arises from his entire ignorance of modern science and mechanical development.

If you look through the Spenglerian spectacles, you are bound to come to a conclusion of extreme pessimism because they obscure the factor which for the first time places in the hands of man the ability entirely to eliminate the poverty problem. And I believe it is our German philosopher's misunderstanding of this immense new factor which leads him to his pessimistic conclusion. Nevertheless, that in no way invalidates his tremendous contribution to world thought.

You will rightly deduce that my suggestion of the marriage of seemingly antithetical cultures leading in the following age of action to the production of a philosophic child of the period, which is expressed in action, has some derivation from Spenglerian thought. But I think I can show you how in actual practice that thesis works out in the Fascist case. I would suggest to you that in the last century, the major intellectual struggle arose from the tremendous impact of Nietzschean thought on the Christian civilisation of two thousand years. That impact was only very slowly realised. Its full implications are only today working themselves out. But turn where you will in modern thought, you find the results of that colossal struggle for mastery of the mind and of the spirit of man. There was a religion which, so far as the West was concerned, had broadly dominated human thought for many centuries. And suddenly, for the first time, that religion and that thought was effectively challenged, and its foundations for the moment at any rate, were shaken. It was denounced with furious energy and with extraordinary genius—fundamentally denounced.

I am not—as you will see later—myself stating the case against Christianity, because I am going to show you how I believe the Nietzschean and the Christian doctrines are capable of synthesis. But at this point it is necessary for me to examine the essential differences in these two creeds, and to see where the differences have accumulated and where the resemblances emerge. Nietzsche challenged, as you are aware, the whole foundations of Christian thought. He said, in effect: 'This is the religion of the slave and of the weakling. This is the faith of the people who are in flight from life, who will not face reality, who look for salvation in some dreamy hereafter—the salvation which they have not the vitality nor the manhood to seize for themselves here on earth. It is derived from a spirit of weakness and of surrender.' He denounced it in a great phrase, if I remember rightly, as 'the religion which had enchained and enfeebled mankind.'

And in place of this faith he created the conception of the superman, the man who faces difficulty, danger, goes forward through material things and through the difficulties of environment, to achieve, to win and to create, here on earth, a world of his own. It was a challenge to the whole basis, not only of thought but of life. And it rocked to its foundations the thought of the world. It must have appeared, to those who were seriously concerned with that controversy at the time, that one or other of those creeds must emerge victorious, and one or other must die; that any combination, any synthesis of those conflicting doctrines was entirely out of the question.

Now I believe, as it so often happens in daily life, that creeds which appear to be so dissimilar are in fact susceptible of some reconciliation when examined more closely, and indeed of a certain synthesis; and I think I can show you that actually, in the Fascist doctrine today, you find a complete wedding of the great characteristics of both creeds. On the one hand you find in Fascism, taken from Christianity, taken directly from the Christian conception, the immense vision of service, of self-abnegation, of self-sacrifice in the cause of others, in the cause of the world, in the cause of your country; not the elimination of the individual, so much as the fusion of the individual in something far greater than himself; and you have that basic doctrine of Fascism—service, self-surrender—to what the Fascist must conceive to be the greatest cause and the greatest impulse in the world. On the other hand you find taken from Nietzschean thought the virility, the challenge to all existing things which impede the march of mankind, the absolute abnegation of the doctrine of surrender; the firm ability to grapple with and to overcome all obstructions. You have, in fact, the creation of a doctrine of men of vigour and of self-help which is the other outstanding characteristic of Fascism.

Therefore we find—I think I can claim—some wedding of those two great doctrines expressing itself in the practical creed of Fascism today. And that, in fact, works itself out in our whole attitude to life. We can bring it down to the smallest details of general existence. From the widest and most abstract conception we can come down to the most detailed things of daily life. We demand from all our people an overriding conception of public service, but we also concede to them in return and believe that in the Fascist conception the State should concede, absolute freedom. In his public life, a man must behave himself as a fit member of the State, in his every action he must conform to the welfare of the nation. On the other hand he receives from the State in return, a complete liberty to live and to develop as an individual. And in our morality—and I think possibly I can claim that it is the only public morality in which private practice altogether coincides with public protestation—in our morality the one single test of any moral question is whether it impedes or destroys in any way the power of the individual to serve the State. He must answer the questions: "Does this action injure the nation? Does it injure other members of the nation? Does it injure my own ability to serve the nation?" And if the answer is clear on all those questions, the individual has absolute liberty to do as he will; and that confers upon the individual by far the greatest measure of freedom under the State which any system under the State, or any religious authority has ever conferred upon the individual.

The nearest approach to that moral test was possibly the approach of Greek civilisation, which in organisation had, of course, a conception of the State not far inferior to the Fascist conception today.

That attitude, that philosophic background imposes upon the Fascist certain very clear rules of social conduct, which amount to a detailed challenge to the existing order of things, though we will not go deeply into this detail, beyond showing that these broad principles are susceptible of reduction to detail. For instance, we regard as ridiculous a system in which a man may be fined if he even risks injury to himself by taking a drink after the hour when it is legal to do so, but who, in his public capacity as a greater or lesser public figure, may with complete impunity take action which may threaten the whole structure of the State. If he risks the slightest harm to himself, the whole force of the law is mobilised against him; yet in his public capacity he may threaten the whole life of the Nation: he may threaten the very pillars of the State.

The Fascist principle is private freedom and public service. That imposes upon us, in our public life, and in our attitude towards other men, a certain discipline and a certain restraint; but in our public life alone; and I should argue very strongly indeed that the only way to have private freedom was by a public organisation which brought some order out of the economic chaos which exists in the world today, and that such public organisation can only be secured by the methods of authority and of discipline which are inherent in Fascism.

To return to the philosophic side, however, we find naturally imposed upon the Fascist by his philosophy a certain discipline in his life, an ordered athleticism, as I would call it, and a sense of trust in leadership, a belief in authority, which are alien to other movements. And here we are brought at once into collision with the fundamental tenets of Socialism and Liberalism. Socialism differs, of course, sharply from Liberalism in its conception of economic organisation; but in philosophy I think there are few Socialists or Liberals who would disagree that they really have a common origin if we go back far enough in the Voltaire-Rousseau attitude of life; and above all the latter. Now may I suggest to you the fundamental difference which here arises between Liberalism and Socialism on the one hand, and Fascism on the other? Rousseau, in our view, either made a big mistake, or was much misunderstood. Rousseau said equality. We reply, If you mean equality of opportunity, yes; if you mean equality of man, no. That is an absurdity. I believe personally that if he is properly read, Rousseau meant equality of opportunity, that the main attack of Rousseau was aimed—and rightly aimed—at the decadent system under which he lived. He said, in effect: “It is preposterous that this idle, decadent nobility of France” (as they undoubtedly were at the time) “should claim for themselves privileges which are throttling the life of the nation. Equality of opportunity is a fundamental thing. Let those rule who are fitted to rule. Let no man rule because his grandfather proved himself fitted to rule.” It was a revolt against privilege, an affirmation that the man of talent and of capacity should be the man to conduct the affairs of a great nation. But that doctrine was seized upon by his later disciples as meaning the equality of man, that all men were equal.

From that construction arises the whole fallacy, as we see it. It is a manifest and clear absurdity. One man, in mind and physique, differs immensely from another. It is not a question, as Socialists often say, of moral or spiritual equality. That is a totally different thing. Morally and spiritually, the man who sweeps the floor of a big business may be vastly superior to the manager of that business. But the question is, which man is fitted to do which job. What is the proper function that he has to perform? Some people are good at one thing and some at another. Certainly we eliminate altogether the social class conception from Fascism because that rests upon the chance of heredity; but we do say that certain people are fitted by nature to do certain things, and others are not. And once you adopt that basis of thought, you challenge the whole conception of democracy.

You challenge the belief that every question in the world, however complicated, can be settled by anybody, however inexperienced; and indeed viewed in that light, it is a preposterous thing that a technician in Government or in anything else can be instructed by people who look at the subject for about five minutes in the year. If I walked into an engineering shop, watched the engineer doing his job, and then began to tell him how to do it, he would tell me—and rightly—that I was a presumptuous ass. Similarly, that a man who has made no study whatsoever of the country's problems should be expected to put down his mug of beer upon the counter and walk to the polling booth and give detailed instructions as to how his country is to be governed during the next four years, seems to us a preposterous notion. "All men are equal and all men are equally qualified to pass an opinion upon any subject, as long as it is a subject so complicated as the government of a country:" that is the interpretation placed by Social Democracy upon the writings of Rousseau and that conception is evidently absurd. It is, however, the philosophic basis of the whole democratic system. We therefore challenge that basic conception that all men are equal to adjudicate upon all problems. We take and make our own the equality of opportunity and we stand—and must stand—against the conception of privileged heredity.

When a man has proved himself, he may rise to the greatest positions in the land, and our whole educational system must be so devised. But he shall not be at the top just because his father or his grandfather was there before him. And so on the one hand we challenge the privilege of the Right, and on the other hand we challenge the preposterous doctrine of the Left that all men by gift of nature are equal. Now you may say, and say perhaps with some truth, that these doctrines have been heard before, that this was the basis of Bonapartism, or to go back still further to its origin, was the basis of Caesarism.

It is, of course, true that Fascism has an historic relation to Caesarism, but the modern world differs profoundly from the forms and conditions of the ancient world. Modern organisation is too vast and too complex to rest on any individual alone, however gifted. Modern Caesarism, like all things modern, is collective. The will and talent of the individual alone is replaced by the will and ability of the disciplined thousands who comprise a Fascist movement. Every Blackshirt is an individual cell of a collective Caesarism. The organised will of devoted masses, subject to a voluntary discipline, and inspired by the passionate ideal of national survival, replaces the will to power and a higher order of the individual superman. Nevertheless, this collective Caesarism, armed with the weapons of modern science, stands in the same historic relationship as ancient Caesarism to reaction on the one hand and to anarchy on the other. Caesarism stood against Spartacism on the one hand and the Patrician Senate on the other. That position is as old as the history of the last two thousand years. But they lacked, in those days, the opportunities for constructive achievement which are present today, and the only lesson that we can derive from the previous evidence of this doctrine is simply this, that whenever the world, under the influence of Spartacus drifted to complete collapse and chaos, it was always what Spengler called the "great fact-men" who extracted the world from the resultant chaos and gave mankind very often centuries of peace and of order in a new system and a new stability. And it was done, and it has been done, by modern Fascist movements, "by recognising certain fundamental facts of politics and of philosophy. Again you have a certain wedding of two seemingly conflicting doctrines. We are often accused of taking something from the Right and something from the Left. Well, it is a very sensible thing to borrow from other faiths; to discard what is bad and keep what is good; and directly you get away from the old parliamentary mind, you of course see the wisdom of any such course. And Fascism does, of course, take something from the Right and something from the Left, and to it adds new facts to meet the modern age.

In this new synthesis of Fascism, coming rather nearer to our immediate situation, we find that we take the great principle of stability supported by authority, by order, by discipline, which has been the attribute of the Right, and we marry it to the principle of progress, of dynamic change, which we take from the Left. Conservatism—to call it by the name by which it is known in this country—believes in stability and supports it by its belief in order; but where Conservatism has always failed in the modern world is in its inability to perceive that stability can only be achieved through progress: that a stand-pat resistance to change precipitates the revolutionary situation which Conservatism most fears. On the other hand, the Left has always failed to realise, thanks to their

Rousseau complex, that the only way to get progress is to adopt the executive instruments by which alone change is made possible.

We have, therefore, come to this conclusion: that you can only have stability if you are prepared to carry through orderly changes, because to remain stable you must adapt yourselves to the new facts of the new age. On the other hand you can only have the progress, which the Left desires if you adopt the executive instruments of progress, namely, authority, discipline and loyalty, which have always been regarded as belonging only to the Right. By uniting those two principles, we achieve the basis of Fascist faith and Fascist organisation.

Again you will say: "This is once more Caesarism or Bonapartism. It has ceased to be a matter of purely individual leadership. The machinery with which we are dealing is much too large for any single individual to handle alone. So it has become a collective Caesarism—the leadership of an organised and disciplined mass, bound together in a voluntary discipline by ideals of national and world regeneration which passionately inspire it. But the basic principles remain the same; and, therefore, while your Fascist movement may perform the purpose which Caesarism has performed before, may bring order out of the chaos which the conflict between Spartacus and reaction has evoked, may for a few years or a few centuries give great peace to the world, it yet carries within itself its own decay, and does not really achieve what we believe to be necessary."

I believe the answer to that case, which is the only really valid case, is that always before, the factor of modern science was lacking. You have now got a completely new factor. If you can introduce into your system of government a new efficiency, and everyone admits that such movements when they come to power are at least efficient: if you can bring to government for even a few years an executive power and an efficiency which gets things done, you can release—and you will release—the imprisoned genius of science to perform the task which it has to perform in the modern world. Whatever our divergent views on the structure of the State and economics may be, I think we must all agree that it would be possible, by sane organisation of the world, with the power of modern science and of industry to produce, to solve once and for all the poverty problem, and to abolish, once and for all, poverty and the worst attributes of disease and suffering from the world.

Therefore, if it is possible to have an efficient form of Government, you have available for such a system, for the first time in history, an instrument by which the face of the earth might be changed for all time. Once the essential has been done, once modern science and technique have been released and have performed their task, once you have changed your political and philosophic system from a transitory and political to a permanent and technical basis, there will be no more need of the politics and of the controversies which distract the world today. The problem of poverty will be solved, the major problems will be banished as they can be, and as everybody knows they can be, if modern science is properly mobilised. Then mankind will be liberated for the things in life which really matter.

Therefore, while it is perhaps true that certain of these phenomena in the eternal recurrences of history have been seen in the world before, and seen with great benefit to mankind, yet never before have the great executive movements possessed the opportunity to complete their task which modern science and invention now confer upon them.

At a moment of great world crisis, a crisis which in the end will inevitably deepen, a movement emerges from a historic background which makes its emergence inevitable, carrying certain traditional attributes derived from a very glorious past, but facing the facts of today armed with the instruments which only this age has ever conferred upon mankind. By this new and wonderful coincidence of instrument and of event the problems of this age can be overcome, and the future can be assured in a progressive stability. Possibly this is the last great world wave of the immortal, the eternally recurring Caesarian movement; but with the aid of science, and with the inspiration of the modern mind, this wave shall carry humanity to the further shore.

Then, at long last, 'Caesarism,' the mightiest emanation of the human spirit in high endeavour toward enduring achievement, will have performed its world mission, will have expiated its sacrifice in the struggle of the ages, and will have fulfilled its historic destiny. A humanity released from poverty and from many of the horrors and afflictions of disease to the enjoyment of a world re-born through science, will still need a Fascist movement transformed to the purpose of a new and nobler order of mankind; but you will need no more the strange and disturbing men who, in days of struggle and of danger and in nights of darkness and of labour, have forged the instrument of steel by which the world shall pass to higher things.

Germany and Her Women
by Anne Seelig-Thomann

DURING my last visit to England many English women have asked me about the position of women in the Third Reich. According to the tales they had heard, they seemed to think we were nothing but slaves. In fact, they said this openly, and added that they pitied us from the bottom of their hearts. I should like to tell you how we German women feel about the New Reich, and I will begin with the wives and mothers.

We all know from history that every revolution is followed by new constitutional forms, and because of the uprising which has produced these new forms, we generally find fundamental changes in the social life of the people as well. The new system in Germany, "National Socialism," came as a welcome change for millions of families, who had suffered terribly from the consequences of the war which had made life a burden for many mothers and their children. It was the task of Adolf Hitler to help them, and bring to an end the disastrous idea that "it is better not to have any children at all."

We must not forget that selfishness was the basis of the old system before the Führer came to build the new Reich. He it was who made German women believe once more that the family is the essential unit of the State, and in it the mother is the living symbol of national survival through her raising of healthy children. Motherhood and womanhood recovered their old meaning and glory.

Service For Mothers

In 1934 the National Socialist League of Women came together for the first time for earnest co-operative work, and founded the Reich Service for Mothers. This service is administered by every branch of the League, and consists of special courses of instruction open to all women, married or unmarried, young and old. Since 1934 no less than 600.000 German women have attended these courses, and have received instruction in house management, cooking and sewing, as well as the elements of hygiene and nursing. Also, as we Germans belong to a nation without colonies, we have to be careful of every sort of raw material, and in these courses the women learn how to turn apparently useless things to a useful purpose. As a rule each course covers ten evenings, with a total of twenty-four hours' instruction.

The cost of such a course varies between two to three marks in the country and three to five marks in the town. Those who can afford it are expected to pay in full, but supplementary amounts are contributed by the Women's Section of the Labour Front and the National Socialist Welfare Organisation for those who cannot afford these payments. Very often the whole sum is paid by the employer for a girl shortly retiring from work for marriage. There are several hundreds of such Mothers' Schools permanently established in Germany, finding a vocation for thousands of voluntary workers as guardians, public welfare teachers, youth leaders and so forth. It is work such as this that gives every German woman an opportunity to take an active part in the life of the National Socialist State, for every woman realises that she must take her part side by side with the men with the same responsibility for the future of our nation.

The Working Woman

Nothing has been more discussed by other nations than the position of professional - and working women in the Third Reich. The opponents of National Socialism have insisted that from the moment Adolf Hitler came to power, all working women would be forcibly removed from their occupations and replaced by men. Nothing could, in fact, be more contrary to the truth, for all active women in industry and the professions are organised within the Labour Front, and those women who were not previously employed, but wished to help in building up the New Reich, entered voluntarily into the League of Women, under the national leadership of Frau Scholz-Klink. In these two organisations we find the housewife, the teacher, the nurse, the midwife, the artist, the lady doctor and all women with university qualifications.

As it is the ideal of National Socialism to preserve the family as the essential unit of the State, it is true that the Labour Front has secured the removal of women from factory work which is unsuitable for the female physique, replacing them by unemployed men. These women have, however, been found more congenial work elsewhere.

German women are still employed in all the trades concerned with clothing, and millions besides are teachers, nurses and domestic servants, while there are numbers of women doctors, women as architects and on the stage and in the films, not only as actresses but as outstanding producers, such as the famous Leni Riefenstahl, who has charge of all photography at important Party Meetings and at the Olympic Games. Also millions of women are employed in general industry, forming a special section, as I have said, of the Labour Front. It certainly cannot be said that German women have been thrust into the home.

Domestic Service

Even those who, as domestic servants or housewives, are peculiarly restricted to the household sphere have received special attention. When Adolf Hitler came to power, the League of Women was given the special task of overcoming the universal prejudice that domestic work is only an occupation for the lower classes. Now every girl, whether rich or poor, on leaving school has to pass a stiff examination on household duties, and in addition to this, most of our girls at eighteen, before starting their own profession, volunteer for the Women's Labour Service, which frequently involves household duties to relieve some hard-worked mother.

The woman's share in the new social order has not been planned on the basis of the old slogan of "Women's Rights," but in relation to the service that woman can bring to the community as a whole—the nation. As the woman's influence has always been greatest in the moulding of the intimate social life of the nation, we are not so much concerned as to where our service is given, but how it is given.

The German Girl

Already at school the German girl joins the B.D.M. (Bund Deutscher Mädel) which is the largest organisation of its kind in the world. Affiliated to the Hitler Youth Movement, the B.D.M. receives detailed instructions in training, and especially in the inculcation of a healthy philosophy of life (Weltanschauung) from the National Youth Leader, Baldur von Schirach. Forty schools have been built all over the country for the sole purpose of instructing girls as youth leaders on these principles.

As future mothers, doctors, economists, teachers, lawyers, etc., all German girls have an obligation to use their gifts to the best national purpose, but they must first obtain, as a foundation, a sure social background. Where can this better be obtained than in the comradeship of the German girls' organisation, the B.D.M.? The first necessity is physical training, and therefore every girl has to undergo a systematic development of her physical standards according to age. At the same time instruction is given in first aid and nursing. There are B.D.M. camps where the girls learn to help on the land, and household schools for training as children's nurses, dieticians and other domestic work.

When the girls leave school they are encouraged to spend a year in the "Land Year Service," doing useful work on the land. This is a parallel organisation to the "Labour Service" for the young men, and performs useful work which does not compete with normal occupations. Indeed, work of great economic value has been found in replacing women incapacitated by illness and giving them an adequate holiday to recuperate. This has been particularly advantageous in the case of the overburdened mother, whose household work has been taken over by girls from the "Labour Service," while her children are cared for in a local "Kindergarten."

Although the mere statistics of this gigantic organisation of the women of Germany are impressive enough, the real value lies in the moral standards created. The German girl in her B.D.M. and "Land Year Service" gains not only great experience, but gathers a sense of social responsibility, as she is given exactly similar lectures and instruction on political and economic problems as the young men in their organisations. Whoever has visited a women's Labour Camp has been delighted with the strong, well-built girls, their eyes sparkling with health and happiness. Many of my English friends have asked me over here, "How is it that the whole atmosphere of your young people is so full of cleanliness and the radiance of strength and life? How did you manage it?" There can be only one answer, "The spirit of Adolf Hitler" !

What Is Socialism?
by Joseph Goebbels

EVERY reasoned modern political conception revolves, whether it be acknowledged or not, round the central factor of all future development—the Social Problem.

Social distress is more than a bread-and-butter question. If it were no more than that, the Marxist would had been right. The proletarian is not international out of any love for international admixing, but because of the tragic realization that, formerly, there was no national solution of his problem of existence. Bourgeois selfishness and Jewish competition worked together, consciously and unconsciously, and produced that thing which steals from the people the very light and breath of life—the Class War.

Social distress breeds the passion for Security. Deep in the proletariat slumbers a love for Home, Soil and Fatherland, which finds its expression in good as well as bad forms, always ready for the noblest sacrifice. Even under Marxism the proletariat feels no hate for the Fatherland, but only for that bourgeois perversion of the Fatherland—the System. This System created indeed a condition in which nationalism and capitalism were one and the same thing. The struggle against internationalism can never be won with phrases. Social distress can only be solved through social action. The proletariat will continue to think internationally so long as they have no share in the Nation. How can one love and respect something which one does not know?

The Social Problem is a question of making the international city-proletariat once more conscious of their fundamental relationship with the soil. Man can only gain root in his own soil. He only feels himself related to that which is his own. The only effective struggle against Bolshevism is the elimination of Capitalism.

It shows the lack of political instinct in the middle-classes that they identified themselves with Capitalism, with which, after all, they had little enough to do. Capitalism is the immoral distribution of capital. Capitalism in economics is the same thing as democracy in politics:

namely, the immoral distribution of power within the State. Both factors, Capitalism and Democracy—their relation is as son to father—are the sworn enemies of a new social organization of the State. Up to the present they were satisfied with ignoring the Social Problem, and evaded the issue as far as possible by a hypocritical profession of philanthropy. That is the tragedy of Liberalism—philanthropy: a conglomeration of bourgeois cowardice, sentimentality, sadism and fear. The whole story of social 'amelioration' unfolds itself before our eyes as a terrible example of Liberal incapacity to deal with the Social Problem—much less to comprehend its depths. The Social Problem has nothing, absolutely nothing, to do with sentimentality and 'Charity'. It is a problem of national necessity. It is not the mere fact that some millions go hungry that gives this problem its world-wide political importance, but that it may cause the collapse of the Nation. That alone gives continuity to social ideas. Sentimentality and 'Charity' are utterly unreliable of themselves. National necessity alone creates fanaticism and the fierce impulse of faith. So it is that the Social Problem is grounded in the structure of future political developments and gives youth new duties and new tasks.

From this realization a truly social concept of the State emerges, which has as little to do with Marxist-proletarian as with liberal-democratic notions. I am thinking in a social sense when I wish for the oppressed classes of my fellow countrymen the attainment of their natural rights, as rights, and not as more or less voluntary gifts. I am thinking in a social sense when I demand these rights not from motives of bourgeois fear or sentimentality, but from the realization of national necessity and social justice.

The Liberal man thinks as a bourgeois; the Marxist man thinks as a proletarian; the Social man thinks nationally, in terms of a national state designed to fulfil a common destiny. For him national and social thinking mean one and the same thing: Love for the Nation; belief in its future; and the will to freedom.

World Philosophy and Foreign Politics
by Alfred Rosenberg

IN every-day life the average man rarely realizes that political and social life are ultimately shaped by philosophical motives. The conception of the bourgeois moral code, the conception of law and all else in daily life which is connected with it are always somehow determined by the inner attitude of man towards them; but it is only on the occasion of great revolutionary events, which affect the life of a nation as a whole, that people become clearly conscious of this fact. It can be said that this is what is happening today throughout the world. No matter what may be the immediate effect of the conflict of 1914-1918 upon the political events of the various nations and states, there is one fact which impresses itself in an ever increasing measure upon all minds whose thoughts are not merely superficial, and that is, that after such a tremendous upheaval men cannot simply return to their previous daily existence just as if nothing at all had happened. Practically every nation in the world has been affected by the great struggles of the World War, or has at least suffered in some measure from its consequences. Millions and millions of men are faced by a fate which overwhelmed them with apparent suddenness and which gave rise to questions vastly differing from those which had mattered for many decades.

Before 1914 the world lived in an atmosphere of optimism. It is true that those in responsible positions in the various countries saw that clouds were gathering again and again on the political horizon, but even among statesmen there were many who believed that, just as on previous similar occasions, the political system of daily compromise would be victorious. Economists calculated with mathematical precision that any conflict between great nations would have such disastrous economic and social results, that a collapse of the world economic structure would be bound to occur and bring about the end of the war within a few months. Intellectual optimists based their hopes on the belief that "world common sense" would carry the day and agreed with the leading economists in saying that the nations would never tolerate the madness of a world war.

But, like nature itself, the life of the people and races did not progress on the straight path of logic, but on the tortuous by-paths of excited feelings and wild passions. It is these incalculable elements which finally unchained the world catastrophe. It is important, I think, that we should recognize today that the year 1914 did not only mark the beginning of a great military struggle, but that on those fatal days of August the entire old world began to collapse. The fact that the nations and their leaders were unable to prevent such a terrible conflict from occurring is conclusive proof that the social conflicts, the whole tendency of world economics of the time and the social structure of the nations, were no longer powerful enough to guarantee a clearly defined peace policy. On the contrary, so much attention had to be given to chaotic mass movements of the lower strata, to political passions and to economic interests, that the helm often slipped out of the hands of the statesmen and the world lurched towards a collision from which it began to recover only many years afterwards, after heroic forces had been spent and enormous sacrifices had been made.

It is natural that this recovery of the common mind, this criticism of the past and present, were bound to manifest themselves first in those countries where military and political defeat made the problems much more evident than in the states which, at least for the time being, could live on the fruits of their war victories. All the fermenting processes, widely different in nature, which occurred in Russia, Hungary, Germany and Turkey, appear to every intelligent observer of world politics as unmistakable signs of the collapse of the old order already mentioned and to an effort to create a new world, in some way or another. This is not so much due to the logical recognition of what is suitable or not, but to an inner change of character which, turning towards the present as well as towards the past, declared: "This cannot continue any longer."

This inner resolution is of greater importance than anything else and cannot be eliminated by any argument. These new mental attitudes of nations, be they in one direction or in the other, are the decisive reason for construction or destruction, as the case may be. The centre of gravity of our present movement in world politics results from the juxtaposition and force of these various mental energies.

We National Socialists see in a well-defined attitude of mind that also which we call "world philosophy" (Weltanschauung). This word, the precise translation of which into other languages is most difficult, signifies in the first place exactly what it states: a particular way of viewing the world, i.e. a clearly comprehensible inner attitude of soul, mind and character towards outer things. An attitude which decides on "yea" or "nay", which, if it is the voice of millions, shapes the mode of living, the structure of the state, the duties and privileges of a race or a people. This attitude is therefore the essential fundamental and decisive factor. If it permeates all the various spheres of life, then we can speak of a united and uniform nation; then we can say that state, people and "world philosophy" have become merged into one. Of course, this happens only on very rare occasions. Most nations under the influence of racial characteristics and political events are affected by diverging currents in the various spheres of life, which frequently give rise to most serious conflicts within the nation.

"World Philosophy" is therefore not equivalent to Religion, but it can include the latter. A "world philosophy" can be given a special character by religion, or by a science; it can be shaped by the artistic or cultural qualities of a nation. If the "world philosophy" of a people is really deep and genuine, it will include and characterize everything. On the other hand, it is spacious enough to include the most widely different mental and spiritual temperaments.

The attitude of various nations and of eminent persons towards questions related to world philosophy, be they of a religious, scientific or cultural nature, has been an important contributing factor in determining not only the intellectual but also the political life of nations through all the centuries of the past, and I am of the opinion that the question what effect on foreign politics during the great epochs of history world philosophy has had, is one of the most interesting problems of world history. I doubt, indeed, whether this question has so far formed the subject of sufficiently deep study, although it should appeal not only to the research scholar but also to every statesman.

May I be permitted to quote some examples in order to demonstrate how decisively a political "world philosophy" may affect the development of history for centuries and millenniums?

When the Christian religion spread from the Mediterranean over the European Continent and one Germanic tribe after another became Christian, it was found that almost all of them did not accept the Roman Catholic dogma but became Arians, i.e. followers of Arius, whose conception of the person and divine position of the founder of Christianity differed materially from that of the Roman Catholic Church. Only one important tribe became Roman Catholic, on account of its leader's convenience, namely the Franconians. These Franconians, however, were also the strongest tribe from a military point of view and had not moved very far away from their original home, like the East-Germans, and thus old Rome was associated with a hard young will-power which henceforth was turned towards the East. This will-power was victorious both in a military and world-philosophical. Arius of Alexandria (died A.D. 336) taught that Christ was not God but created by him. His doctrine was banned by the Council of Nicaea and thus Europe did not become Arian as seemed likely at first, but Roman Catholic. Here we have, then, a victory of one idea over the other, accompanied by immeasurable consequences from the point of view of world history. If the other, Arian, tribes had vanquished the Franconians, Europe would have taken an entirely different spiritual aspect and the whole Protestant movement which materialized later would not have made its appearance; at least not in the same form.

A second example showing how a "world philosophy" based on religion imposed its will on whole nations, is provided by Islam. This belief united countless Bedouin tribes who, strong in their faith, conquered the whole Northern part of Africa and invaded Southern Europe. Although repulsed by the Europeans who fought for their independence, the Mahomedan religion has imprinted its mark on a considerable part of the inhabited earth: from Gibraltar across Africa, Palestine and so on as far as India. Political movements and bitter feuds, continuing to the present day, show how a given "world philosophy" acts as a continuous driving force, compelling all the nations who are under its sway to propagate and defend their particular " world philosophy", their mode of living, their conception of government, their culture.

After the Universal Church had remained victorious for many centuries, violent revolts against it broke out in many parts of Europe. These evoked from the people protests which shook the world and were based upon a common ideology. For centuries the fight of the various Protestant peoples against the Universal Church and its military representations raged over Europe. But in the midst of this struggle the European collective mind turned in an entirely new direction in a most characteristic way: from being an essentially religious or dogmatic struggle, the controversy became national. The protection of a national structure will displace ethical values, even if their representatives are of the highest order. Perhaps the best example of this turning towards a new epoch is the case of Cardinal Richelieu. He saw in himself the leading minister of Louis XIII and the successor of Louis XI, in carrying out the plan of a national unification which the latter had conceived; on the other hand, he was a bishop and later a cardinal of the Roman church. At the Court of Paris the Roman Catholic influence held sway and was represented primarily by the Spanish party. The policy of Rome undoubtedly favoured Spain and the Hapsburgs, and the completion of the Hispano-Hapsburgian victory over France would certainly have resulted in a purely Catholic supremacy in Europe for a long time to come. But Richelieu, although he demanded freedom for the Roman Church in all his pacts with his Protestant allies, transferred his support to the other side and did his utmost to mobilize the world against the Hapsburgs, and to break the power of Spain, neutralizing at the same time the temporal power of the Pope. Against all the papal friends at the French Court he enacted all the measures for consolidating the supremacy of France; in order to ensure its independence he annihilated the Protestants in his own country but formed alliances with Gustavus Adolphus and with Bernhard, Duke of Weimar. He even ordered the French guns to fire on the Papal soldiers. I think these shots, fired against Rome's army by order of a Roman cardinal, symbolize the turning of Europe to a new attitude which, since then, has never ceased to be present in the life of our Continent.

In the nineteenth century this attitude underwent a change towards a new form of European Nationalism. Everywhere in the world the national idea was the liberating thought of life. Proof of this is found in many writings of the time, and in the persons of Washington, Bolivar and Garibaldi. At the same time, however, science and commerce assumed an ever-increasing importance and Walter Rathenau's saying: "Fate is decided by Economics" became the "Leitmotiv" of the elaboration of most social problems. Another important factor was the population figure of the several states, which caused them to seek markets for products and raw material supply anywhere in the world. This attitude was sponsored and propagated principally by a people spread all over the globe. It was advocated that a "World Republic" should be aimed at, and that the previously existing National-economic systems were to be replaced by a so-called world-economic system, preferably under a central control.

It is true that at the turn of the century there were some national states of a military-political character, but considered from an economic point of view there existed an almost hopeless confusion of many different economic groups, commercial and industrial trusts, and international banks, which opposed one another and the success or failure of which were bound to affect so many people that the national policy was forced to subordinate itself to these private interests and recognize them for the greater part as of national importance.

As a protest against the social effects of this purely economic system in every way, millions of people arose and listened to the doctrines preaching social freedom by means of a movement embracing all the nations, i.e., the Marxist-Communist International. All these currents and tendencies, which were continuously complicated and increased by new side issues, brought about an obstruction at the end of the Nineteenth Century and it can safely be said that Friedrich Nietzsche has been the most sensitive seismograph of these tremors which shook the whole world. He did not indulge in a sentimental philosophy but experienced a foreboding of the events to come, which were to affect hundreds of millions of people.

The realization that the social fabric would collapse into Nihilism under the impact of both civic and Marxist forces, and at the same time the hope that from this catastrophe would arise a strong race, characterize his aphorisms and all his writings. At the same time men like Paul de Lagarde and Richard Wagner felt that the world was drawing to its end and that a new world was to be born. In Russia, Dostoyevsky painted in sombre hues the end of Russia. And while the feeling of extreme insecurity became universal, these ideas, lacking any shape, found acceptance in the capitals of all nations. Russia fell, and those tendencies came into power which Dostoyevsky predicted in his "The Brothers Karamazov" and "Demons". Communism was victorious in Russia against all social theories, not through a proletarian mass organization of the towns, but by the fact that a will which had been broken already came under the influence of a strong-willed non-European character.

If we survey these various world-philosophies, which often seem to oppose each other in deadly antagonism, we find that they all have one feature in common. They all arise from a well-defined doctrine, whether the latter be of a religious, a scientific, or a social-ethical nature. On these doctrines or confessions of faith they build a programme, gather together all those who believe in this programme, and endeavour with all the political and military forces at their disposal to carry out this doctrinal programme.

Speaking generically and politically, this attitude is related to what may be called "universality". This universality exists, no matter whether an individual is appointed as supreme master from whom a world-movement receives its laws, or whether it is founded on abstract society or on any particular theory. Indeed the past fifteen centuries of European history show that all nations move somewhere within such a universally conceived "world philosophy" and that all the great struggles between nations followed their course within a doctrine which had a universal character. This doctrine was characterized by religious universality in the Roman Catholic "world philosophy"; and the same characteristic existed in the Protestant dogma, although in a different form and in spite of individualistic results; in the system of Liberalism we find a social-ethical universality, such as was preached during the French revolution; and it was a Nihilistic universality which characterized the offshoot of the Marxist movement, World-Communism, which no longer recognized nationalities and states, but only a Union of Socialist Soviet Republics, to which at any time other Soviet Republics would be added.

The decisive and radical world-philosophical change, as we see it today, consists in our firm conviction that the coming struggle will no longer have the same character as before and that national struggles will not be fought within any given "world philosophy" of a universalistic kind, but that these struggles will be fought out within a nationalistic "world-philosophy". In other words: the tendencies which formerly were purely statal, become wider and are considered from a world-philosophical angle, developing into a decisive factor in regulating life in its widest concept. At the beginning of our present era the rule of a universal church was the highest religious and political element. When the first revolt occurred, two religious confessions opposed each other. At a later stage of this struggle these principal factors were transferred from the religious to the statal-political arena, which at first took the form of monarchy and finally that of a republican idea.

At the end of the nineteenth and the beginning of the twentieth century we find that the class idea stood highest in the minds of millions of people. And each of these different factors formed the fundamental political principle of one of the various parties, particularly in Germany. The principal factor of the middle ages was represented by the Centre Party; the dynastic idea by the former Conservative groups; the economic idea amalgamated with the republican idea by the democratic party; and the class idea by the Marxist groups. In opposition to all these groups existing in Germany, the National Socialist Movement proclaimed a new, and yet old, principal factor, namely—the ideal of national honour.

All the struggles of the last fourteen years, until 1933, have been fought under this banner. If, however, it assumed a mystical strength, this was only possible because a great nation, conscious of its honour, had suffered a collapse, after which only one decision remained to be taken. Either the old political groups had to be tolerated still further as representing the old- world philosophies, or a new political philosophy based on new principles had to be created as a foundation of the German people's life. I need not point out that the idea of National Honour is not a novel idea which arose suddenly; indeed, ever since a German people existed, its whole art and literature revolved around it. The "Hildebrand Epos", the "Nibelungenlied" and the "Gudrun Saga" prove this, and so does the whole of German heroic music. Besides this, this idea was at the root of the legal codes of the old German "Saxon Laws" and the "Civic Law" (Stadterecht) which for many peoples became the foundation of many factors which ultimately produced unification. Nor is it necessary for me to emphasize that what I am saying here is not intended as a reference to, or a criticism of, other nations.

My sole aim is to explain what has happened here in Germany, and to show that we are not dealing in this instance with one out of many revolutions but that the decisive revolution in German history had begun: a revolution which did not begin suddenly but one whose principles can be found in the German Peasant Wars, in the legal enactments of the old "Free Cities", in Frederic the Great, in the Leaders of the German Wars of Liberation of 1813, and in the great thinkers at the turning-point from the eighteenth to the nineteenth century.

And may I be permitted to declare here, that this fervent German Nationalism is indeed not a menace to the legitimate nationalism of other peoples, but that on the contrary it is precisely this German Nationalism which, by its spiritual superiority over all other issues can alone give the guarantee for that just balance for which the whole world is longing. The Authoritarian State, based today on the National Socialist Movement, is in a position to eliminate an unjustifiable cultural propaganda amongst people of other races, as well as a lawless economic expansion which otherwise might well lead the German Nation from economic conflicts to political strife with other nations.

German Nationalism, a "world-philosophy" based on race and soil, is not a dogma related to universality; neither its premises nor its conclusions include the presumption that it should influence other and therefore different nations and races. On the other hand, we think that our philosophy constitutes also a return to a reverent admiration of Nature and its laws. The National Socialist "world-philosophy" therefore means to us a deliberate turning away from those forms of national life which do not give due importance to the characteristics of the various peoples and races; a discarding of those cultural-scientific doctrines which claim to apply to all nations equally; and finally we look upon it as an attempt to achieve a higher and at the same time deeper consciousness of our own driving forces in these same spheres. Our new "world-philosophy", far from despising others, is an essential element in bringing about a reciprocal genuine respect between nations and cultures.

For this reason, for example, the National Socialist Movement has the greatest respect for an entirely different race and statal constitution, both having their own peculiar characteristics. In the two great nations of the Far East we see structures which have been built on their own foundations. To us Japan, the history of which goes back for thousands of years, is admirable in its religious expression, in its subordination to state authority and its devotion to national interests. The Chinese nation has also developed from one form of "world philosophy", economics and social ethics, which, although it seems broken up today, may yet revive. And we shall watch this attempt to reorganize with the same interest and respect that we give to all the noble ambitions of other nations.

It is typical that the era of a practically uncontrolled expansion of many nations all over the globe led to a conflict and to the realization of the fact that after this period of economic expansion, a period of contraction has set in. In this every nation will find its true form. That this struggle exists in all nations without exception is demonstrated by violent clashes of a social or world-philosophical nature the whole world over. They prove the existence of an almost universal lack of faith and show that the actions of nations are not governed ultimately by a well-defined idea, but that a number of different systems are fighting for supremacy without coming to a lasting decision.

If we interpret the signs and tokens of contemporary politics rightly, it seems that the mental struggle of all nations centres on the desire to replace all the systems which are waging an indecisive war by a particular one of these systems, or by an entirely new one which surpasses them all.

Germany may well provide one instance in this world struggle— and not necessarily an exemplary instance — for strengthening the possibility that a so-called "fateful" development is not by any means bound to end in Communism, but that a determination born of a strong character can overcome the outlived mode of thought that is no longer in keeping with present-day conditions. The free and secret plebiscite in the Saar has shown the whole world how deeply the new conception of life has permeated the entire German nation in spite of all the opposing currents, which were allowed to exert their influence without any hindrance. We ourselves, at least, are convinced that the German system, in that it prevents any private political or private economic interests from gaining power, is alone capable of defining for the German Reich those limitations which are essential in the vital interests not only of Germany but also of other States. This makes it possible, for the first time in many long years, to differentiate between private interests, be they never so strong, and the vital interests of the nation as a whole. At the same time, however, we have the possibility of a stable foreign policy which we conceive to be of such a nature that the natural driving forces connected with the life of the various nations can no longer be directed arbitrarily against each other, but will stand back to back both in the interests of the individual nations and in those of an organic collaboration of all nations. In this complex of great Powers it will then become possible for numerically smaller nations to be no longer the instrument of narrow egoism but units endowed with equal rights in the organic activities between Great Powers. May I add that when speaking of "small nations", I allude only to their area and population and do not wish to minimize in any way their intellectual and cultural importance.

Thus the National Socialist "world philosophy" and the re-birth of the national ideal give rise to a new conception of State and national economy; a new well-regulated state control of the individual which alone can produce real freedom, in clear contrast to misuse by individuals which, in the absence of control, affected many spheres of life, poisoned and corrupted the feelings and thoughts of whole nations, to the disadvantage not of the corruptors but of the nations.

The establishment of accord between the various forms of life, agreements between an authoritative State regulating all branches of national activity and other States, and between the groups ("komplexe") of States thus formed and other units determined by political, racial and geographical factors—in contrast with the haphazard elements which characterized the nineteenth century—all this constitutes the decisive change of our present era. And National Socialism is prepared to serve these purposes in the interests of all nations. Thus we find that the new "world-philosophy" has a decisive shaping influence on political thought and ultimately on economic and foreign political activity.

We believe that the considerations submitted in this short summary are worth closer study from the angle of their possible practical applications and effects; bearing in mind the words of a German who fought for freedom a century ago: “Respect the fatherland of others, but love your own”.

Fascism, Women And Democracy
by Norah Elam

"Experience shows that in all countries today democracy can develop its nature freely, the most scandalous corruption is displayed without anyone considering it of use to conceal its rascalities . . . Democracy is the land of plenty dreamt of by unscrupulous financiers." — Georges Sorel, *Reflexions sur la Violence.*

TO a genuine cynic who lived through the struggle for votes for women from 1906 to 1914, no spectacle is more diverting than the post-war enthusiast whose one obsession seems to be the alleged danger to enfranchised women in a Fascist Britain.

This unsuspected solicitude finds its most insistent champions in unlikely places, and those who were so bitter against the pre-war struggle have today executed a complete *volte face.* Our new-found patrons are second to none in their determination that women shall be denied nothing in principle, even if in practice they are to be denied most things essential to their existence.

To the woman who took part in that historic fight, and, regarding the vote merely as a symbol, believed that with its help a new and a better world might be possible, this kind of patronage is as distasteful as was that of a generation ago. She thinks, and with some justification, that it is humbug that those who in all those weary years never raised a hand to help her, but on the contrary were wont to describe her as an unsexed virago or a disappointed spinster, should in the hour of success endeavour to exploit her sex in the interests of a reactionary and decadent system. Such effrontery is possible only because those who resort to it entirely misunderstood and still misunderstand the meaning of that struggle, and construed the demand for political liberty as a desire for personal licence.

The time has come when the principles which underlay that remarkable and determined manifestation for ordered change, not only in the position of women but in the accepted attitude to them, should be restated.

What was it, then, which underlay the passionate stirring that moved the hearts of thousands of women, and guided their heads, in those stormy years? It was not, as so many imagined, the ignoble desire of individual self-interest, nor a struggle on behalf of women for their own sex alone. On the contrary, from the leaders to the most humble of the rank and file it was the fundamental belief, that in a world peopled by men and women and under a political system controlling the destinies of both sexes, the country which shut out from its councils the influence, viewpoint and talents of more than half its people, would be to that extent handicapped in working out the best system of government. If men were the victims of chaotic economic conditions, women suffered with them. If the social conditions under which men dragged out an almost hopeless existence were intolerable, they were equally so for their womenfolk.

Looking round on the great cities of their land, from north to south and from east to west, they saw housing conditions which man and woman agreed were a disgrace to modern civilization; watching the labour market, they gazed with apprehension on the spectre of insecurity which haunts the wage-earner and which is inherent in the old system. In the political field, they noted that, both in Home and Foreign policy, affairs were being conducted in such a manner as to strike terror into the heart of any person who cared deeply for Britain or realized, the decadence that had already begun its erosion upon all parties of the State. They rose to demand that women should be called in on equal terms with men, to lend a hand before it was too late.

This uprising was in short a challenge to the old antagonisms and a call for co-operation in the corporate body of the State.

In this conception of practical citizenship, the women's struggle resembles closely the new philosophy of Fascism. Indeed, Fascism is the logical, if much grander, conception of the momentous issues raised by the militant women of a generation ago. Nor do the points of resemblance end here. The Women's movement, like the Fascist movement, was conducted under strict discipline, and cut across all Party allegiance; its supporters were drawn from every class and Party. It appealed to women to forget self-interest; to relinquish petty personal advantages and the privilege of the sheltered few for the benefit of the many; and to stand together against the wrongs and injustices which were inherent in a system so disastrous to the well-being of the race. Like the Fascist movement, too, it chose its Leader, and once having chosen gave to that Leader absolute authority to direct its policy and destiny, displaying a loyalty and a devotion never surpassed in the history of this country. Moreover, like the Fascist movement again, it faced the brutality of the streets; the jeers of its opponents; the misapprehensions of the well-disposed; and the rancour of the politicians. It endured the hatred of the existing Government, and finally the loneliness of the prison cell and the horror of forcible feeding. Its speakers standing in the open spaces and at the street corners were denied the right of free speech; it champions selling their literature spat upon and reviled; its deputations were manhandled. Suffragettes became the sport of any rowdy who cared to take the law into his own hands. To make the analogy the more exact, no calumny was too vile and no slander too base to set about the moral character of its leaders, or the aims and objects of the women who owed them allegiance.

Thus it came about that women welded together in such association had no illusions about political and party shibboleths, and when the sacred words "Democracy" and "Individual Liberty" were a commonplace on the lips of their detractors, they remembered that these things were done under a Liberal Administration, and by the champions of a Party which had made the democratic system the summit of its political wisdom. That under it, they were classed with criminals, lunatics and children. They argued and with some cogency, that if this were democracy then women had little to hope for from it.

Their experience as outlaws from the democratic system was as nothing compared with that which faced them, when they found themselves honoured citizens under its doubtful protection. They had earned, it is true, the right to individual liberty for a very brief space once every five years, but when they had put that fatal cross upon the ballot paper and closed the door of the polling booth behind them, from that moment they found themselves completely helpless before the democratic machine.

Though we shall be told that this was what we had fought for, a moment's reflexion will show that this was regarded as but the symbol. Women never made the fatal error of imagining that because men voted they were necessarily free. It is the mark of the unintelligent woman today to suppose that a woman is free because she also votes, or that democracy can ever offer anything but the careful and organized exploitation of men and women who suffer it to exist.

Given the vote on a limited basis at the close of the War, women were also granted the right of entering Parliament, and the election in the late autumn of 1918 gave them their first opportunity. The Party system was already beginning to show the first signs of decay, and by the inexorable law of retributive justice, the Party which had given birth to democracy in Britain was in full retreat before its ungrateful offspring. Nevertheless, women in the first flush of their triumph turned to the then existing parties either as voters or prospective candidates.

My own distrust of Party politics made me chary of turning in this direction, and I preferred to stand as an Independent, going down with all the other women candidates on this occasion, save one. The exception was the Sinn Fein Countess Markievicz, who though a notorious and avowed enemy of Britain, found it a perfectly simple matter under the democratic system to secure election to the Parliament of the country which she had openly boasted that she would destroy, disintegrate and discredit. She was, if I remember rightly, returned unopposed. The next example was hardly more encouraging, for the first woman to be elected for an English constituency was an American-born citizen who had no credentials to represent British women in their own Parliament, save that she had married a British subject who found himself forced to the Upper House on the death of his father. Detractors of the Women's Movement, pointed with a hardly disguised satisfaction to this denouement, and were at pains to hold up this lady as a sorry specimen of feminine irresponsibility. They need not have been so personal, for she was no better and no worse than any other woman elected to the British House of Commons, as a result of the years of effort and struggle of the militant women. It is a sorry fact, though none the less true, that the subsequent election of Party women to Westminster has not made one tittle of difference either to men or to women, and though many able women have joined the ranks of our elected representatives their influence has been wholly negligible on the destinies of Britain or her Empire. They, like their men colleagues, are simply cogs in the Party wheels of the democratic system, marching into the lobbies at the crack of the Party Whip, helpless before the Juggernaut of the official machinery which rolls on, crushing all initiative and independence before it, and reducing every person who owes it allegiance to a mere cipher for the carrying through of its policies and its measures. And if this be true of Parliament—and who can deny it?—it is even more true of the woman voter. She too, is caught up in this inexorable system, a veritable slave to her Party organization.

To those who challenge this, the question must be put: What power has the woman member or the woman voter, under the present system, to alter any one policy of any government yet elected? Does the most enthusiastic admirer of the present system allege, that women, no matter to what party they belong, are satisfied with the existing position of this country? Are they willing to see economic conditions whereby the employment figures have reached the incredible total of between two and three millions remain unchanged? Do they rest content with the spectacle of those derelict areas which strike despair into the heart of every living person? Are they indifferent to the decay of the agricultural districts and the plight of the farming industry and unconcerned with the appalling housing conditions which all parties alike deplore?

Turning to the vast field of Imperial and Foreign politics, is it to be contended that the bulk of British women desire to see the disintegration of the Empire, or the orientation of the present foreign policy of the alleged National Government, whereby pacts and commitments are being made in their names and in secret with the avowed enemies of this country, while at the same time we are being left defenceless, not only for the purposes of our own immediate defence, but if the need should arise to honour those commitments? Do we indeed know to what we are being committed; what this policy of collective security involves, or what is the sinister power which dictates it? “Democracy is the land of plenty dreamt of by unscrupulous financiers” says Georges Sorel. Have enfranchised women any power to check a Home or a Foreign policy dictated for the purpose of making that dream a living reality? Let it be remembered that when the time comes to foot the bill, we shall be driven as sheep to the slaughter, helpless before the results of these policies. What is the value of so-called freedom if it cannot give us the power to alter these momentous issues?

If it be true that the average woman voter wants none of these things, why, if she be free under the democratic system, does she permit them? If she possesses this freedom, is she not doubly and trebly guilty in suffering them for one hour longer? This is the test of her claim to a responsible part in the government of her country. If she has gained the necessary power and liberty under the existing system, the charge that she is incapable of playing a citizen’s part in the affairs of her country, and is in fact unfitted for responsibility, is proved up to the hilt.

None of these things is true. The truth will be found in the fact that there is no freedom either for men or for women under the present antiquated system. What fetters both men and women is that the

Party system is in decay, and this is the more noticeable since the granting of adult suffrage under an unbridled democracy. Throughout the world the same decadence has set in, by the inevitable march of time and circumstance, the change from a world of poverty to a world of boundless plenty makes ordered planning not only requisite but vital to existence. Under these changes the methods of the old world are obsolete and must give place to the new. If women are to be worthy of their place in the councils of the nation, they must face as realists the new world conditions which are gathering round them. Sooner or later they must choose. The decision is momentous, for upon it will depend the status of women for a considerable period of time. It is therefore no light matter that they should weigh well in the balance the history of the world.

There are two courses open to woman. The first is that she should struggle on with the decaying system of the old world, content to be the handmaid of the professional politicians of the various parties to which she attaches herself. Of this it may be said that she has given it a long and faithful trial, and that if under it she could have accomplished any practical change in the direction of social, political or economic freedom, she has lamentably failed. She must now consider whether the fault lies within herself or within the system to which she still clings. In this connexion she will note that the separate parties are themselves gradually disappearing. The Liberal Party has passed into the twilight of the past; the Conservative Party is in rapid disintegration, and we know upon the assurance of its own Leader, that there is no hope of its regaining its independence. The same fate awaits the Socialist Party, since it too must travel along the same road, which has sucked the other two parties under the quicksand of Social Democracy.

She must therefore look for some better system; one more in accord with modern conditions. What is to take the place of the tottering edifice of the past?

Every student of politics realizes that the issue now lies between Fascism and Communism. So far as British women are concerned, Communism makes little appeal. To go no further, it is the philosophy of destruction, and is the negation of the natural instincts of womanhood. It is the antithesis of every principle and practice which women value and require.

Fascism seems to be the only solution. It has within it every principle peculiarly suitable and adaptable to the genius of the British character.

It offers real freedom and liberty to all men and women of goodwill towards this country. Lest there should be any misunderstanding, we shall define these so often loosely-used terms, in words with which no democrat will quarrel, for they are taken from that apostle of unadulterated democracy, John Stuart Mill.

"The sole end," he wrote, "for which mankind are warranted individually or collectively in interfering with the liberty of action of any of their number, is self-protection. The only purpose for which power can be rightfully exercised over any member of a civilized community against his will is to prevent harm to others."

This is precisely the Fascist conception of individual liberty, and it is obviously a conception that so far as women are concerned gives them every opportunity that they can legitimately require in their future status as women citizens. In no other system are these principles embodied. Moreover, in the machinery of the Corporate State, Fascism assures women an equal status with their menfolk, for it holds within it the only means whereby they will be enabled to direct and control the conditions under which they shall live; thus Fascism alone will complete the work begun on their behalf by the militant women from 1906 to 1914. In addition, it will rescue them from the vitiated atmosphere of corruption inherent in the Party system, and for the first time it will give an opportunity, through the machinery of their own special Corporations, tackling with some hope of success those great questions which so closely concern their own and their children's lives.

In the economic field it will assure security with equal pay for equal work, that eternal bone of contention which has rent the sexes asunder with such dire results to industry.

In the social sphere, it removes all class barriers, while in the political, it gives justice and equality for the first time in history of the Women's struggle.

And most important of all Fascism comes to lay for ever the haunting spectre of war, by removing the fundamental causes, which exist and have their being in Internationalism, an instrument forged for the purpose of enabling "unscrupulous financiers" to take advantage of that "land of plenty" called "democracy" of which they dream.

To enable all this to be accomplished, Fascism will require that women equally with men should offer a disciplined cooperation in the welding together of an ordered State, and Fascism will rightly lay upon all the citizens of the State the responsibility and the duty of working in harmony, not in the interests of any section or class, but for the benefit of all its people. It will call upon women as upon men, to subordinate all selfish individual privileges, that the less fortunate may under its protection be safe from exploitation.

This is Fascism. All else is mirage. Is it to be said that British women cannot rise to this great occasion in the history of their country? Those who would bid them reject this opportunity are the enemies not alone of women, but of all progress and of civilization. Those women who endured the ordeal of the great struggle of pre-war days, have at least earned the right to challenge the people who once again would enslave them in the subjection of the past, and fetter them within a system which denies them all opportunity to play an honourable part in the necessary reorganization of their country. British women have never failed or faltered when Britain has had need of them. They too, with the men of their generation, will raise aloft the banner of British Fascism, and bearing it high above the turmoil and sordid quarrels of the Party system, will hasten that day which shall see their nation reborn. In that triumphant hour, they will have truly earned the proud right to pay homage to a regenerated and Great Britain, and to rest at last within the Peace, Security and Prosperity of her Sovereign People.

Precious Acres
by Jorian Jenks

THOSE who may be tempted to assume that because Britain has no land policy she has no land problem will do well to consider carefully these disquieting facts.

With the exception of Belgium and Holland, Britain is the most densely populated country in the world; and since the proportion of naturally infertile land (e.g., mountain) is much higher in these islands than it is in the Low Countries, it seems indisputable that we have less food-producing land per head of population than any other country.

Britain is the only civilized country in the world without a settled policy of land conservation, reclamation and improvement. Not a single government has taken any step whatsoever to check the annual loss of farmland, which now amounts to over 2 million acres, or 7% of the total, since the close of the Great War.

Britain is unique in the high proportion of her people who are divorced from all contact with their native soil, and in the high proportion of stale, preserved food in the national dietary. Scientists are beginning to discover the results of this artificiality in terms of malnutrition, nervous disorders and social unrest.

A foreign observer might be forgiven for concluding that we are trying in our perverse British fashion to make ourselves the subject of a highly dangerous experiment, namely, to discover whether or not national life can be healthily maintained in a wholly urbanized and virtually parasitic community, dependent for the very necessities of life upon the exertions and the goodwill of other nations. He might further assume that so precarious a situation had been forced upon us by the inclemency of our climate or the poverty of our soil. And his attitude towards us would be one of pity rather than one of admiration.

How painful it is then to have to confess that this alarming situation arises from one cause, and one cause only, namely callous and persistent neglect of first principles. Let there be no mistake about this. Ours is not an inclement climate; on the contrary, it is one of the most equable in the world. Ours is not a poor soil; on the contrary, it is, on the average, one of the most productive in the world. But we have, for our sins, a political system which refuses to look further than the next election, which is bearded by every vested interest with an axe to grind and every misguided economist with an academic reputation to maintain.

It is the profoundest mistake to assume that it is our natural destiny to be manufacturers, carriers and bankers to the rest of the world and that such a situation implies a constant tribute of raw materials and food. For a brief period, certainly, this hypothesis was rendered colourable by the fact that a series of fortunate coincidences gave us a considerable start over other nations in the development of those services for which the world was at that time prepared to pay almost any price. But the swift and well-nigh universal advent of industrial and financial nationalism has swept away our temporary monopoly and has rendered the hypothesis not merely untenable but positively dangerous. The longer we cling to it the less able are we to face the facts of modern life. Every gesture towards the irrevocable "recovery of international trade" postpones the inevitable day of reckoning when we must stand on our own feet and take stock of our own resources.

Because it is the prime source of vital necessities, its careful and enlightened development is a prerequisite of national prosperity. Because it is a national heritage, cultural as well as material, its preservation is a solemn national duty.

It is worth remembering that until comparatively modern times these facts were generally recognized, if not always correctly interpreted. Land-ownership was held to confer not only great privileges but great responsibilities, social as well as pecuniary. The ruling classes were drawn almost exclusively from the landed families. Agriculture was recognized as the great basic industry, and its welfare was a matter of national importance.

It was not until an impoverished landed aristocracy had been supplanted by the upstart and largely alien plutocracy which sprang out of the chaotic finances of the Napoleonic period that the national attitude towards the land underwent any serious deterioration. And it was not until Victorian export-capitalism began to draw its huge import-revenues that British agriculture failed to keep step with the development of British manufactures. But once the doctrine was established that the profits of organized capital are the measure of national prosperity, unorganized agriculture could look in vain to Westminster for assistance or leadership.

And so today a study of the British countryside is almost a study of an extinct civilization. Deep-cut lanes that have not carried wheels for a generation, sprawling hedges that have not seen iron for a decade, ancient plough-marks still visible in thick-turfed pastures, barns and cottages in every stage of decay, churches built for congregations five times the size of the present parishes, silent water-mills and crumbling manors: all speak of a lost rural population once actively engaged on the manliest of all tasks.

It is true, of course, that the better land is still being farmed, and often farmed well, though the number of those with a direct interest in it shrinks year by year. And here and there one finds plucky adventurers staking their all on pigs or poultry, fruit or milk. But over a great part of the countryside there hangs the blight of hand-to-mouth methods born of lack of confidence and expressed in neglected pastures under-stocked with nondescript cattle. So apathetic is the atmosphere that even the wasteful and unlovely incursions of the speculative builder are accepted with hardly a trace of the resentment which such desecration would have aroused a few generations ago.

It is important to realize the extent of the damage which has been done to an irreplaceable national asset. Theoretically land is indestructible, unless, of course, it is washed away by the sea, a process which can, by the way, be witnessed at several spots on our coastline. But several things can happen to it which will render it virtually useless from the viewpoint of food-production, and that is the most vital viewpoint for the nation.

In the first place, cultivated land, whether arable or pasture, can rapidly sink into a derelict condition in which it produces nothing but a scanty picking for store cattle and sheep, and even they go short if the rabbits arrive first. The ominous increase in the acreage returned as "rough grazings" during a period when the farmed area has been steadily shrinking shows clearly enough what has been taking place. The bulk of our rough grazings are, of course, mountain-tops and moorland. But the whole of the recent increase, and a good deal more besides, consists of improvable land of a type which would be farmed in any other European country or even our own Dominions, but which cannot be farmed here in the face of persistent official neglect.

Politicians of the Inskip type like us to believe that this abandoned land can be brought into production in an emergency. Apparently the disillusioning experiences of the last war have not taught them that land cannot suddenly be rushed into productivity by tickling it with a few tractors and some unskilled labour. Land-reclamation is a highly-skilled job requiring some years of patient labour before results can be achieved. It can very usefully be incorporated in a long-term agricultural policy; but as a means of producing food in an emergency it is practically valueless.

In the second place, building operations, whether residential or industrial, use up a great deal of land every year and sterilize fully as much as they actually use. Since 1929 England and Wales alone have lost 421,000 acres of farmland, of which only 159,000 acres have re-appeared as rough grazings; nearly the whole of the remaining 262,000 acres have passed into the maw of the builder, much of it level and fertile arable land in a high state of cultivation.

It should be remembered that the loss of agricultural land does not stop at the area actually occupied by factories, houses and gardens. Roads and recreation grounds must be provided, and there are always, especially in newly developed areas, large blocks of waste land. Moreover, farm land on the fringe of a built-up area or farmland which has been sprinkled, in the modern fashion, with isolated dwellings, suffers considerably. Sparrows and rats come in their thousands; gates and fences are broken down; stray dogs harry livestock and petty damage increases enormously. With the advent of cheap road transport and the consequent outward thrust of suburban development the area thus affected, though still returned as agricultural land, must amount to hundreds of thousands of acres.

It is impossible to escape the conclusion that Britain is squandering her national heritage at a time when the course of world events is making it of vital importance that she should conserve every acre. Those who may consider this an alarmist statement are advised to study carefully Professor R. G. Stapledon's recent work, *The Land; Now and To-morrow*. The authority considers that "our agricultural acres are dwindling rapidly, and dwindle they inevitably must, and, unless some decision is made as to the minimum acreage that should at all costs be retained for food production and appropriate action taken, no more than two hundred years hence may see the farm lands of England reduced to one half."

Two hundred years may sound a long time, but is there anyone bold enough to suggest that our children, much less our grandchildren, will be able to draw unlimited food supplies from the Americas and the Antipodes? Do we wish to go down to history as the generation which dissipated the national estate and left our descendants to face the elementary problem of starvation? Victorian export-capitalism has bequeathed us the Distressed Areas; are we to be responsible for a new set of Wasted Areas?

Further consideration of the nutritional and economic aspects of our land problem would lead us deep into a discussion of the many functions of agriculture as an integral part of national life. It is necessary, therefore, to break off in order to discuss the equally important cultural aspect.

This aspect, it is true, is already receiving some attention in a spasmodic and one-sided fashion under the town-planning movement. But the very name of this movement reveals its limitations. A community which has been encouraged to forget the significance of its agriculture and to regard imported food supplies as a natural phenomenon has come to regard countryside as a mere adjunct to the towns, a sort of glorified public park. There is, indeed, a great danger that rural England may become a character-less "open space" in the same way that a huge slice of the Home Counties has become a featureless garden-suburb.

The innate craving of an urbanized people to escape from the noisy, contaminated atmosphere of their cities can evoke nothing but sympathy. That these people will cheerfully spend half their Sunday swallowing petrol fumes on a congested main road in order that they may spend the other half in fresh air is pathetically significant. The pity of it is that so many of them seem incapable of grasping the fruit of their enterprise without spoiling it.

For the countryside cannot fulfil its cultural function unless it is allowed to preserve its own character, and that character is inseparable from its material or agricultural function. The town cannot escape the town, if it takes the town with it, any more than the intellectual can give his mind a holiday, if he takes his arguments with him on his country walks. The sight of a village suburbanized by those who have come to "live in the country" is as pathetic as the sight of a band of intellectuals striding along in full spate of talk while around them are ten thousand activities more interesting and important than their own. As a farmer put it not long ago, "I don't so much mind 'em walking across my fields. I don't so much mind 'em exercising their fool dogs at my expense. I don't even mind 'em scrambling over gates that a child could open. But when I think that they've walked over two miles of good farming land and never once thought to look what was going on, I feel my courtesy's been wasted."

What we may term the "public park" attitude finds expressions in ways more serious than indifference to rural activities. Just as the urchin thinks it no harm to throw stones at the ducks when the keeper is not looking, so there are thousands of educated adults who see no harm in petty trespass when there is little or no chance of detection. And the cumulative effect of petty trespasses is creating an unpleasant situation in districts favoured by urban escapists.

In Germany fruit trees are planted in roadside hedges and the land is cultivated right to the edge of the metal. In England, such a procedure is utterly impossible, for the trees would be stripped by organized raiding-parties and the crops trampled flat for a chain's width. The Briton is not necessarily less honest or more destructive than the German; he has simply been de-ruralized to such an extent that his sense of values and his code of moral behaviour cease with the last lamp-post. Persons who would be shocked at the idea of filching a penny pencil from a shop-counter will see nothing immoral in breaking through half a dozen hedges in order to steal mushrooms.

The countryside has so much real wealth to offer its visitors that the obvious way to overcome present deplorable tendencies is to show people where this wealth lies. Even now there are many who can and do appreciate the healing balm of solitude, the spiritual comfort of peace and security, the absorbing interest of the ever-changing fields and woods; but they are all too few. No one will willingly injure or deface that in which he feels a keen personal interest, and the first step towards the preservation of the countryside is a national drive towards the development of what Professor Stapledon calls "rural mindedness".

A Fascist Government will naturally have to face the land problem in its entirety, for the land is one of the bases on which is built its conception of living nationhood. Indeed its avowed policy of agricultural development will itself create an urgent problem by stimulating speculative activity in the estate market, and this activity will have to be severely dealt with before agricultural policy can be fully developed.

The Fascist attitude towards the land can be set forth in a few sentences.

Land must no longer be regarded as a speculative commodity. Its value must be fairly appraised, and all increment must be shared by those who have helped to create it, including the State.

Land-utilization must be the subject of careful long-term national planning. So far as possible, building activity must be confined to areas of low agricultural value.

Land-ownership must be as widely diffused as possible, the object being a large number of small, secure family freeholds. It will, however, also entail responsibilities, and those who misuse their land will be regarded as social enemies.

Public access to the land must be improved by the extension and better definition of field-paths, camping-sites and roadside halts. At the same time the law of trespass must be revised and the rural community given better protection against interference and damage. Possibly it may be necessary to establish a corps of wardens.

War must be waged on such pests as rabbits, rooks and pigeons; and while there will be no discrimination against field-sports, such sports must not be allowed to interfere with either agricultural or recreational activities.

The public must be educated to respect and appreciate the countryside and to take an intelligent interest in its activities.

We are not as a race much given to sentimentalizing about the land. We use the word Motherland but seldom, Fatherland never. A century of *laissez-faire* Liberalism and financial Conservatism has bred a short-sighted commercialized attitude towards our soil.

Yet the Britain of our dreams, the physical embodiment of our national spirit, is not a Britain of streets and factories or even of parks and public buildings, but a Britain of smiling valleys and rolling uplands, of tilled fields and snug homesteads. A city is a city the whole world over; and the cities of the world are tending yearly towards standardization. But rural Britain is peculiarly our own, inseparable from our national character. We must preserve it jealously, not in the museum-like atmosphere of a Stratford-on-Avon but in the natural vigour of productivity.

Few of us are more than a few generations removed from the soil. A little re-education by Press and radio would make us countrymen again, at least in our leisure moments: not the education of the professional schoolmaster, whose "agriculture" consists of useful but rather dreary elementary science, but the education which would send us out into the lanes and field-paths with open eyes and enquiring minds. An introduction to the history and everyday life of the countryside would not only encourage the townsman to appreciate the problems of agriculture but invest his rural outings with absorbing interest. Intelligent rural-mindedness could be made the finest possible antidote to the stress of urban life, for Mother Earth can provide comfort for the soul as well as for the body.

Hitler's Berchtesgaden an Idyll of New Germany

by Joan Morgan

EVEN if you know Bavaria well, and even if you bear in mind that the Wittelbachs with all Bavaria and the Führer with all Germany to choose from picked on Berchtesgaden for their summer houses, nothing quite prepares you for this place that contrives to be at one and the same time both the heart of the old Bavaria and the soul of the new Germany. All that you dreamed of Bavaria at its most fairy-tale and National Socialism at its finest is compressed in this mountain-locked market town that boasts about the same population as London's newest block of flats.

After the train leaves Bad Reichenhall it runs deeper and deeper into the mountains until you feel that they will completely envelop you as you wind up the deep valley that is a wedge of Germany driven into Austria. (It is possible, and rather a thrill, to walk to Austria in any of three directions.)

The first impression is one of movement. Everybody from two years old upwards is on his toes in a sort of expectancy. Whether this is due to altitude, Bavarian high spirits or the fact that the Führer may drive through at any moment, I have never discovered; the fact remains that the air tingles with vitality.

Here in this adorably musical-comedy setting National Socialism seems very good fun. Except at occasional meetings, which are simple and strangely inspiring, you are not so aware of the deep mystical seriousness of it all; the immensity of the task accomplished and the task ahead.

You feel that the S.S. with its attractive uniform, contact with the Führer, and a healthy life in lovely surroundings is a very pleasant occupation, and the S.S. is indeed a splendid organisation, open to all ages and classes on the common ground of patriotism.

Here, more than anywhere else in Germany, you see how everyone from the oldest S.S. member down to the youngest child selling Winter Relief badges has a stake in the country; no one suffers from the soul-destroying agony of feeling unwanted. Every achievement is their achievement; every setback theirs. You realize how National Socialism, in restoring hope, revitalizing faith in the future of their country, has given the people something to live for.

The centuries-old life of the place goes on as it always has, plus National Socialism; and therefore, life in Berchtesgaden is a non-stop show. When the curtain falls on one act, up goes another. You hear a monotoned hum past your window stream a hundred peasant women in national dress with the little black-green-red knitted coats they call Berchtesgadners. With them is a priest, and they move slowly, chanting, with downcast eyes. Later you hear the shrill voices of the young B.D.M. (Hitler girls) marching along in their short brown coats, or a troop of Hitler Jugend, huge virile boys carrying banners. There is always a marching song in the air.

When all else fails, they have fire-drill. A hundred firemen (or one to every thirty inhabitants) in tunics, helmets and plus-fours perform daringly in front of your window. Sunday is, however, the day. In the Markt Platz, which is the apex of the town, the peasants assemble; the men, vying with each other in the immensity of the brushes in their green hats, on one side of the fountain with its Bavarian lion, on the other the women with flat black hats perched on their coronets of plaits. At ten they adjourn for beer and sausages-in-soup to Neuhaus (that small brother of the Hofbrauhaus) with its beer-garden under the chestnut trees, where they air your bedding on the fence of the Wittelsbach Schloss, its *bierstube* with its unsurpassed gemütlichkeit, where Party Leaders rub shoulders with guides; vital centre of a vital town.

The Grand Hotel, grand enough for anybody. The Kurhaus with its excellent orchestra and visiting players from Munich. The Peasant Theatre, with its crude wit and attractive music. There are the dance places; Hofschaffer with its intimate atmosphere, its pocket-handkerchief floor packed beyond the dreams of a London *maitre de hotel,* and the Kur Cafe, where the immense, elegant boys of the S.S. Bodyguard dance in what was once a Royal villa of the House of Bavaria. There are the artists, Fritz Richter with his strange inspired woodcuts, and one of the first-class landscape painters of the modern Alpine school.

To come out into the open: first, there is the Führer's house, on top of the world, with a wall of glass looking out on to a procession of mountains, perched on such a precipitous site that it seems to be leaning back. The house dominates the valley as the Führer dominates the town.

There is Konigsee, loveliest of all Alpine lakes, deepest green with sheer mountains hemming it in on all sides. There is the Zauberwald, a magic wood, where the stream from Hintersee dashes through green plush rocks.

There is the salt mine where (in this land of uniforms) you dress up in a black tunic and white plus fours (which is not nearly as *chic* and becoming as it sounds) and toboggan down to an underground lake with a necklace of lights and a swastika at the further end. There is the Schloss Platz with its war memorial.

There are the Alpine meadows with Nature's succession of colour schemes, pink one week, blue and yellow the next, which would drive to envious distraction the florists of London, Paris and New York.

There are the forests, uniform, marching straight and strong up to the snow line. The mountains; lovely Watzmann, second highest in Germany; bleak Goll and rugged, legend-haunted Untersberg. For the stout hearted there is the floodlit ice-hole, six thousand feet up inside Untersberg, and also there is Almbach Klamm, a roaring, stunning gorge, where you seem to go down far more than you went up, which ends only when you have given up hope and comes under the heading "Emotional Experience" and not "Scenery".

In Berchtesgadener Land they greet you equally with "Grass Gott" and "Heil Hitler!" No wonder, Greetings to God for having created anything as lovely and Hail Hitler for having saved it for the people who love it more than life.

A Nordic World Federation by Vidkun Quisling

Leader of the Norwegian Nasjonal Samling

AN old world falls, a new is being born. Simultaneously with our third annual rally in Stavanger last year, the seventh World Congress of the Communist International was opened in the former "noblemen's club" in Moscow, after an interim period of seven years since the last world congress in 1928.

The congress lasted from July 25 to August 21. Its primary purpose was to review what the Jewish international Marxist conspiracy had accomplished during those seven years inside and outside Soviet Russia with regard to the execution of Stalin's programme for the Bolshevizing of the world, which had been the subject of discussion at the previous world congress.

Secondly, it confirmed the tactics of its programme to destroy the forces of national resistance and light the fire of the Communist world revolution. Emphasis was specially laid on the tactics of the so-called united and popular front, which we have seen developing in France, Spain, Belgium and elsewhere. We are also well acquainted with it here in Norway in the so-called "crisis agreement" with the farmers' party and in the new camouflage tactics of the Labour Party through its adoption of a bourgeois and national disguise. Another matter which touches our country directly, namely, the participation of Soviet Russia in the League of Nations, is also a symptom of the same popular front tactics which have long been incorporated in the programme of the Komintem.

This year, while we of the Nasjonal Samling are met together for our annual rally, we see the summoning of another world congress.

This time the shareholders of the bankrupt concern of the League of Nations are holding their Special General Meeting to discuss the liquidation of the undertaking or its possible reconstruction in the autumn, when the assembly holds its customary annual meeting.

I mention these events, which have occurred simultaneously with our two last national rallies, not only on account of their great importance, but because these things illustrate very markedly the foreign political situation which faces us today.

On one side we have an untiringly active world Bolshevism, which, from an historical point of view, is simply an alarming symptom of the passing of the old world, and a persistent effort of sinister powers to force world evolution into their own way of destruction, that is, towards a universal materialist republic under Jewish dictatorship.

On the other side we find the aimless attempts of the old world to solve the imperative demands of the present day, the demands for peace and cooperation among the nations. The whole affair is frustrated by the clash of individual interests, just as the internal national collaboration which the situation demands is being wrecked by class war and selfish party conflicts. This process of disintegration is accompanied by unrest and crises, war and civil strife. The internationalist powers intervene and the whole concern lapses gradually into Marxism and destruction in just the same way the bourgeois-liberal state is being gradually consumed, by Marxism, as we see so clearly in our own country. Amidst all this the ever-youthful stock of humanity is putting forth fresh shoots; national movements of renaissance and unification heralding the new age, bringing in a new State and a new world order. The new order is under way in this country also.

Sanctions And The League Collapse

Another significant fact is that the collapse of that bourgeois parliamentary capitalist institution, the League of Nations, is not due merely to its own unsoundness and the subterranean activities of Marxism or to the fundamental and formal errors in the organization of the League.

It has been wrecked by Fascist Italy, one of the representatives of the organized communities of the new age. In spite of the fifty sanctionist states and the opposition of the whole democratic and Marxist world, and the world opinion which was mobilized against Fascism and Italy, national unity proved to be the strongest force.

Without in any way identifying themselves with Italian Fascism or Italian interests, the leaders of the Nasjonal Samling have, from the very beginning, taken up a clear and definite standpoint towards the Ethiopian conflict. They have stood for the neutrality of Norway and against her participation in the so-called sanctions.

In this we were solely influenced by consideration for the interests of our country. I believe, however, that public opinion here, as in many other places, was the victim of propaganda which in reality served quite other interests than the high ideals which it pretended to instil.

Our movement, however, took no sides. We demanded Norway's neutrality, and demonstrated the hypocrisy and aimlessness of the whole sanctionist game. We can say today that we judged the situation correctly.

From a military point of view we were right. In spite of the general opinion we valued correctly the significance of modern war materials as well as the power of resistance of Ethiopia and England, and not least the immense moral and material strength created in a people organized for a united effort on an historical and national foundation.

Politically also we judged correctly. The uselessness and the serious miscalculations of the sanctionist policy are now evident. Look at the tragic discomfiture of mighty England on account of its short-sighted League policy; it is the greatest moral and practical defeat which the British Empire has suffered since it lost America.

Soviet Russia, that new and remarkable member of the League of Nations, saw in the sanctions policy a possibility of picking a quarrel first with Mussolini and then with Hitler, but when their calculations began to miscarry the wily Bolshevik Jews retired quietly into the background and, getting off scot free themselves, left the British Government to bear the blame and suffer the disgrace.

Nationalist Policy And International Cooperation

For the first time since the world war Norway has had to face real hard facts in foreign policy, which make it very difficult to carry on the usual parochial politics.

In this connexion, I wish to emphasize a fact which is sadly underestimated in this country: namely that the lives of the people are dominated by foreign policy and not by home politics. Next to a nation's own "will-to-live" its internal conditions and its structure are dominated by international conditions of economy and power. These conditions are created by the primitive and peremptory needs of peoples and states, by their struggle for existence and for space to live in. But the influence of a state in foreign politics always corresponds to the degree of development of its internal strength.

Thus the necessity of self-support in case of war and, above all, the remaking of the structure of world economy simply force communities to organize themselves on an economic basis as national Workers' States. The altered conditions throughout the world force every nation to deal with its neighbours as an organized economic unit with full and capable control of all its resources and power to utilize them in the best way possible. To this extent the present crisis is mainly a crisis of readjustment in world production and trade.

There is, however, no inherent opposition between the demand of the age for these united and strongly characterized economic national units and the demand for planned international cooperation, which is driven forward with irresistible force by economic causes as well as by the consideration of the maintenance of peace.

It is just the formation of such organized national personalities which will bring about honest and effective international cooperation, free from either partiality or oppression.

Two Hostile Camps In Europe And In The World

The situation is that in the world and especially in Europe two hostile camps are being formed in the same way as before the world war. Soviet Russia, France and Czechoslovakia, backed by international Jewry, which is inciting them to war against National Socialist Germany, are already presenting a united front against that country and are seeking to encircle Germany still further, both politically and militarily.

Under these conditions the position of Norway is extremely exposed, situated as it is at the crossroads of Russia, Germany and England and with its internal policy already in the power of Marxists.

Russia, from being a great European power with Asiatic interests, has become a great Asiatic power with European interests, especially towards the Atlantic. But, above all, it is the base of the world revolution.

World Bolshevism is attempting to turn Norway, and with it Scandinavia as a whole, into the right wing of its European front of attack against Germany and England. This plan contains sinister possibilities for our country. In the event of a conflict between

Germany and Soviet Russia the whole outlook of the Labour Party will drive Norway to take the side of the Bolsheviks in opposition to Germany, and this will be contrary to our pledge of neutrality. Tranmal, the irresponsible dictator of the Labour Party, has recently spoken clearly enough in this direction. As long as Norway and Soviet Russia are members of the present League of Nations and Germany is not, it appears that we are seriously threatened with war in this direction, for we are bound to allow the Red Army and Air Force free transit through the country in case of a German-Russian conflict.

Under the present conditions in Europe the possibility also exists that Germany and England may go to war. This may occur, for example, in connexion with a conflict between Germany and the triple alliance of France, Czechoslovakia and Soviet Russia, Czechoslovakia being an almost more sensitive spot than Austria. That France will then go to war against Germany would provide England with reason for war, which is even more certain now than before the enormous development of aviation.

Such a war between England and Germany is a catastrophic possibility for Norway, for since the world war the whole situation is now totally changed.

Through the League of Nations as an instrument of British world policy we should then be forced straight into the war and, even if the League of Nations falls to pieces, we should, according to such an authority as Lord Lloyd, be certainly exposed to a punitive bombardment if, as was the case in the world war, we allowed our merchant fleet to carry goods for England, which she for her part would undoubtedly insist on now as she did then.

The Norwegian Labour Party—The Government Party —is actively assisting this policy aimed at Germany. If Norway agrees to this, it means that we are irretrievably drawn straight into this war policy against the wish of at least 99 per cent, of the Norwegian people. Norway cannot and will not march unless our own freedom and our own boundaries are in danger.

Peace With England And Germany

I have already emphasized that peace between Germany and England is a vital necessity to our own country. What we must, above all, prevent, is that Germany and England should be on opposite sides in a new war. To us this would be fatal; indeed, it would mean destruction.

Therefore, it depends on us to do everything in our power to create peace and understanding between these two countries who, like ourselves, are of Nordic descent and outlook. Even if we are unable to do a great deal in this respect and have to be careful not to interfere in the affairs of other countries, it must be our immediate duty by all just means to oppose those who are attempting to stir up dissension between these our kinsmen, usually on false and dishonest grounds.

We know the powers for whose interests these efforts are really being made. One is world Bolshevism. To work for peace and conciliation between Germany and England should be our aim for Norwegian foreign policy without consideration of party interests. It is in the highest degree apparent that the interests of Norway demand this. The only way in which we can escape war and chaos depends upon the maintenance of peace and understanding between these great neighbours of ours to the south and west, with whom we have also the largest trading connexion.

About 40 years ago there was, as there is now, an opportunity for an honest attempt to create a lasting understanding between the great Nordic peoples. The opportunity was neglected or turned down, and the catastrophe which followed this omission involved the whole world. Anyone who now dares to promote the same catastrophic policy must do it with his eyes open.

But everyone who understands the times in which we live must bestir himself to take strong and positive counteraction.

Another decisive consideration brings us to the same conclusion as to the main lines of our foreign policy. Decadent liberalism and its offspring and heir, Marxism, have their aims directed against national communities, primarily against the Nordic.

Consciously or unconsciously, the aim of this policy is to break down the natural national organization of the peoples in order to realize the international world republic.

Then the inner cohesion of the nations will be destroyed. They will be the prey of that nation which, in contrast to all other nations, is dispersed over the whole earth and lives as parasites upon the other nations; for that very reason it needs such an arrangement in order to *effect* its passionately desired mastery of the world. For in that mastery lies the secret of Jewish nationalism and imperialism.

A duel between Judaism and the Nordic spirit is inevitable, since Marxism and internationalism are in reality Jewish nationalism and imperialism, a conspiracy inspired and led by Judaism against the definitely Nordic European civilization. It is clear that the decaying processes of the present day are the most serious menace to ideals of life and that the most powerful antagonisms of our time have been narrowed down to a struggle between Judaism and the Nordic-European principle. This being the case, we must realize that the most effective remedy for the present decadence and the subterranean activities of Marxist materialism will be found in a national renaissance for our people on the vitalizing or vital foundation of the Nordic race and characteristic temperament.

And, on the other hand, there must be in the widest sense closer cultural, economic and political collaboration between the Nordic and Nordically determined peoples all the world over: in the Scandinavian countries, in Holland, Flanders, the British Empire, Germany, and in other countries where members of the Nordic family are comparatively less numerous.

The meaning of the word "Nordic" is, therefore, not restricted to the Scandinavian peoples but applies to all the great Nordic races, and we are not now considering an insecure northern collaboration.

On the contrary, it is, on the one hand, a necessary consequence of the realization that to uphold national character and organization is the most important life-issue for all creative peoples. Only in this way is it possible to secure a free and peaceful development for Norse culture and characteristics, both in the national and the universal spheres. At the same time, it is one of the conditions of a deeply-rooted recognition of the value and cultural contributions of other races and it will thus fortify all nations against dissolution and chaos.

On the other hand, it is an inevitable consequence of the fact that the international collaboration which must be built up in these times should preferably be based upon the Nordic peoples who are so closely related in race, language, culture and interests. They have the same standard of living and a similar view of life, and are also grouped together geographically. Economically, too, they are one another's best customers.

A Union Of Nordic Peoples

A block-formation of these peoples, a union of Nordic peoples, will be unconquerable. Such a union will be much more able than the bankrupt liberalist-Marxist League of Geneva to act as a bulwark against world *Bolshevism* and create guarantees for the peaceful development of the world. The way to organized humanity will be found in a union of the great Nordic family of peoples in such a block-formation with a common currency, internal free trade and a common customs policy; it will be their aim to draw other countries and groups of powers into this system.

Such a foreign policy will be the best guarantee of Norway's position in the world and against Bolshevism. And for the benefit of ourselves and others it will create a field of activity abroad for the surplus of energy which must be expected in this country if our own resources are inadequate.

Cooperation Founded On National Movements

While emphasizing the Nordic common destiny we must not underrate the significance and the accomplishments of others or of our common humanity; and, above all, we must not under-value the importance of ordinary European and universal cooperation. But this international fellowship must be founded on a system of national states. It must be created by the national uplift of peoples in Europe and throughout the world and not as the result of liberalist and Marxist experiments such as the League of Nations, Pan-Europe and Soviet Russia, the seat of the world Soviet Republic.

The history of life shows that all progress is dependent on union of freedom and discrimination with fellowship and organization. Universal monarchies and world republics end in anarchy and dissolution. The hegemony of a single nation is disastrous to others and to itself. A Babel-like compound of all nations and races, which is the aim of liberalism and Marxism, spells destruction to the individual characteristics and values of each one. History teaches us that true harmony is the result of segregation and development.

Mankind's instinct for organized formation is directed towards national life and the cooperation of national unities. For this reason all the international institutions which have proceeded from liberalism and Marxism have failed in their alleged aims, which were to secure a good understanding between the nations and promote their progress.

A Nordic World Federation by Vidkun Quisling

In view of the failure of liberalist League ideas and of international Marxism, it is urgently necessary to create a new fellowship of the nations with a European and worldwide character, founded on the new ideas for the organization of the communities which were laid down by the congress of the new order in Montreux on December 16 and 17, 1934 the first consideration of the congress is that of respect for spiritual and national values.

In place of the hypocritical and technical methods of the old diplomacy there must be evolved a spontaneous and honourable collaboration between all young and healthy national movements, and the national states re-created by them in order to obtain a general spiritual renewal and a political and economic recovery throughout the world. But within the framework of this universal plan the nations who come of one stock and share the same culture and civilization must group themselves together in accordance with their closest interests.

The Nordic World Movement

The main principle on which the Nasjonal Samling takes its stand is that our politics, besides meeting the demands which modern changes have made imperative, must be in harmony with everything needed and desired by our family of nations. It is useless to expect national recovery unless we rekindle the fire of the Norse spirit and build on a spiritual and responsible view of life.

No progress can be expected if we do not keep the Nordic strain unmixed; if we do not preserve our distinctive character, we shall lose it and go on towards national extinction.

The so-called Nordic idea, that a Nordic people can only be restored by building a new state in accordance with modern demands and on the double foundation of a national stock and a spiritual outlook, has a steadily growing influence and currency in the respective Nordic countries and already plays an important part in practical politics.

The seed and the soil for a pan-Nordic collaboration are thus already in existence. But, in order that the idea may spread quickly enough, it must find a definite and adequately organized expression.

In these circumstances, I consider that the time has come for us to proceed to promote a cultural, economic and political collaboration between the Nordic peoples and others with a Nordic outlook throughout the world with the following aims:

- The creation of an international Nordic movement.
- The formation of a Nordic Union of peoples.

Active participation in work for the organization of the world and its peaceful development; and for ensuring the place and contribution of our own country under the revolutions and new constitutions which are now in progress. This collaboration must start, as usual, in the field of ideas, in order to be politically achieved upon a solid economic foundation.

If, therefore, the existing basis of currency could be expanded into an established currency union between the Nordic peoples, and if through political fiscal collaboration a Customs Union could be effected between these peoples, the foundation would have been thoroughly laid for the political realization of our avowed aims: a great union of Nordic peoples in the world-fellowship.

This ideal has for a considerable time formed part of the Nasjonal Samling's programme. It follows that the Pan-Nordic collaboration actually implies a further intensifying of the cooperation of the Northern states in the narrower sense: Norway, Sweden, Denmark, Finland and the Norse islands in the North Sea. The position of Denmark and Finland is so much more exposed than that of Norway and Sweden that Norway, at any rate, is excluded from voluntarily linking her fate to these countries without the support which would be obtained from a peaceful and assured relationship with England and Germany. But, this having been safeguarded, it is also desirable that the Northern countries should take their place as a natural group in the Nordic world - collaboration alongside of Britons, Germans, Netherlanders and the rest.

In this connexion, I wish to emphasize the fact that it does not alter the case if many people in this country find that they must disagree with various details in the British and German policy. The conditions which today necessitate cooperation with and between these kinsmen of ours are more important than those which may tend to separate us.

There may also be those who object to our having any foreign policy at all, and consider our own affairs to be quite as much as we can manage. I would remind them that the characteristic feature of our time is the fact that the world is becoming one great economic unit and that no country can any longer be sufficient unto itself; it is dependent on the others; and, if such collaboration in current politics is of vital interest to our country, it is equally so to our movement. As the forces working for our national destruction are internationally organized, we are obliged to meet them with an organization which aims beyond national interests. A fully effective organization of this kind can only be built up on the common vital basis of our peoples, the Nordic principle.

The Nordic Principle

The Nordic Principle rests on Nordic traditions, Nordic thought and constructive cooperation, in contrast to Jewish liberalism and Marxism, which promote their destructive purposes by means of hatred, envy and class war for their own ends. One is allied to the Divine; the other to the diabolical.

The spiritual power of the Nordic principle is, therefore, stronger and deeper than the Marxist-materialist view of existence which is threatening our race and civilization with destruction. It is in reality our intrinsic national Principle to which we must adhere and which we must realize with inexorable consistency.

It is also my conviction that, when we recognize the profound truths of the historic past as well as the historic present, and see the great things accomplished by peoples of Nordic race from the beginning of history until our day, when they are more powerful than ever before; and when, at the same time, we are convinced that the Divine Will is revealed in the historical course of world development, we must, without under-estimating the importance and contribution of others, be permitted to believe in the continued historical and divine mission of the Nordic peoples in the world. As in times past, it must be the mission of our great family of peoples to do away with an obsolete world and create a new world which can place the whole human family on the upward grade.

The Nasjonal Samling invites all people of Nordic race and outlook in every country—Norwegians, Swedes, Danes, Icelanders, Britons, Germans, Dutch and all others of Nordic blood and spirit—to unite in a Nordic World Movement to create peace and cooperation between all Nordic peoples throughout the world and to carry on the struggle for the salvation and progress of our civilization.

An Interpretation Of Fascism
by Claud Sutton

FASCISM, in the sense in which it will be used in this article, is an awkward and inconvenient term to describe the world movement which has emerged in our time to compete with Marxism and Liberal-Democracy for men's allegiance. It should undoubtedly be confined to naming the special form which this movement has taken in Italy. Nevertheless, the popular mind, feeling that in Italian Fascism something new and of worldwide import had emerged, persists in using the term in a wider sense.

Fascism is not international as Communism is, in the sense of being a dogma to be thrust down the throat of every nation, regardless of its history and circumstances. It is rather an underlying similarity of outlook which can be detected in various modern national movements, and which may be seen to emerge with a kind of necessity from the situation in which our European culture finds itself at present. We in England share in the common cultural inheritance of Europe; just as we were most profoundly affected by the ideas of the French Revolution, so we are bound to be deeply affected by the ideas of the Fascist movement, and to react to these ideas in our own particular national way.

The two factors which are everywhere giving birth to this movement are the decay of Liberal-Democracy and the rise of Marxism.

It needs but a slight acquaintance with history to realize that there is nothing inevitable or eternal about Liberal-Democracy. Compared with other forms of government, democratic governments have neither been common nor stable, nor have they contributed as much of enduring value to human culture as have aristocratic and monarchical governments. Of course it is possible—and often done—to define Democracy in such a way as to include in it all tolerable forms of government whatever,—for instance, to describe England under Queen Elizabeth or under Pitt as a democracy. But this is a gross misuse of language and a debasing of the intellectual currency. "Democracy" should not be used to denote every government which rules by the consent of nearly all the governed; nor one which consciously pursues the welfare of the whole people; nor one which is tolerant of a variety of opinions and encourages free discussion; nor one which rules according to settled and known law, impartially applied. Many democratic governments have failed conspicuously in these respects; many non-democratic governments have exhibited these virtues in a high degree. It is absurd to call "democracy" any government which is not tyrannical; democracy is one particular historical form of government, which has sometimes worked to the general satisfaction, sometimes not. Its chief feature would seem to be the decision of all important questions by majority vote, either of the whole people or of large representative assemblies.

Democracy as we know it in Western Europe and America—which I shall hereafter term "liberal-democracy" —is a special product of the French Revolution, and based upon the peculiar theories of certain influential thinkers of that era. The underlying philosophy of human nature on which it is based has not always been accepted by thinking men, and there is no reason to suppose that its sway over men's minds will be eternal. On the contrary, there is considerable evidence that this philosophy of the "Rights of Man and of the Citizen" no longer carries conviction, and that the system of government based upon it is therefore doomed to pass away.

Like other political philosophies, it did not win general acceptance without a struggle. But today, who can detect any difference between Conservatives, Liberals and right-wing (non-Marxian) Labour in respect of their ideals or the general character of the methods by which they propose to realize them?

What are the philosophical assumptions, or axioms, of this system of Liberal-Democracy? The first is, that all men are equal, at least to the extent that they must have an equal share in government. The second is, that government only exists in order to prevent any man interfering with the equal liberty of others (J. S. Mill); or as more forcibly expressed to me by a student: "government only exists to enable every man to go to hell in his own way". The third, that such individual liberty results in the greatest possible satisfaction of all. [1]

1 This third axiom, as M. Haldv has pointed out, takes two forms. On one version, maximum social satisfaction results automatically from maximum individual liberty, whatever the laws and institutions of the society. On the other, certain legal restrictions are necessary to achieve this greatest sum of satisfactions. Most writers do not stick quite consistently to the one version or the other; but they have no doubt about the end, nor about the means—individual liberty restricted as little as possible. (E. Halevy :

Fascism is based on the denial of all these principles. To the first it replies that all men are not equal in their capacity for cooperative enterprise,—and government is a cooperative enterprise. Men differ markedly in respect of their courage, fairness, loyalty, veracity and other qualities of character which are required for any corporate undertaking. Such qualities are not the monopoly of any class, nor dependent on education in the ordinary sense of the word. Some men are markedly deficient in them—all the Old Bolshevik leaders for example, if we are to believe their confessions; anyone of us would try to exclude them from power in any organization for which he was responsible.

Political representation must be based on a selective system of real groups whose members are personally acquainted with one another. A good political system should not even try to ensure that all opinions have equal weight.

To the second principle it observes that equal liberty is impossible, for men do not all want to do the same things; that every system of law presupposes some positive ideas as to what is objectively good or bad for everyone; that the principle is either meaningless or disastrous.

To the third, that owing to the nature of man and society, the greatest possible sum of satisfaction cannot be achieved by the system of maximum individual liberty; nor is this "greatest happiness of the greatest number, everyone to count for one and no one for more than one"[2] the end of life. Men are and should be more interested in the welfare of their own family, their own profession, their own neighbourhood, their own nation; and good government should take account of this fact. We shall return to these points later.

Liberal-democracy is a lazy philosophy. Instead of making up one's mind what ought to be done and fighting tenaciously to get it realized, the good democrat waits and sees which way the majority will jump, secure in his belief that the voice of the masses is the voice of God. We must not even seek to persuade people of today the driving power of Liberal-Democracy has everywhere run down. Few people wholeheartedly believe in its slogans. Half its present-day advocates are really timid Marxists. Their avowed end is equal wealth for all, and democracy merely a means to this. They fondly imagine that this end can be achieved by mere voting, without force, at least in the

Growth of Philosophic. Radicalism.)

2 J. Bentham: Principles of Morals and Legislation. Follett: The New State, p. 27.

distant-future. They frequently betray their contempt for individual liberty as such. They are envious, but they care for their skins. Such are the Lib-Lab Social-democrats.

What is the philosophical basis of the unholy alliance between Communists and Democrats, wherever Fascism appears on the scene? To this problem we must now turn our attention.

Communism—or better Marxism, for there are many Marxists outside of the Communist Party—is altogether a product of the individualistic, equalitarian philosophy of Liberal-democracy. Frequent in history have been revolutionary movements of the less fortunate classes; this one has taken over the peculiar ideology of the early Victorian era in which it was born. It too conceives the community as a collection, and social happiness as a sum. It accepts the first two principles of Liberal-democracy; all men are equal —though there is no God—and therefore they ought to have not merely equal political rights, but equal wealth.[3] Again, happiness is to be achieved by giving everyone equal wealth and then letting them do what they like with it; when once economic equality is achieved, the state is to "wither away". But it most emphatically rejects the third principle of Liberal-democracy, that this happy condition of things comes about by letting people alone. *Laisser-faire* is the ultimate aim, when once economic equality has been achieved; but this has to be achieved by the forcible dictatorship of the proletariat, that is, of the unskilled factory-worker.

Its central doctrine is the Class-war between proletarians and capitalists. It persists in herding all mankind into these two pens, although no economist any longer takes seriously the "surplus-value" theory upon which the distinction was based. How unreal the two pens are! There is indeed conflict between groups, and such conflict is of the essence of a live community. But a large proportion of the inhabitants of the modern state, who live on the joint proceeds of their work and of the property needed to make that work fruitful, cannot be squeezed into either pen except by a tour-de-force. And are not the conflicts of interests between townsmen and countrymen, between manufacturers and financiers, between craftsmen and unskilled labourers, between racial groups and religious groups, just as real and vital as this alleged one between capitalists and proletariat?

---

3 Contrast Aristotle. *Politics* III, 9 and 12: " Justice is giving equal treatment to equals, and unequal treatment to unequals. Men omit one factor or the other, as it suits them; for they are not good judges in their own cause." But this should not free us from the duty of judging as well as we can.

The keynote of Marxism is the class-war, in which all methods are allowable. That is why, wherever it raises its head, politics become so embittered and so dirty it destroys all sense of the moral unity of the nation which previously mitigated conflicts between groups. That is why it must be fought to the death.

But, it will be said, has nothing of any value been achieved through the Communist experiment in Russia? And is there no resemblance between the "dictatorships" of Communism and Fascism?

It is impossible to understand the development of Communism in Russia, unless we distinguish the present stage of "Bolshevism in Retreat", as it has been termed, from the earlier stage in which doctrinaire Communism had full sway. This earlier stage was marked by an unparalleled destruction, for the sake of the class-war theory, of the human and material resources of the nation—of farmers, technicians and teachers, of cattle, machines, buildings and art-treasures. The same phenomenon has manifested itself in Spain and elsewhere, wherever Bolshevism has seized power. When after some ten years production had reached such a low level that it seemed the limit of human endurance had been reached, the doctrines were largely abandoned; and with the help of capitalist credits, foreign technicians and machinery, and Stakhanovist driving of the workers, a beginning was made to build up again. Certainly the change of heart is far from complete. One symptom of it seems to be the present conflict between Stalin, the robust and undoctrinaire brigand from the Caucasus, and the Jewish gang who hitherto controlled Russia and are now largely eliminated. Russia has not abandoned the Comintern and the Marxian ideal of world-revolution. But for herself she seems to have tacitly abandoned the equalization of wealth and the dictatorship of the proletariat, and to be building up a powerful nationalistic state. Under Stalin, there are signs of a sort of shamefaced Fascism with a guilty conscience emerging. If this was to be the end, at what a cost has it been achieved! [4]

"Fascism" has arisen out of the decay of Liberal-democracy and in response to the menace of Bolshevism. Unlike Bolshevism, it was not the putting into practice of an academic theory; it arose in response to an actual situation, and can therefore only be understood in the

4 Stalin himself seems a very different type from the " Old Bolshevik" Jewish bosses of Russia. It is striking that the two really big men the Russian Revolution has produced 'have not been Jews. But we do not know the extent of the influence of Stalin's father-in-law, Lazarus Moiseivitch Kaganovitch, who seems to be the second man in the state.

light of the two world-movements which it is destined to supersede. Originally it was a kind of instinctive reaction of European man to the forces of disorder, materialism, plutocracy and cosmopolitanism. It is at one with Communism in denying absolutely that there is a pre-established harmony which makes the greatest happiness of all result from the greatest liberty of each. But this is all that it has in common with Communism. It takes a radically different view from both Communism and Liberal-democracy with regard to the "happiness" which the state is to secure. For it conceives the nation as an organic unity of many different functional groups; each of these represents a certain unique contribution to the nation, with its own type of life which must be fostered. If the right relationships between these groups are disturbed, there can be no enduring happiness or soundness in the state. "We could," said Plato, "make our potters much happier by allowing them to lie on couches before the fire, eating and drinking, and turning their wheel when they felt like it . . . But do not advise us to do this, for our potters would no longer be potters, nor our farmers farmers."[5]

Moreover, it conceives the nation, in the words of Burke, as "a partnership not only of the living, but of the living with the dead and with those that are yet unborn". If it is something that endures, with human and natural resources, which may be wasted or which may be made more fertile.

A movement has come into power in each of the "Fascist" countries with a will to make the best out of the national estate, as the old noble landowner did out of his own family and estate. This is what has been called the religion of Blood and Soil.

It is evident that these movements cannot admit the unlimited rights of majorities. They cannot for instance permit a present majority of townsmen to wipe the countrymen out of existence, nor to enjoy the utmost possible present wealth at the expense of future power. The evils which the rule of short-sighted majorities brings—the decay of public honesty and the spirit of self-help, the decay of the family, of mental and 'physical fitness, the decay of lands, forests and ships—can only be cured by giving great scope and independence to leaders.

Fascism evidently must, and does, devote its chief efforts to strengthening the weakest links in the national chain, that is, in improving the conditions of those groups which are hardest pressed.

5 Plato: Sep. 420e. Burke: Reflections on the French Revolution.

It cannot however admit equality between the lazy and the active, between imaginative and routine work, even as a far-off ideal. "Fascism affirms the immutable, beneficial, fruitful inequality of men." (Mussolini.)

Liberal-democracy is paralysed by the rivalry of functional groups, whose existence it pretends to ignore. Fascism recognizes these and bases its representative system upon them, believing that it can master their potential conflicts through the strengthened national sense of unity, and the "leadership-principle", the principle of individual responsibility. "Democracy"—the principle of control by anonymous majorities—" is on its trial in the industrial no less than in the political field."[6]

In the economic sphere the aim of Fascism, conforming to its general outlook, is to achieve the utmost possible security and stability for all producers—not the maximum freedom of choice for consumers. To this end international trade must be reduced to a subordinate and auxiliary position, in the interests of national planning. And ethical considerations—considerations as to the kind of life which should be encouraged or discouraged—must often override economic.

There is nothing in Fascist nationalism which is incompatible with the well-understood interests of other nations. Its foreign policy is based on the principle of minding one's own business and being really ready to fight for certain well-known vital interests and only these. It is naturally opposed to the democratic, equalitarian and universalistic principles of the League of Nations. It wants friendly cooperation with those coordinate nations with whom it actually has interests in common, based on the planned elimination of possible causes of friction. It wants leadership in international affairs as at home. In Europe its task is to rebuild the Concert of Europe which the founders of the League of Nations destroyed.

Finally we may attempt to answer the objection so often heard that Fascism subordinates the individual utterly to the state, a living being to an unreal abstraction. The answer to this is implicit in the foregoing. Government, the Fascist conceives, does not exist merely to increase the happiness of the individual citizens. It is a trustee for the enduring national culture and for the material resources which form its necessary basis. Without this the individual would be nothing; nor

---

6 Miller and Campbell: Financial Democracy, a recent research by two economists of Liverpool University into the operation of British industrial companies.

can he divest himself of it even if he leaves the territory of the state; it is the whole sum of ancestral traditions which differentiate him from a Stone Age man. A government which secures the harmonious development of the different culture-bearing groups and prevents them annihilating one another has a claim on our allegiance. But the state is a mere piece of machinery, a mere "container", as Hitler said, for the people, conceived as an enduring biological and cultural entity. Fascism is not *étatiste;* unlike the Hegelians, it does not worship ' the state as such.

Historically considered, it presents analogies with the ancient European state-form as it was "before the Orontes began to flow into the Tiber"—before the rise of abstract individualism and the desire for salvation in another life. Again, it presents analogies with Feudalism, with its conception that government must be based on the personal loyalty of man to man—the primeval Teutonic idea of the *comitatus.* Further, it reminds one of the aim of the medieval guilds to regulate production in the interests of all categories of producers. Like every big movement, it has its roots in the past. But it is no mere harking back to outworn systems. It is unintelligible apart from the essentially modern conceptions of Nationality, Race, Voluntary Trade Associations, the Divorce of Ownership from Management, the idea of Liability without Fault, interacting Cultures as opposed to a "one-track" Civilization—and many others.[7] It is through and through modern, and a creature of our time. Five years ago, it seemed to many of us that there was no choice except between the not very palatable alternatives of individualist liberal-democracy and Marxian Socialism. Now there is a third alternative.

---

7 A. Toynbee: *A Study of History.* Vol. I, p. 149 fl.

The War In Spain
by Major-General J. F. C. Fuller

HAVING as a soldier or as a journalist taken part in four wars, namely the South African War, the World War, the Italo-Abyssinian War and lastly the present Spanish War, I have found each to be extraordinarily different.

The reason for this is obvious, it is that their causes differ; yet, in the popular mind, it is not so obvious that in turn these causes largely influence the form a war takes.

For instance, in the case of the last of these wars, it is generally accepted that its causes are political; that is to say, that it is a clash between two systems of government holding clearly defined yet incompatible views. Is this true? I do not think so; because, though politics play a by no means insignificant part, surely the star turn is played by culture, which, should I be right, means that the causes of this war are far deeper than the political froth which covers its surface. Therefore, I am of opinion that we shall fail to understand what is happening, unless we look upon it as a clash between cultures as well as a clash between political theories and armed forces. Of these cultures there are three:

First, the reactionary Spain of history—a stagnant church, a faineant aristocracy and a moribund bourgeoisie. Secondly, revolutionary Spain—the reaction against this inertia as represented by the socialists, anarchists and communists who have largely borrowed their ideals from foreign sources—Marx, Bakunin, Trotsky and others. Thirdly, the hypothetical Spain of the future; not dreamed of by Primo de Rivera, who was little more than a military dictator, but by his son Jose Antonio who a short time back was assassinated by the Red Government.

In 1933 this young man, though he did not actually create the Spanish Fascist Movement, consolidated the *Falange Espanola de las* J.O.N.S. (Juntas Offensivas Nadonal Sindicalista—Committees of active national syndicalists) and gave it life and form. Its charter he elaborated in twenty-seven points which may be condensed under four main headings as follows:

National Foundations. Spain is the supreme reality of all Spaniards. All separatism is a crime. Therefore the unity of Spain is the goal, and not only does this unity admit of neither international isolation nor foreign mediations, but it demands the inculcation of military virtues, and the creation of a powerful army and fleet.

Political Foundations. The State is to be totalitarian in character, in which all political parties will be abolished. The corporative system is to replace the parliamentary. Political discipline is demanded, yet private initiative is essential so long as it is compatible with the collective interests of the National-Syndicalist State.

Economic Foundations. The capitalist system "which ignores the necessities of the people, dehumanises private property and reduces the workers to shapeless masses exposed to misery and despair" is repudiated. So also is Marxism. The strong no longer are to dominate the weak. Private property is recognised and also the right to work. The standard of living of the peasantry is to be raised by establishing family holdings and agriculture and cattle breeding are to be rationalized.

Moral Foundations. The foundations of the State are unity, discipline and military training. Education is to be organised "so that no talent is lost for lack of economic means." The Catholic spirit, freed from politics, is to be incorporated, and life is to be considered as a duty "to be lived in a spirit of exalted service and sacrifice."

The War In Spain

Contrary to much which has been written in the British Press, this Movement had little to do with the outbreak of the rebellion in July last year. At the time it was still in its infancy, yet during the last eight months its growth has been miraculous. Today its members and sympathizers run into millions, of whom 180,000 are formed into a Militia. The extent of this growth is well illustrated by the fact that the Movement now publishes nineteen daily and thirty weekly newspapers.

When the rebellion broke out, General Franco's object seems to have been somewhat vague. It was a revolt against intolerable conditions—in fact of order against anarchy; for life and property were no longer respected and churches were daily being looted or burned. His aim, it would appear, was almost entirely a military one, namely to reinstate order, but for what form of government is uncertain. Had his victory been rapid, in all probability it would have led to the establishment of a military dictatorship of the Primo de Rivera type.

On landing in Spain he was faced not only by a complete confusion, but by an utter lack of unity and aim amongst the factions which sought his support. For example, the Accion Popular, or Gil Robles Party, were fervently Catholic and soused in Christian Socialism; it possessed no defined policy, was politically amorphous and the tool of the Church. Then there were the Requetes, or Carlists, whose motto is, "God, Country and King". They believed in absolute sovereignty, the Corporate State and were violently anti-parliamentarians. Besides these there were Monarchists - and other factions, the most important being the Falange. All these various parties and movements he had to absorb.

For the time being this was not difficult, for the Reds compelled consolidation. A mixture of democrats, republicans, communists, anarchists and what-nots, their sole enemy Spain is therefore drawn towards Germany and her ally Italy, just as France is drawn towards Russia and her semi-ally England. In fact, once again an occult war is in process of being fought against Germany in order to secure France, as it was fought a year back during the Italo-Abyssinian conflict.

Of this inner struggle little is heard in the Press; but its name is "non-intervention", which in reality means non-cooperation with Burgos and French cooperation with Valencia in order to strike at Germany. If the international "blockade" of Spain were impartial, there is little doubt that it would favour the Nationalist cause; but it is far from being so, as honesty is not a characteristic of modern France.

Though it is always most difficult, especially during wartime, to ascertain the truth, there can be little doubt that French aid of the Reds has been excessive and profitable, for every assistance has been paid for in gold. Wherever one goes in White Spain the same story is to be heard, namely, that French assistance to the Reds has been far more important than Russian. That since July last France has passed over the Pyrenees thirty to forty thousand red international fighting men, and that this traffic is still going on. That the French have printed Spanish passports, in Bordeaux alone, and that they provide pre-dated contracts for "specialized" workers to enable them to enter Red Spain. Further still, that large numbers of internationals are passed over the frontier as repatriated refugees, or are sent to the ports of Catalonia as members of the cargo boats they travel in. Munitions are sent through Andorra; lorries carrying petrol daily cross the frontier; there is a Red aviation school in France, and arms are smuggled to Bilbao.

In spite of all this, the chances definitely are that National Spain will win; because Franco's policy is creative whilst the policy of the Reds is not.

General Franco's Speech

Broadcast On October 1st, 1936, On Assuming
The Powers of Chief of State

GREETINGS to all of you, listening in your homes to the war news, or at the front, thinking of your homes, or in the Red areas, looking with longing for the arrival of our troops, or beyond our borders, following our fortunes anxiously—greetings from the microphone of Radio Castile!

I am not going to speak of the war, for the obligations of State which I am assuming make it necessary to tell you something of the work ahead of us.

We need not discuss any Utopia, nor divide up the accomplishment of our hopes into rigid stages. However, to speak of our intentions it is necessary first briefly to examine the past, both to profit by our experiences, and to implement our decisions usefully.

Spain, whose name I invoke with all the devotion of my soul, has suffered for many years from many ills, not the least pernicious of which has been the influence of unbalanced intellectuals, who have tried to lower the prestige of the thinkers of our race, and have looked beyond our frontiers in order to bring into Spain all sorts of exotic and destructive ideas which were taking root in other countries. Demoralizing literature, demagogic doctrines, bitter racialism, the infiltration of defeatist ideas, and the perversion of history—all this and much more served to shake the foundations of our patriotism, so that we lost the main characteristics of our people, becoming ashamed of our present, forgetful of our past, and afraid of our future.

Having achieved the moral downfall of the race, it was not difficult for these people to put the country up for auction, and to sell it to the highest foreign bidder. Our trade began to show a debit instead of a credit balance, and the fruits of our soil were treated as if they were those of some conquered colony, while a pseudo-pacifism was encouraged, in order to weaken the sword-arm of any possible deliverer. False prophets arose who, while sowing hatred and class-war, promised the land to the peasants, dictatorship to the workers, and autonomy to our Provinces. Utterly cynical, these people, had they obtained power, would have taken the land from the peasants, liberty from the worker, and all hope of autonomic flexibility from the Provinces.

And now our New Spain, taking count of the magnitude of her task, goes forward to her liberation, determined to show, in a spirit of social collaboration, that the re-establishment of law and order is the prior condition and the sure path to liberty, whose benefits will flow to all her people, within and without the limits of the mother country.

Spain is organizing herself largely under a totalitarian concept, in which her native institutions will ensure her nationality, her unity and her continuity. The application of these new methods of authority does not mean that our regime will be of an exclusively military character; on the contrary our system will establish a hierarchical regime in which all the capacities and energies of the country will find their expression.

The personality of the Provinces of Spain must be respected, in conformity with the old national tradition in the time of our greatest splendour; always provided that this contributes to national unity.

The Spanish municipality will reassume its historic importance, in order that it may perform its ancient functions as a unit in our public life.

Having abolished universal suffrage, with its disastrous local and national effects, and its oppressions through unions and political interests, we shall see to it that the will of the nation expresses itself through those technical and corporative organs in which the needs and ideals of the country are best developed.

As the force of the new Spanish State grows, so will decentralization be achieved, so that districts, municipalities, associations and individuals will enjoy the most ample liberty possible within the supreme interests of the State.

In its social aspect, labour will receive an absolute guarantee that it will not be a slave to capitalism, provided that it does not adopt those bitter and combative methods which make mutual collaboration impossible. The labourer is worthy of his hire: not only will security for wages be established, but all advances in wages hitherto secured will be maintained. With the rights of the labourer hereby recognized, will stand his responsibilities for loyal cooperation with the elements that create the national wealth.

All Spaniards will be obliged to work according to their capacities. The new State cannot admit any parasites.

The State will give to the Catholic Church its due rights and privileges, thus respecting our tradition, and the faith of the great majority of the Spanish people; but the State will not admit the intrusion of any outside power into the specific functions of Government.

With regard to revenue, the State will organize the just distribution of taxes, seeing to it that their burden falls on the shoulders best able to bear them.

With regard to agriculture, family holdings will be realized by establishing the cultivator on the land, not by any hypothetical system of ownership but by direct and constant aid, whose aim shall be to give the peasant his independence. A permanent feature of our work will be directed to this end. The agricultural labourer shall receive a part of what the city absorbs today in payment for its commercial and clerical services.

With regard to international affairs, we hope to live at peace with all peoples, opening up a wide horizon of friendship with all the world. To this there is one emphatic exception: we shall have no contact with the Union of Socialist Soviet Republics, whose policy has had such disastrous results for humanity and civilization.

I am sure that this land of heroes and martyrs, in meeting her difficulties, will write yet another glorious page of history, and will find a solution that shall be derived neither from the east nor from the west, but shall be genuinely Spanish.

Spaniards, long live Spain!

Towards An Economic Orthology
by Ezra Pound

DOUBT about the nature of the *so-called* orthodox economics, i.e., as to whether it should be considered as sincere enquiry or as a criminal and misleading fake, can today be said to be out-of-date by at least 50 years. Today the followers of orthodoxy can include only the simple, the blind and the careerist acting in bad faith.

Anyone who seriously investigates a subject cannot take 15 years to become aware of visible and common phenomena.

To say that economics is not a science is mere defeatism, and can only cause confusion. In the middle of last century aeronautics and radio could not yet be called sciences (though a certain Loomis at the end of 1864 succeeded in transmitting electric signals from one boat to another without the use of wires).

What serious men can do today is to distinguish between that part of economics which is science (field of knowledge—episteme) and that part which is *techne* or the field of skill (too often of knavery).

It could be said that the art of running a ship is not a true science: yet the science of navigation exists and is being perfected: from the simple ship's compass to the gyroscope.

It seems natural enough that confusion abounds in economic papers when one considers that the study of economics has actually been done by empiricists, by men who lack a serious terminological preparation. For example, consider the serious and honest writers of the Anglo-Saxon world who have built a live economic science. Soddy, Nobel prize in physics; Douglas, engineer, head of Westinghouse in India; Larranaga, road engineer; Orage, journalist converted by Douglas; Kitson, inventor of the Kitson lamp; Gesell, business man; etc. All practical men! To say that they have discovered the moon would mean nothing, but they have rediscovered the real moon, while the professors continue their childish game with a stage-prop moon; illusionists, able to gull the public only inside their booths.

To get an idea of the mentality of the founders of so-called orthodox economics let us take, for example, a phrase from Ricardo (without blinking the fact, of course, that he recognised the value of paper money): "There is no commodity which is not subject to require more or less labour for its production." It would seem that David Ricardo had never been in a hen-house, and that the egg had been excluded from his economic system. Simply as a measure of nutritive value (life value) the egg preceded the price index. By direct observation of natural phenomena the average man comes less into error than by having his head stuffed with logarithms and banking mythology. And I'm not joking! The value of the egg grows and diminishes in relation to hunger and satiety.

Aristotle bequeathed us a word of obscure and complex significance: *Xpeia,* utility, desirability, which Rackham, naturally from Cambridge, translates demand. The scholiast does not enlighten us. Aristotle was right, but intended to say that the value of a monetary unit "is worth what you can get for it." Absolutely true, but you can't call it scientific terminology.

The student can go to the library and consult 500 pretended treatises on economics without finding one which begins with a Euclidian table of definitions of the most common, basic, and necessary terms for the discussion of economic questions.

Let us begin, for example, with the term "Money." Aristotle defines it badly, or rather doesn't define it at all, but speaks of it without truly defining it. And man has remained for 20 centuries in this state of semi-obscurity.

I shall try to give a few definitions, though aware that they can be of no great use until some academy or congress, or better still, a group of serious and authoritative specialists, recognise the validity of this lexicographical work.

Uncoined gold is not money; the exchange of monetary gold against other goods is at bottom a kind of barter: barter of a certain quantity of goods or a certain weight of merchandise, for metal which has been weighed and measured in advance.

The essential quality of money is that it be measured and be able to serve as a measure. Even in bartering a disc of precious metal for goods, it is the imprint of the State that determines its being money. A government that said, "We cannot construct roads because we have no money" would be as ridiculous as a government that said, "We cannot construct roads because we have no kilometres."

Let us try to define what money is. "Money is a measured claim." Money is a title or measured claim. "Money is a general claim." Money is a title which is not specific (like a railway ticket, an inn-cheque, a steamer ticket which carries the right to transport, food, cabin, etc.). It is general. Money is, moreover, exchangeable, that is, it can be transferred from one person to another without formalities. It does not bear interest as does a state-bond, a railway-bond or the bond of any "societe anonyme."

Let us consider the term "credit." It is said that a man has credit when it is believed that he will be able to pay in cash and when it is supposed that he will not seek to evade or put off payment. "Debt" is not precisely the opposite of "credit." In fact credit is often the possibility of making debts, and does not always necessarily mean the opposite of a debt already made. We are, therefore, faced with an ambiguous term.

Finally, let us consider "inflation." Among the half-truths of orthodox pretences some few are based on natural and repeated phenomena. So-called inflation must first of all be distinguished from true inflation, which takes place when money is issued "corresponding" to goods or services which no one wants or in excess of the desired quantity. Money has no value when it is issued "against" (that is in pseudo-correspondence with) goods or services not deliverable or procurable. For example, to issue money "against" a shell which exploded in 1917 would be inflation, and the money itself would have no value, since no one wants the shell, and no one can deliver it.

A brief list of valid definitions would allow the average man to escape the deceits and the absolute damnable and rotten perfidy of the great usurers and monopolists.

In fact, with a definition, or rather with a serious and just concept of *money,* Soddy, after publishing a quantity of obscure books (obscure, that is, for the reader, though extremely profound and dear for Professor Soddy) writes in *Tomorrow's Money* "Just as it is unthinkable that private people should have the power to levy taxes, so it is preposterous that the banks, in the teeth of all the constitutional safeguards against it, should by a mere trick usurp the function of Parliament and, without any authority whatever, make forced levies on the community's wealth."

Let us distinguish between the Italian situation today and the situation of the Anglo-Saxon countries. Let us distinguish between countries where abundance of wealth creates crises, and countries in which there is a serious lack of certain materials; let us turn back a little to outline the history of the "new economics," which yet includes so much of old knowledge or consciousness.

There are four live currents in the economic thought of today: (1) Douglasism; (2) Gesellism; (3) canonic economy which has its origins in S. Ambrose and evolved with S. Antonino; (4) Corporative economy with its policy of improvement (swamp drainage, etc.), la battaglia del grano, savings, family cheques, food cheques, work cheques, state control, amass, etc.

The orthological economics which we should initiate must consider certain facts obscured by so-called orthodoxy. Goods are of unequal durability, chairs, cheese: the works of Pheidias, Praxiteles or Botticelli have diverse durabilities. Primitive man used one instrument where civilised man uses a dozen.

We must, it seems to me, make a list of the serious men who are collaborating today in a science of economics, even if they are empiricists, even if they have made one lone discovery in their activity, and are not in the process of co-ordinating it with history, and with the just and valid ideas of other schools, or of other times, or other economic sects.

Let us recognise at once that so and so observed the power of steam to raise the cover of a tea-kettle. This is of value, even if the inventor did not publish an encyclopaedia or a voluminous treatise on physics.

Let us recognise that C. H. Douglas on his own discovered the insufficiency of purchasing power distributed by (and within) the industrial system. His factory distributed purchasing power more slowly than it created "prices," that is, of goods thrown on the market. Hence was created a quantity of prices in a month greater than the purchasing power which was distributed.

The delinquent, the imbecile, and the monopolist, who live on the starvation of others, would like to cut man according to his coat. Douglas saw, instead, the possibility of issuing purchasing power corresponding to the quantity of goods deliverable and desired by the people. In that there was little that was new and much that was honest. David Hume had already seen that prosperity did not depend on the quantity of money possessed by any given nation, but on the fact that this quantity should be increasing. Let us specify that the increase must be slow and constant.

Among useful writers let us name MacNair Wilson, who has educated his public to recognise that the banks do not lend money but only promises to pay. *(The Promise to pay.)* Gesell, starting from the point of view of free exchange, re-evoked the *bracteates* of the mediaeval bishops. With his demurrage charge (the stamps, which must be attached to the note every month to maintain its declared value), he intended to stimulate the velocity of circulation, and Mayor Unterguggenberger at Wörgl demonstrated the efficiency of this system.

Gesell destroyed the dead part of Marx by his lapidary phrase: "Marx never questioned money." That is, Marx never questioned the nature of money, nor analysed it.

The advantages of the Gesell system are at least the following: (1) in pseudo-democratic countries it can free the nation; that is, the government and the people (including all the producers, be they employers or employed) from the power of the banks and of usurers.

Yet no pure-bred Gesellite has ever considered demurrage money from, the State—and Corporative—point of view.

With a stamp proportional to one per cent of the value of the note added monthly, a circulation of 8⅓ milliards would give the State a revenue of one milliard a year, with practically no expenditure for collection, which would be automatic and almost entirely free from bureaucratic monkeying or interference.

Instead of heaping up debts (astronomical debts) with national bonds as Roosevelt has done, every State debt, every title to the State's wealth, would, instead of doubling be cancelled in 100 months. (The English are still paying taxes for the battle of Waterloo.)

Treasury bonds could continue to be held in private hands, as a mode of saving for those who want to provide for old age and for their families, but they would be considered a State dividend to a worthy class of citizens, not as an inescapable necessity for a government that wants to use its credit.

I insist: the State need not pay "hire" for its credit; that is, it need not borrow from the great professional usurers, as is done in almost every country, through ignorance and preconceived prejudices; for example, in my unfortunate country, in France in its present grave moral crisis, in England through the power of traditions accepted without cognisance of new events in the world.

The second generation of social creditors, after the empiricists and the inventors, has produced Butchart, who, stimulated by A. R. Orage, published the first book of economic orthology, *Money*. With his second volume, *To-morrow's Money*, Butchart has been less successful; he has, in fact, collected seven writers differing in opinion, all of them praiseworthy, but he has failed to make the individual authors read each other's essays and correlate them. The book is of value chiefly for the reprinting of some of the writings of Douglas and for a page of Soddy already cited in this article.

Among popular writers, Irving Fisher and Christopher Hollis must be named. But one must distinguish; Fisher is a journalist (officially a professor, but at heart a journalist) who writes well. Forty pages of his *Stamp Scrip* merit the attention of every serious man, as well as of professors. Fisher does not engage himself very deeply in the battle. Perhaps he is optimistic and seeks to persuade the great American usurers to content themselves with a half a pound of flesh instead of Shylocking the last bit and gramme.

Christopher Hollis has written a book of great value, *The Two Nations*, and has continued the fight for the public in diverse books, in which he can be said to have a happy touch; he is, in fact, among the few economists who succeed in treating monetary science and the various problems of usury in such a way that their books sell and reach a third edition.These phases belong to popular education, necessary enough in countries where so-called "majority" governments persist.

Wyndham Lewis calls the English Government *fake antique*. Though primarily a man of letters, a satirist, he has recently contributed a book of high sociological value, intended for a select public: *Count Your Dead, They Are Alive* (preparation for another Great War about nothing). I do not cite it as economics, but to suggest the rhythm with which these problems are penetrating the work of living writers of the first rank. The four best American poets today are concerned about monetary problems (no longer with the old "pink" Webbite, Fabian, Manchesterian or Villardian) as, in fact, were the great writers such as Dante, Shakespeare, Aristotle, Hume, Berkeley, Montesquieu, etc.

Another current of thought which is directed on these ideas appears in the writings of those who invigorated the foundations of the North American republic, that is, the writings of Jefferson, Jackson, Van Buren. My *Jefferson and/or Mussolini,* the books of W. L. Woodward, A New *American History,* the articles of Father Coughlin and of Buck or more specifically the best part of Coughlin's book which is called *Money* (pp. 211-213).

It would be difficult to say which English and American reviews a foreigner should read, for intellectual life in these countries has its manifestation in ephemeral publications which last only two or three years (or even less) and then suddenly cease to exist or degenerate into a kind of literary or ideological bureaucracy, assume a protective colouring and take their ease in manufactured ideas. However, we must remark that the English Fascists a year ago began the publication of a socio-economic periodical of high vitality: *The Fascist Quarterly.* This is the only English review in which I have been able to read the writings of the other contributors, among whom are General Fuller, Joyce, Wyndham Lewis, A. K. Chesterton, J. Jenks.

Hugo Fack, who has the great merit of having published in Texas *The Natural Economic Order* by Geseli, at his own expense, when the big publishers didn't think that such publication was good business, tints his little paper, The Way Out, with the ideas left over from Scarcity Economics, notwithstanding the publication of Loeb's Chart of Plenty (see Odon Por's rescension in Rivista del Lavoro, March, 1936).

Freedom of speech does not exist among these sects of liberal breed. Neither the publications of the Gesellites nor the official publications of Douglasism permit open discussion of economic ideas. They seem to be hypnotised and rigidified like decadent musselmen. They quarrel among themselves. Douglas thinks the stamps on demurrage money constitute an oppressive tax—useless and perpetual, though more comprehensible than the "cancellation" of Douglas credit or than his discount and other means of cancelling the credit issued.

Gesellites are almost sadistically enraged at the thought that the whole race can profit from the work of those already dead, and from scientific discoveries. (Value is derived from work but a great quantity of work has been done by our predecessors who ate not here to consume its fruit.)

The *Fig Tree* (Douglasite) does not point out the progress of non-

Douglasites—to Gesellites or to the corporative system. *The New English Weekly* is submerged in the English suburban temperament, and is hence discoloured by that pallid life rather than by a specific and defined ideology. *New Democracy* (New York) was useful, but no longer exists. Coughlin is performing a work of popular education through a weekly for the general public, not for the initiated (*Social Justice)* But in the month of June anno XV, I find in his paper news that is either not printed elsewhere or is given a few lines only, hidden among columns of scandal and camouflage. From editors of the periodical Press of a general character I often receive the invitation: *Can't you write about anything except economics?*

I crave the serious reader's indulgence: I have spoken of too diverse things.

This article consists of two parts: in the first I have almost begged economists to consider the urgent need for an exact terminology; in the second I have briefly indicated certain works, fragmentary but sincere, chosen from a number of scattered writers, that are not, but could be, co-ordinated, if a nucleus could be found composed of technicians ready to assume a lexicographical responsibility.

I say most emphatically that without a sound ethics there can be no sane, no scientific economics. To consider mere dynamism, without taking into account the end and object of a monetary policy, would lead to chaos. The direction of the will is one of the components of study in the science of economics. Badoglio saying, "Our gold is the will and the arms of our soldiers," is more an economist than all the professors in London.

Causes of the Slump
by A. Raven Thomson

I HAVE written on several occasions *in the Fascist Quarterly* and *British Union Quarterly* on the coming depression, which was bound to follow the short-lived recovery boom boosted by the old gang economists. I showed how the trade cycle of boom and slump had been in operation for the past hundred years, ever since capitalism was founded, and had shown a regular period of nine years on the average, falling, occasionally, to seven or rising to eleven. On average the next crisis year should have been 1938, with probability of postponement to 1939, owing to the unusual depth of the depression. Actually, the crisis has been precipitated a year earlier than usual, and the next slump has already begun in 1937.

This has come as a surprise even to those of us who were convinced that "prosperity" could not last. Only in the last issue of the *Quarterly* I discussed the effect of rearmament and cheap money upon the coming crisis, and although I recognised that excessive speculation had created a premature boom, I considered that the impetus of rearmament would carry us through until the autumn of 1938 at any rate, when I argued that a war to consume accumulated armaments would alone prevent a slump. Indeed, I warned against the danger of financiers deliberately seeking war as an alternative to slump.

Actually, I had underestimated the weight carried by American economics in the shrinking world of Financial Democracy, and the absence of any large rearmament programme in America. It is from America, as in the last slump, that the new depression is radiating, and all the encouragement of rearmament profits is insufficient to prevent Throgmorton Street from reacting to the dramatic collapse of share values on Wall Street.

Although this premature slump, like that of 1907, may be of lesser intensity, and thus be a lesser blow to capitalist stability than a later and more intensive setback, it has one advantage, that it has arrived before the warmongers have been able, for all their efforts, to plunge us into war. As the depression intensifies, public interest will return from foreign affairs to pressing home problems, and the danger of international conflict will diminish. Already the danger of war as a preventative of slump is passing.

Panic On Wall Street

Despite the endeavour of our Press to cover it up, the panic on Wall Street has been quite as bad this autumn as it was in the autumn of 1929. The decline in the demand for steel for capital works has been the decisive factor, and United States Steel and other steel shares have led the fall in values. Early this year U.S. Steel was quoted at 129¼ for the $100 share. Even after the gold crisis in April the value was well over 100. The steady decline in September brought U.S. Steel to 80. Then came the October slump, with values crashing day after day. Down went U.S. Steel through the 70's to 68. A short rally, and then on "black Tuesday" panic selling sent the price to 54. Since then there has been a further recovery, which brought U.S. Steel back to about 65, but already in November the price is sagging again into the 50's on fresh reports of reduced steel output, which is now less than 50 per cent of capacity.

All this cannot be dismissed as mere Stock Exchange "jitters." There are fundamental causes behind the Wall Street slump. Demand for consumption goods may be well maintained as yet, but demand for capital goods is falling rapidly. Over-production, if not yet actual, is at any rate potential, and industrialists are ceasing to extend plant. As a result, producers of capital goods, into which steel now enters in increasing proportion, are already badly hit, and the fall in the value of steel shares, which has disorganised the market, is no mere market manoeuvre, but reasonable anticipation of reduced profits on lowered output.

Can Roosevelt Help?

In the steel cities, like Pittsburgh, unemployment is already growing, which will, of course, have its effect upon demand for consumption goods, with redoubled repercussion upon investment. America is well on its way into a classic depression once more, before it has properly recovered from the last. If Roosevelt intervenes, as he seems reluctant as yet to do, he will be swimming against the tide, as Hoover strove to do in 1929 to 1932. This time it will be no easy task, as it was in 1933, to set America upon the tide of general world recovery. This time the mighty President will have to exert his full strength.

Monetary manipulation, public works, and so forth, will be insufficient to meet the crisis, indeed, within his terms of reference Roosevelt can only help by gigantic state purchases, which may have to be so intensive as to place the bulk of American industry in Government ownership. As Roosevelt has no power to enforce the Fascist alternative of state control of industry, his New Deal being discredited and largely destroyed by Supreme Court decisions, he may well be forced to the Communist method of introducing state capitalism. How far his Jewish advisers are working in this direction we have yet to see. U.S.A. and U.S.S.R. may gravitate even more closely together as the two great materialist republics, in which Jewish control is paramount.

British Reaction

Our Conservative politicians, despite all the evidence of a Stock Exchange collapse, assure us that there is no sign of a coming "recession" (special word coined for the purpose of reassuring the public), that Britain is not affected by the same economic troubles as America, and that rearmament will carry us through. All this is nonsense, as all financial democracies are closely linked by international finance, and Wall Street is, and remains, the financial centre of the world. Whatever happens there is bound to have its repercussions elsewhere, just as much in 1937 as in 1929. Have we not, after all, stressed the "union of the great democracies" by a Tripartite Agreement? Is not our Government, amid the applause of the "old gang" parties, negotiating closer trade relations with America? This last manoeuvre seems about as useful as a swimmer, deliberately embracing a drowning man, good if our object is the rescue of Judaic-American finance, bad if we wish to save Britain from sinking in the waves of a new depression.

As to rearmament, far from saving us from depression, it has undoubtedly precipitated trouble, not only here but in America. Speculators, who, of course, enjoy the full liberty of Democracy, saw in rearmament and the possibility of war untold opportunities of profit, and, taking advantage of exceptionally cheap money, proceeded to buy up stocks of all kinds which they conceived the rearming nations as requiring, or which might become scarce in time of war. As a result, prices of all commodities, especially metals, rose within eighteen months by amounts reaching 100 per cent in some cases: a speculative boom unprecedented in history during a period of peace, surpassed, indeed, only during the worst periods of the last war.

Luckily for us, the speculators over-reached themselves. The war they anticipated was restricted to Spain and China, despite the efforts of the Left warmongers, and, like all who attempt to corner products, they soon became embarrassed by renewed production, attracted by more profitable price levels. Indeed, they completely underestimated the immense productive capacity of modern industry, and were swept away by the flood of commodities which the higher prices produced. Very little stimulus is now required to produce over-production relative to present consumption. The immense stimulus of an unprecedented rise in prices has completely swamped, not only the speculators themselves, but legitimate trade as well, which cannot cope, despite rearmament, with the glut. Indeed, there are already renewed demands for reduced quotas of production, before the depression is even fully under way. How such reductions will react in unemployment, and consequent lack of purchasing power, we leave our readers to imagine. Already there are 80,000 more unemployed than in August.

Underlying Cause

Beneath all these outward symptoms, with their reaction to rearmament and war scares lies one fundamental cause, which is the chronic disparity between modern industrial production and general popular consumption. As long as this absurd discrepancy exists our economic system is obviously subject to an inherent instability, which involves it in the recurrent booms and slumps of finance capitalism. Indeed, as science ever increases the power of production, and trade unionism is powerless further to increase workers' wages against the growing resistance of the financial combines, the discrepancy becomes ever greater, and, as Mosley has pointed out, the booms become shorter and shorter, and the slumps longer and longer, as capitalism declines.

The fundamental cause of this, as of every depression, is a lack of purchasing power in the hands of the masses of the people, and the crisis is precipitated unusually early on this occasion by the unprecedented rise in prices, which has not only encouraged a glut of production, but has further curtailed the purchasing power of the people, whose wages have failed to keep pace with the increasing cost of living. The resulting slump can only be permanently corrected, not by economy and wage reductions, as the "old gang" believe, but by public works and constructive wage increases, until State and people consume between them the production of modern industry. True the State is at present, through rearmament, consuming production at an unusual rate, but even this does not by any means offset the lack of purchasing power of the bulk of the people, impoverished as they are by recent increases in commodity prices.

Remedies

The remedies generally canvassed are monetary reform and economic planning. The first has lost its strongest argument, as money is as cheap in 1937 as it was dear in 1929, and yet the slump is as bad as before. Monetary problems are obviously secondary to the primary problem of economic maladjustment of consumption to production, and no form of monetary theory is any good that does not explain how the money is to reach the consumer. Social Credit has its interest in this direction and deserves consideration, but Social Credit supporters must recognise the need of extreme authority to overthrow the present financial dictatorship. In this connection, the measures taken by the Social Credit Government in Alberta to control the banks, and even the Press, are highly significant.

Economic planning is obviously necessary, but again authority is required, and the question arises as to how this authority is to obtain its title. According to the financiers, who favour, like Israel Moses Sieff, of P.E.P., the industrial and distributive combine, the authority to plan is to come by capitalist purchase and amalgamation. *Planning by purchase* in fact. According to the Socialists, who favour nationalisation of the means of production, distribution and exchange, the authority to plan is to come by State confiscation under the civil service. *Planning by confiscation* in this case.

British Union favours a less materialist means of gaining authority to plan, not by combine capitalist purchase, or State capitalist confiscation of private property, which are very closely akin, but by authorisation from the people to impose an economic plan upon private and public enterprise alike. *Planning by consent.* The means by which State authority and private ownership are merged into a largely self-governing economic system may be studied in a number of books, already published, on the Corporate State. What must, however, be grasped, is that the Corporate State exists to distribute the products of industry to the people, and finance is entirely subordinated to this principal aim. Especially is all speculation and excessive return upon capital prohibited to prevent instability, and to enable the fair share of the product to pass to the producer.

Insulation From Further Slumps

Not only must the Corporate State balance production of capital and consumption goods, ending the instability of speculative investment, and enabling the people to consume the production of modern science; it must also protect the nation against external competition by cheap foreign labour such as at present comes from Japan. For this purpose an Insulated Empire policy must be introduced, reserving Imperial markets for home and Imperial industry, and offering dominions and colonies a fully protected share of the home market demand for raw products.

Only by these means can a full plan for our economic affairs be implemented, and only thus can we guarantee our people against a recurrence of the appalling slump with which they are now menaced. Never again should a panic on Wall Street be allowed to throw British industry into depression. Let us insulate ourselves, as Germany has done, against the insane fluctuations of the capitalist world, and plan our affairs in the full knowledge that no unknown factor outside our control can suddenly wreck all that we have done. British Union policy of the Corporate State within an Insulated Empire alone offers security from boom and slump, and the distribution of the fruits of modern scientific invention to the British people.

Revolution Betrayed
by Ezra Pound

THE revolution that has been betrayed is, basically, "our" American Revolution of 1776, not in its local and particular phases, and certainly not as an wholly unnecessary split of the English RACE.

Whatever good may have come or not come of that scission, the scission was utterly unnecessary and, in great part, involuntary. It certainly was no benefit to Britain. It was, perhaps, the first great wound inflicted on your country by the pawn-brokers let in by Cromwell.

The Nineteenth Century was all that La Tour du Pin called it, all that Maurras and the French Royalist clowns have tried to forget that La Tour du Pin called it. It was the century of usury. It was the century of decomposition. It was a century baser than any other I can think of in being the age of the BETRAYAL of terms, the messer and befouler of the meanings of words.

The REVOLUTION BETRAYED is no revolution betrayed in a year or two by one or two false steps of Joe Stalin or of any one government.

The revolution betrayed was the revolution born of the Leopoldine reforms in Tuscany, and quite manifest in the Jeffersonian process which culminated with the victories— all too ephemeral— of Andy Jackson and Martin van Buren.

Before them the Leopoldine reforms had evolved into the concept of autarchy, and into a belief that a nation's GRAIN existed primarily in order that the nation (in the person of each and all of its citizens) should EAT.

That revolution has been quite clearly betrayed by the generations of Dan Websters, Biddles, Morgans, Baruchs, camouflagers of all shades, Trotskys, Wallaces, Perkinses, the two shoals of Roosevelt's advisers, organisms like Morgenthau, steeped from the cradle in usurious preconceptions, the pinch-penny aryio-kikes.

This term I insist on. The Semitic poison is in the Semite tempered by Semitic instability, by the Semite's wobble from one excess to another.

This instability makes him a peril to static and paralytically-minded races. But in all Roosevelt's hideous, dangerous and subversive entourage it has been the Jew, M. Ezekiel, who has toddled first toward the economy of ABUNDANCE in his *2,500 Dollars a Year.*

This book is unpleasant, it is as evasive as any Semitic writing can be, it dodges the real money problem. It is Jew compromise, it has all the J. Simonic desire for a smooth deal and general quiet, BUT it is better than Wallace and Perkins. And any reasonable objective anti-Semite will admit also that the facts wherewith Mordecai Ezekiel is trying to compromise emerge from the report of a committee headed by the sporting Jew, Loeb (Mr. Hemingway's cock-shy).

If you believe that a whole race should be punished for the sin of some of its members, I admit that the expulsion of the two million Jews in New York would not be an excessive punishment for the harm done by Jewish finance to the English race in America.

Whatever comrade Wyndham Lewis may have said about Jews governing England rather well, Jews do NOT govern America in a satisfactory manner, but the Jew financier is not our worst evil.

Our worst evil is the aryio-kike who is able to take a dirty line and stick to it without deviation or shadow of turning, with none of the Jews' moments of pity, excitement or need of opulent display.

A race may possibly be held responsible for its worst individuals. The Jewish race has not for ages taken the responsibility for the enforcement of its own law. In the Gospel story, whether you take it as fact or as illustrative fiction, the execution of Jesus was achieved by passing the buck. The law enforcement was up to the Romans. If a man is going to be anti-Semite, let him be objectively anti-Semite. Let him gather as many facts as he can, and not blink them.

The Jew has brought anti-Semitism on himself by LACK OF ORGANISATION, by refusal to undertake responsibility.

If the Jew wishes to live in a neighbourly world among ENLIGHTENED peoples, he must undertake the discipline of the less pleasing breakers of Jewish law. So far as I know, he has for 2,000 years been quite unwilling to do this. No other race asks to have a country run for it, or conquisted for it, at least, not in the Occident. If Brahmins do, they deserve the name "dirty niggers," and so, perhaps, do some Chinese epigons, non-Confucians.

Roosevelt's cabinet has two diseases. New York usury, which is linked up with all the usury in London and thence to Basel and the sewers of Paris.

But it has also the aryio-kike meanness and stinginess of the Perkins. This is the meanness of the "roundhead" and has the roundhead's persistence, the false morals of stinginess, born quite probably of envy but at any rate damnable.

The "dozen economists" whom the *N. Y. Tribune* listed in November, 1937, as advising Roosevelt to end the slump, deserve no human pity for the advice they gave, whether it were given from brute ignorance or sheer malice.

"Bolster pubic confidence," etc. These men had the chance to tackle the problem of equating the public purchasing power to available needed goods, and failed to take it, and they are as little worth compassion as Neimeyer, Baruch, or any son-in-law of incorporate usury.

Look upon this and on that!

Turning to the organised state, we have a levy on INCORPORATED capital.

This tremendous move caused hardly a ripple on the kept Press in pseudo-democratic countries. The snivelling Reds did not hail it as a triumph of ideas. The loan-capital papers passed it off as if it were a levy on private property.

NONE of the great dailies has distinguished between property (land, houses, furniture) and a claim against "interest plus property" or against interest "and to total possession if the interest be not paid promptly." Naturally, they have not done so, they are a legacy, a dead and putrid hand from the grave, from the common ditch of the XIXth century.

That century was the betrayer of words. It befouled every luminous idea of the century before it. Voltaire, the deist, was passed off as an atheist.

LIBERTY,- which meant the right to do what does NOT injure others, was dressed up as the right to bleed others.

EQUALITY in Jefferson's mouth meant that men had the same rights at law; that no man was born with an insurmountable handicap. It had a flavour of Burns' "a man's a man for a' that," but it did not, in Jefferson's time, mean even universal suffrage. Suffrage could be a reward of merit. It wasn't defined as strictly as party membership, but it was not cast upon swine unawares. Before these sanities could be bitched and defiled it was necessary for the usurers horde to betray the very means of communication. Language had to be torpedoed. Each word that had been ennobled had to be hollowed out to cover the skulking gangsters of bank-issue, 'Leihkapital.

LIBERTY is impossible without order, and order comes of organisation.

An agricultural nation, such as Jefferson's mostly was, did not immediately need a guild organisation as the medieval cities had needed it and evolved it. No system is fool proof and time proof. Evolve a perfect social mechanism and put it into action, and the sons of hell will start chiselling; leeches will start sucking blood and vermin will infect corners left unattended.

The extent to which the kept Press has befuddled the Anglo Saxon reader in England and the U.S. is apparent in a letter come yesterday and now on my desk, from a man by no means an imbecile. I quote it to show what can be:

In his latest book Christopher Hollis says that Mussolini has given Italy a decent money system by taking from the private bankers the power to create money or credit arbitrarily with a fountain pen. He implies that the government controls and *causes* the issue of money there. Reluctant to take his word alone for such a revolutionary reform in national economy, which must be fought tooth and nail by the bankers, I am asking you if such is the case. If so, Italy should be a place to go.

This is dated November, 1937; i.e., two years after the Italian bank reform. The facts are there, but the young man has been so conditioned by the Leihkapital press that he just can't believe 'em without personal word from a friend.

Gent just seen at Cafe below, just out from England, he didn't know the levy was on INCORPORATED capital, not on private capital. He thought he knew what had happened. He had read the brief unaccented notice in his London paper.

The Russian revolution was the END of cycle. It continued the XIXth century betrayal of words, it used hoax verbiage, as in "dictatorship of the proletariat," to mean dictatorship of a few people, etc. The Bolshies won't even now define words. They do not want revolution. At least none whom I have encountered in print, or in days when they asked for replies, do. They won't take up the fight for clear terms, for the clear definition of meanings, so that however much one may have disliked some things they were out to destroy, one simply cannot continue to stand still, anchored with them.

We can't, or at least I can't, at the present moment, get any clear information from Russia as to what Stalin means monetarily. No one even claims that he, Stalin, knows. At least I have not seen any such claim, and his opponent, Mr. Bronstein, is no clearer. Hence the pink intelligentsia.

They do NOT go in for defining words. They do NOT go in for collecting information. They do not seek to report on actual events in this peninsula, such as Rossoni's acts and clear statements.

"In the *ammasso* of grain there is, further, a political reason: Bread should be guaranteed to every Italian, without absurd jumps of price, without immoral speculations." Rossoni admits that this is not a new economy, or rather his words are "we do not achieve a new economy." We HAVE, however, quite definitely got ON from carrot-before-the-nose-ism (*"pursuit"* of happiness).

In one sense this is more or less a return to the nine fields system admired by Mencius. On the negative side it does not DIRECTLY equate money to a mass of consumable goods. But, on the other hand, it is effective, because every honest control of price for the public, and the public good, affects the purchasing power of such money as is in existence. Two years ago an Italian, as well known as Rossoni or perhaps better known, but not in the Cabinet, wrote me:

"The two diseases of modern society are the legalisation of usury via the banks, and the legalisation of theft in the limited liability company laws."

It was a private letter and I had never quite known whether I was free to quote it. I now feel quite free to do so, as such an idea is no longer imprudent. Whether the letter was originally a private opinion or an indication of what was about to be public at suitable time, the root idea has gone into action IN ITALY.

You can measure the Fascist course by degrees :

1. In the Consegna, anno XII: "discipline the economic forces and equate them to the needs of the nation."

2. The Milan speech the following autumn: "production solved, economists prodded on by the State should solve problem of distribution."

3. Autarchy. C. H. Douglas' doctrine. Analogy with Jefferson's policy. The bases of sound economics have been the same for millennia. 'Certainly a nation can NOT properly and honestly pay a dividend until it has that which to divide.

The various possible methods of distributing purchasing power would need a whole issue of this journal to describe them.

To keep praise in true measure, the anti-democrat must admit that the U.S. Constitution gives the U.S. Government full right to central its own currency. It is nothing but Rooseveltian slobber and Baruchian bunkum to puff up balloons about constitutionality. The U.S. Congress, were it honest and supposing it to contain a few dozen men among its hundreds of apes, COULD tomorrow fix the purchasing power of the dollar at one bushel or whatever of wheat, at six pounds of best beef steak, at two yards of serge or four pounds of wool of a certain grade, or whatever were found just after proper survey of national resources.

No one but a liar or a man jockeying for personal political advantage can seek to obscure this. In the U.S. it is NOT a defect of the Government's verbal instrument but a root rottenness of will or a sheer bestial ignorance that impedes these reforms.

If such reform be Fascism, it must be Jacksonian Fascism. Any country needs some form of order. The Spanish American war, when we kids (kids of my time) were being drilled, introduced a jargon about open order. It may be that the ultimate isles and the American continent demand an OPEN order, not adapted to Europe as continent. But at any rate let us try to see what is, and what has been, and let us try to keep these realities separate from what Milords Bunkum and Wunkum tell us, and have us told in their papers.

The discipline of troops in open formation differs from that of the troops under Braddock, who tried to fight Indians back before 1776. I apologise for military comparisons if it be manners for me to do so. But I should like to make my point somehow. I should like to establish a true demarcation for the words "liberty," "order," "responsibility," "shiftiness."

Mussolini's recent statement that "Capital is at the service of the State," is the answer to Adam Smith's sentence: "Men of the same trade never meet together without a conspiracy against the general public."

The damnable thing about the kept Press, and hired pseudo-economists is that they never light up the real greatness of the writers whom they profess to admire, and to whom they attribute their deleterious theories. That sentence of Smith's was real.

The XIXth century never faced it. It needed a hundred years and the blacksmith's son from Romagna to find its answer and balance. Hence various corporazioni, or high central guild organisations, including the corporazione of "Foresight and Credit." Credit proclaimed to be as the life blood.

The rest of this article is applied to answering miscellaneous statements of honest writers. Someone must tty to correlate current thought, must try to eliminate certain misunderstandings, even if *they don't all belong* to the same part of the subject.

As footnote in answer to the letter enquiring about Italy creating her own money. Italy creates her own money, but credit is a natural human product. So long as any one man trusts any other, no state can ever TOTALLY prevent small patches of individual credit springing up as the grass, by nature, beneficent and fraternal.

Italy has NO state-olatry. The phrase "worship of the state" has been coined in ignorance, and for purpose of propaganda.

You can get it straight from the fountain head. The state in Italy is not here to suppress individual initiative, but to prevent abuses and to find a just measure when contending interests have not in them sufficient, sense to find their own solution.

In reply to a dozen correspondents and to the tag ends of two dozen conversations, YES, there are defects in the Italian corporate state at this moment AND they are due to the superstition, the leftover, the dirty habits of former monopolists. There are in Italy, as in all countries, human swine, and torpid and slothful minds which still go on in the old slough, trying to sabotage, trying to gyp their neighbours, preventing simple and naive persons from getting maxima of result for themselves and for as much of the public as their activities could affect.

But it is my firm belief that these defects will be tackled in due order. I have never yet found any tendency to discourage anyone who sets out to fight these diminishing obstacles, or "windmills" on his own.

"The Roman donation is measure," by which I mean that the Roman genius for 2,000 and more years has been a genius for measure.

There are limits to the power of the state (whatever theory it be run on), some things the state can NOT do. The immoderate Russian experiment is now busy illustrating what happens when the state tries to load up too far over its Plimsoll.

The XIXth century state tried to do without ballast. Mussolini's Italy is perhaps the first state seriously to ask itself how much freedom can be left in private hands without being seed of ruin. I mean that no other state ever seriously examined this question.

Jefferson's lot were attacking the evils of privilege and the wet-rot of centralised financial tyranny. They knew that for their time they would be unable to get too far toward the opposite.

If I did not believe that Fascism in Italy meant the fullest development and the maximum field of individual liberty compatible with a sane social order I should be as antifascist as the pink-tea boys and French pseudo-literati, who don't yet know that something has started in Italy. One is permitted to believe in liberty through order. You are much more likely to get it with decent traffic regulations than via chicken-headedness or disinvoltura, as of the hero who managed to shoot his own camel during a camel charge.

I am as worried now by lack of transmission of economic and political news, or say of news re the state of economic thought, as I used, 25 years ago, to be about the lack of real news about books. There was, then, no place where one could conveniently know what was being written abroad. A serious anti-Fascist would today want to know what he was up against, and whether his pet hates corresponded to an extant and objective reality.

"There is," says Karl Winter, in the October issue of Civilta Fascista, "an anti-Fascism in the democratic world which is just position and bad faith; there is also an anti-Fascism ignorant and in good faith."

I recommend that article of Winter's, and what he has to say about the left as a constructive element in totalitarian countries. Beniamino de Ritis also contributes to that issue of "C.F." with an article on the disappearance of hostility between (North and South in the U.S.A., an article which might lead one to think of the possibilities of a new and healed Europe.

I have said repeatedly that anyone who wants to love or hate the new Italy intelligently, must read at least a few of the Italian monthly magazines, such as Rossoni's *La Stirpe, La Revista del Lavoro, Critica Fascista*, or *Rassegna Monet aria, edited* by Prof. Spinedi, Senator Bevione and Furio Lenzi.

Lastly, there is one expression in Montague Fordham's admirable article in B.U.Q. of December that I should like to see more clearly defined. When he "doubts the value of special money issues to consumers as such," I am not quite sure what he means. Might not some readers think such issues were a part of Douglas' essential thesis? They are not.

As a mere matter of equating total purchasing power to available wanted goods, the discrepancy, when there is one, could theoretically be made up in the immediate market by anyone who could create and would spend new money (or credit).

Plenty of anti-Douglasites have seen that distribution to the most needy means the quickest spending. The British (damned) dole is certainly given to people NOT engaged in production, that is, to pro tem nonproducers. The "pro tem" is pretty thin theory in the cases of men eight years without work.

But the Douglas dividend is given, as I seem to recall the Major has told us, to shareholders, as such, in the nation. It is given in respect to work (mostly inventive, but also plant-construction work) performed by our forebears, that is, by workers no longer present to eat food and use houses.

I don't know whether Mr. Fordham considers the allowance for children, in Italy, as made to future producers or to non-producers pro tem; it is made certainly to immediate consumers and pro tem non-producers.

There are at least the following alternatives, which carry the following conditions.

Credit issue- if not made as a direct issue of non-interest-bearing "measured claims" i.e. state notes (as understood at least by 1816 by Jefferson and by all informed economists since then) is issued by borrowing and paying interest, and I should like to know who Mr. F. thinks should receive such interest, even if it be as low as that Mr. Roosevelt is supposed to pay to supporters of old ideas.

Issues of borrowed credit are recorded as debt.

Issue of unborrowed credit are money issues.

Mr. Fordham says "special money issues," and I don't want unfairly to read into this the meaning "issues of special kinds of" money.

I do, however, want to make it clear that an issue of moneta d'Avigliano or Gesellite scrip with its demurrage charge is an issue of measured claims which fade out in 100 months, leaving no debt.

Douglas calls the monthly stamps a tax, but I again point out that the state, in providing a measure of exchange which is also an exchangeable claim, does perform a service and that the monthly stamp can be regarded as a recompense for such service. It, at any rate, eliminates the need of other taxation up to an amount equal per year to 12 per cent of the scrip in circulation.

It is more easily understandable than any of Douglas' cancellation schemes. Its pedagogic value is enormous. I mean that even quite simple people who have used such money have a much clearer idea of what money IS than have the general run of Cambridge students of "economics."

There are numerous alternative schemes for demurrage charges on unused purchasing power, but none of them are as generally educative. The Milhaud plan, for example, would educate only a few exporters and importers and a few of their clerks.

Naturally, if you issue credit or money or even special kinds of money in excess of available WANTED goods you have an inflation, that is, a disease, which defeats the aim of the issue, UNLESS you have government price fixing, as demanded by Douglas and OPERATIVE in Italy today.

Devaluation is cheating and, moreover, it is a drastic reduction of the amount of purchasing power at large. The man who chooses the time of a devaluation can always rook someone else. Even if his intention be decent, he tempts and almost forces speculation by crooks and by hard-pressed men struggling to live in the wallow of merchantilism and hell of a mercantilist-usury milieu.

The gold owners, being by a long shot more clever, wily, and blood sucking than the general public, have, quite naturally, and (if we weren't such asses) instructively, set up stabilisation funds, so as to take care of THEIR interests.

A SLAVE is one who waits for someone to free him.

Marxism, the Doctrine of Decay by Francis Mcevoy

MARXISM is the doctrine of universal destruction propounded by the German Jew, Karl Marx, which has found political expression in Russia under the label of "Communism." This latter imposture, stripped of its pseudo-scientific jargon about dialectical materialism, and its mumbo-jumbo for dupes—dictatorship of the proletariat, brotherhood of man, and the rest—reveals itself as nothing else but a regime of despotic state-capitalism, maintained by assassination and terror. In its system of collectivisation, collective vampirism is the dominant factor.

Needless to say, the utopian equalitarianism of the denationalised intellectual has never existed anywhere, but it is not political so-called communism which threatens immediate danger to this country. That would be the final consummation, but before the oriental commissars can come into their own, the minds of the prospective victims must be prepared for the event, that is to say, perverted and poisoned to the necessary degree of receptivity. Herein lies the task of cultural Marxism, the preliminary bolshevisation of the mind, facilitated by the indiscriminate toleration-psychosis of liberalism, inherent in Social-Democracy, and leading to its final inevitable collapse.

Thus, in Russia Marxism has, for the present, political ascendancy, and thereby controls every sphere of activity, whereas here, and in the other, democracies, its corruptive influence is, as yet, chiefly apparent in social and cultural life. This is far more insidious and fundamentally destructive than any mere doctrinaire political activity, for the creed of subversive materialism, subtly introduced into the life of a people, is the annihilator of all spirituality, moral values, and national culture. It is, to quote the words of Mommsen, "an active ferment of cosmopolitanism and national decomposition." Many people, both opponents and dupes of political communism, as well as large elements of the superficial masses, drift unwittingly into the Saragossa Sea of cultural bolshevism upon the many unhealthy currents which infect contemporary life.

Numerous are the flowers of evil which allure the seekers-of-sensation, and the hedonists of the modern cities, with the iridescence of their putrefaction!

Compare what goes by the name of art today with the entrancing achievements of the Elizabethan era, or with those of other and lesser epochs, even down to the beginning of the present century. The stultification of the *folk-mind* set in seriously with the advent of the industrial revolution, and the concomitant destruction of the peasantry. Having now become amorphous, it is incapable of reaction against spiritual infection. In spite of everything however, the 19th century could still show in its decline some great writers and poets, good painters, and capable composers.

What is the intellectual food of the people today, the ambrosia of our blessed democracy? Surrealistic painting and sculpture, an orgy of morbid and distorted imaginings, which finds its cacophonic counterpart in crooning and hot-rhythm—jungle music tainted with the neurosis of the night club. Films charged with titillation, cosmopolitanism and propaganda. Books and magazines either sensational or sexual, or both. Papers replete with mendacity, trivialities, and photographs more calculated to attract attention to the bodies of females than to their faces. It is peculiar that so many "beautiful and glamorous Miss so-and-so's" should pull their skirts up to be photographed.

In the economic sphere liberalism, which is the philosophical leit-motiv of all the democratic parties, gives unhindered play to predatory instincts, and the domination or extinction of the weak and less cunning by the strong. The apocryphal humanitarians who indignantly decry any resort to physical force, call for no restraint upon the exercise of massed money power, or the economic tyranny of unscrupulous "business ability." And yet there can be other and more despicable forms of bullying than crude physical violence.

Slavery and subjection are not always only physical. Individuals who have not one saving grace, and no talent beyond mere mercantile cunning, can, and do, force other infinitely more worthy and gifted people into a state of abject economic dependency. They have brought the fight on to the terrain where they know they are sure of winning, where the code of Mammon is all prevailing. Under the money dictatorship profit is necessarily the first and final aim, and mass standardisation in every phase of life offers the most rationalised and therefore lucrative method of draining the public milch-cow.

The nation finds itself increasingly dominated by the financial and commercial chain-system from the cradle to the grave. Moral, spiritual, and cultural ideals are not "paying propositions." They cannot be "bulled" or "beared" on the stock exchanges. Also people who possess them lack the necessary docility and apathy to become the go-alongs of standardised exploitation and dupery.

Thus Marxist spiritual subversion marches hand in hand with commercial materialism, "cashing in" on folly and decadence. One precedent broadening down into another (a phrase which crystallizes the breakdown of the modern democratic mind) license begetting still further license, and culminating in uncontrolled abuse. The classical thin end of the wedge thrust in here, there, and everywhere, and the breach widened, until the "real" nation totters to its downfall.

The apostles of decay term this "progress." It is, but progress on their own appointed road to Gehenna. The rake's progress of spiritual bolshevism, the rot-gut of Marxism corroding the vital organs of the nation—a sinister aphrodisiac administered by the witch doctors of decadence under the various labels of democratic liberty, self-expression, and advanced thought. "One must move with the times" is the futile catchword, as though the present social anarchy were the result of "force majeure," and it had become the irremediable fate of the British people to succumb in a welter of cosmopolitan degeneracy.

Accompanying the moral and cultural rot, the doctrine of racial atrophy and mongrelisation enters the contemporary field, and the same distillers of poison are foremost in the campaign for race limitation and the abolition of the colour bar. The people of the countryside, the source of national health and culture, are economically strangled, and the barrier of their instinctive opposition removed. The last remnants are garnered into the cities for an artificial and unnatural environment to make of them part of the uprooted megalopolitan mass, divorced from nature, and swelling the number of the passive purblind victims of financial democracy for the greater profit of the international chain shops and cinemas.

Neither week-end trips to the country or to the sea, nor the habitation of semi-detached villas in garden-suburbs, can compensate the wholesale deracination of the people, the almost total destruction of the English peasantry, for apart from the economic dangers, the moral, physical and cultural effects are incalculable. In face of the crying need for a complete reorientation and replanning of our national economy, social democracy gives us "green belts," and "national fitness" campaigns. Puerile palliatives, sand castles and make-believe. The week-end fugitives from a mechanised civilisation take the city with them in their minds, and reflect it in their subconscious actions. It accompanies them in their speech and literature, their jazz records for the portable gramophone, and their wireless sets, in their town slickness and their affectations. Smart Alick replaces long-forgotten Amyntas, and a steatotic Jewess in shorts is his Amaryllis. ("Oh Singer of Persephone.") Seeking Arcadia they find a road-house. They hear not the pipes of Pan in leafy glades, but wail a negroid jazz song, or the Internationale, in derelict fields awaiting "development," from which the fairies have fled.

In such an atmosphere of decay, Marxism flourishes like Dead Sea fruit, while human, weakness, greed, vanity and vice are pandered to and exploited. Unhealthy tastes and tendencies are excited by suggestion and "giving the lead" propaganda, and then cynically called "public demand." The fairest of our girls display their allurements on films, in international dancing troupes, or "strip tease" in foreign cabarets before the multicoloured scum of humanity.

The apotheosis of national degeneration, if unchecked, is control by political bolshevism. The Marxist plan is to impose it furtively under the mask of a pseudo-idealistic socialism, when the collective mind has been sufficiently poisoned by the virus of collective decay. The minions of Marxism undermine with the intensity of a plague of musk-rats, and every irresponsible pleasure-seeker, every apathetic egotist, and every fatuous imbecile who thinks it fashionable or clever to decry everything traditional, patriotic and wholesome is helping to increase the momentum of our national decline.

The writing is on the wall. Have the people eyes for nothing but stock-exchange reports, sports results, the daily programme of paltry pleasures, atrocity and persecution mongering, and the anti-fascist litany of hate? It is significant that it is precisely against those who have seen and understood the portent of that writing, that all this hyena-like snarling is directed.

Marxism profits by every folly and weakness, seeks the joint in all armour, and demands tolerance and yet more tolerance, until the time has come for the imposition of its own immeasurable intolerance.

Even should its work of evil remain but half accomplished, surely the destruction of the soul of Britain were too great a sacrifice on the altar of Anti-Christ.

The Enemy Is Liberalism
by J. K. Heydon

Part One

THE nation is a natural unity, functioning as a living organism by virtue of a common love which binds together the individuals who compose it. It exists by nature, for man is by nature social as well as individual; it exists for the common good, which, as Aristotle recognised, is more sublime than the individual good; and it therefore constitutes a life which in some respects transcends the lives of the individuals who compose it at any particular moment.

I say "in some respects," because the truth is ever balanced between errors which exaggerate one aspect of it and disregard another. It is an error to say, with Hegel, that the nation transcends the individual in all respects, just as it is an error to say, with the Liberals, that the nation is no more than the arithmetical sum of its individuals. The truth lies between these errors. The nation is a unity composed of parts, and therefore it has greater being than its parts; because that which is composed has greater being than that of which it is composed. It has a principle of composition, in the present case love, which actualises the potentialities of its components, and so constitutes greater being. Moreover, the greater being of the nation is evident in many ways. The nation has a certain natural immortality which its individuals have not; it has a certain measure of the power of creation, vested in its fundamental units, the families; it has the right to take the life of the individual for a sufficient cause, which no individual has. Hence it is manifest that the nation, the perfect community, transcends the individuals who compose it.

But all this applies only in the order of nature, which is the order in which the nation exists. Man, the individual, unlike the nation, is a supernatural being. He has no natural end, strictly speaking; he has only a supernatural end, to which all his natural life, whether personal or social, is subordinate. Hence it follows that the nation, which is in the natural order only, is subordinate to the individual in respect of finality. It exists by nature, precisely in order that its individuals may come to be, and may then be enabled to attain the supernatural end for which they have come to be.

This matter is of the utmost importance and Fascists will do well to keep it quite clear in their minds, else they may jeopardise the very kernel of the strength of their case. The use of the word "totalitarian" is to be deprecated, for it is very ambiguous, especially if the distinction which I have just drawn is not clearly in mind. Whereas Communism is strictly totalitarian, denying that the individual has a supernatural end or any rights against the Civil Power, Fascists are sometimes content with a condescending manner towards religion, as if they could justly claim an absolute totalitarianism but magnanimously waive it in the case of religious practices. If this represented their real attitude, it would shatter the whole strength of their cause, justifying the accusation that Fascism does not differ from Communism in essence. Let us keep it as clear as noonday that we hold the national organism to be greater than the individuals, only in the order of nature and to the end of the common good, which common good is to be understood in the light of the supernatural destiny of the individuals.

Even with this made clear, the use of "totalitarian" is still to be deprecated, as leading to misunderstanding. It suggests that the State, in the sense of the civil power of the ruler, could claim the right to do such things as removing children from the control of their parents, if thought fit, even though the parents may have done nothing to forfeit their natural right to bring up their children. No such right can be claimed by the State, of course, for it is against nature to destroy the family, and therefore it cannot possibly be for the common good. Fascists do not mean to make any such unnatural claim as this; but they call themselves totalitarian sometimes for emphasis, meaning to claim total authority to rule for the common good. This use of the word is defensible; but it is too open to misrepresentation, and even to innocent misunderstanding. Moreover, the intended emphasis is quite unnecessary. The sound doctrine of Civil Power needs no emphasis, for it is that the ruler has *full* power for civil good by natural law. No power can be fuller than full, and there the matter is best left, save to consider what is meant by civil good.

In this regard it is to be noted that the national organism is not without internal structure. On the contrary, it is organic throughout its mass. Love, is its life-principle, from conjugal and parental love in the family up to patriotism which gives personality to the nation as a whole; and between these limiting manifestations it forms intermediate concentrations of every sort and kind, political, cultural and economic, corresponding to the needs of the nation, or to the needs of the individuals in various social but sub-national capacities. A man may be at once a husband, a voter in national and sub-national politics, a doctor, a shareholder in several companies, a golfer, a naturalist, an art lover, and many more things; and in each capacity, some of them of national importance and some not, he finds himself united with other individuals by the bond of a common love.

Some of the organic concentrations within the nation are of such vital importance that we can only liken them to the major organs of a human being, while others are more ornamental. Thus, the Ruler is clearly the head of the nation, Agriculture and Industry are its hands, and Transport is its red blood; Publicity is the national ear, and the Army is the protective skin; the Police are perhaps the phagocytes, and so on. The Royal Academy, on the other hand, is a comely dimple, desirable and serving a purpose for health and happiness, but of less urgency.

Such being the life of the national organism, it will follow that liberty consists, for each individual, in his having the opportunity to effect a harmonious balance among all the aspects of his life that are proper to him in view of his general and particular nature, whether these aspects are individual or social, important or unimportant. And what is more, opportunity in this connection is to be understood in a positive sense, since love is the principle of social life. Opportunity is not a mere *laissez faire* to make an adjustment that may be a practical impossibility, but the community must afford every facility and encouragement for a man to effect a harmony of all aspects of his life, so that nothing but his own lack of love can prevent him.

Opportunity, in the other sense of mere absence of active prevention, may perhaps be called freedom, but it is far from being liberty. For example, ethics affords various criteria whereby we can estimate, at least approximately, what is the just wage of a workman in given circumstances. This wage cannot, under any circumstances, be less than the wage which will support the man and his family in frugal comfort, and it will be more than this if the wealth produced, in part by the man's labour, is more than enough to afford a bare recompense to all the human agents involved in the production of the wealth. But Liberal theory disregards the just wage of ethics and regards labour as a commodity to be bought as cheaply as possible in the labour market; it reckons that a natural wage will arise from the free interplay of supply and demand for labour; and this is the theory of wages which is embodied in the whole of the Liberal organisation of England today, even though absolute *laissez faire* has been considerably restrained by social legislation. In these circumstances it may not be pure nonsense to say that the workman is *free* to refuse the market wage and to demand the just wage, that the employer is *free* to pay the just wage and to disregard the market wage. Economists speak of the wage contract as a free contract, and this may have a meaning, just as it has a meaning to say that I am free to climb up to the moon. The workman is free to accept an unjust wage or join the unemployed; in our free country it is not a punishable offence to be unemployed. And so is the employer free to pay an unjust wage or succumb to the free competition of his rivals and cease to discharge his social function as an employer. But neither workman nor employer can demand or give justice and still continue for long to discharge his social function. Therefore neither of them enjoys liberty. Liberty requires as its barest minimum that justice may be done in the discharge of social functions, for justice comes before love. If love is the life-principle of the social organism and it cannot display itself in bare social justice, then, clearly, the social organism must be diseased and liberty impaired. Liberty is social health, a social environment in which the individual has every facility and encouragement to effect a harmony of all aspects of his life.

This is the true theory of liberty and let us compare it with the false Liberal theory, amid the death-agony of which Anglo-Saxon civilisation is still manfully and pitifully attempting to thrive. At its best the Liberal theory does not identify liberty with *laissez faire;* this identification was a natural development from a theory which was originally less obviously false. At its best and most presentable, the Liberal theory regards liberty as a balance between personal freedom of action and obligations arising under a social contract which the citizens are deemed to have entered into among themselves for the sake of good order, the terms of which contract are to be ascertained by reference to public opinion, for the voice of the people is the voice of God. Individual self-interest is the only force recognised as operating, namely, ordinary self-interest when personal freedom is being considered, and an enlightened kind of self-interest when the necessary restrictions of personal freedom are being considered. Love does not enter the case at all, because all the sacrifice of personal freedom that may be necessary for the sake of order is regarded as sufficiently accounted for by enlightened self-interest.

Now, this theory might work very well if men were perfect. It would be artificial and simply false in its formulation, but I see no reason why it should not yield the same results as the true theory; because self- interest, in its perfection, has the same end as love, namely choice of the highest good.

But we are not perfect. We are essentially good and truth loving, but not perfect; we are definitely warped towards self-interest of the kind called selfishness, which is the opposite of love. The warping is not enough to make us otherwise than good and beautiful by nature, but it is a distinct and undeniable taint. Nobody does or can deny its existence, whether he adheres to the Christian doctrine of the fall or regards us as evolving from apes towards supermen.

This being so, you might expect the Liberal theory to depart from perfect working by as much as, but no more than, mankind departs from perfect enlightenment in its estimation of self-interest; and you may ask what better working hypothesis can we expect or hope for in an imperfect world. It is all very pretty to talk of love as the life-principle of society; but since the working of the love theory will be affected by our tendency to selfishness just as much as the enlightened-self-interest theory, what do I gain my substituting one theory for the other?

Such reasoning might be specious, but it would be false, for the love theory is true whereas the enlightened-self-interest theory, what do I gain that the false theory works better than a simply false theory should, because love remains to help it out; and I admit that the true theory will not work as well as it should, because love is contaminated by selfishness. But for all that, it is still true that the Liberal theory is a false theory, and a false theory in human affairs must needs, since we are imperfect, lead to ruin in the long run. It must be so, from abstract principles.

But I do not need to rely upon abstract reasoning. The Liberal theory has been with us long enough to permit us to observe the ruinous process actually at work. When first formulated, perhaps the imperfection of its operation was no greater than the imperfection of mankind. In fact, it had no considerable operation at all; it was only as the theory found expression in economic doctrine, and in political action based thereon, that its operation grew to be the Liberal organisation of society which now has us almost helpless in its grip.

The expression of the purely theoretical hypothesis of Liberalism in economics, and in the politics based thereon, was a matter of reasoning; and that reasoning was the start of the degenerative process. As long as the heart was free to override the false theory, there could be no results baser than the baseness of mankind; but reasoning upon a false theory can proceed to baseness without limit. At first, perhaps, the supposed balance between personal freedom of action and sacrifices for the sake of order was only a little warped towards the side of personal freedom; but as men got used to that false balance and began reasoning about the matter, their streak of selfishness easily found excuses for throwing the balance a little more in favour of personal freedom. And so the process went on until we arrived at naked *laissez faire,* which was solemnly enunciated as the highest economic and political wisdom.

By that time we were the slaves of the false theory, at least in our capacity as individuals. It was no use a man being kind-hearted; unrestricted competition was the order of the day and was protected by the laws of the land and the entire organisation of society; a kind-hearted man could only sigh and tell himself that business was business, that the laws of economics were the inexorable laws of the jungle—eat or be eaten.

But human nature remained good and beautiful, and the results of *laissez faire* were openly shocking. The individual could do nothing to alter it, but the community as a whole could restrain the law of the jungle; and thus it came about that men turned to political action, from which before they had demanded that it leave industry alone, calling upon it to intervene more and more by social legislation.

Thomas Carlyle - National Socialist
by William Joyce

THOMAS CARLYLE ranks first amongst British thinkers who preceded him showed in their writings some of the main tendencies of Fascist philosophy, and of their number Shakespeare and Goldsmith contributed much; but in all the vast extent of Carlyle's writings there is nothing that could be regarded as other than the product of a National Socialist mind. He himself had the spirit of National Socialism long before the name existed. His words are always the words of a patriot. His passionate love of country might, in his own day, have failed to satisfy the tests of patriotism, because it was no abstraction that he loved, it was the people; and herein precisely lies the fundamental difference between the old patriotism and the new. The old concerns itself with ideas, and outer lineaments: the new concerns itself with the very reality of the people, and is patriotism because it is socialism in the only honourable sense that may be attached to the term.

The purpose of this short article is not to write about Carlyle, to criticize him and add to the already ponderous mass of generalizations which must inevitably be woven round any great writer. Still less is it our intention to discuss what the unwary would describe as "Carlyle's politics". Let those who have a superabundance of time on their hands embark upon researches designed to show that the great author was a Whig or a Tory. To show that he was either would be difficult; but apart from the difficulty, it would be useless because these ancient terms connote nothing which exists in British politics today. Instead, therefore, of trying to prove our thesis, we will simply introduce Thomas Carlyle once more.

To those who, unwisely, may have taken a long leave of him, let him speak for himself, and his words will provide for the National Socialist both an inspiration and a confirmation of Fascist theory. Every advocate of Fascist National Socialism is aware of the charge constantly brought against his movement: that he is conspiring to destroy liberty. Perhaps, indeed, no accusation is more frequently levelled against the National Socialist creed.

Glancing through the pages of *Past and Present,* we read:—

> "Liberty? The true liberty of a man you would say consists in his finding out, or being forced to find out, the right path and to walk thereon. To learn or to be taught what work he actually was able for, and then by permission, persuasion, and even compulsion, to set about doing of the same. That is the true blessedness, honour, 'liberty' and maximum of wellbeing. If liberty be not that, I for one have small care about liberty."

There has probably never been a clearer statement that without discipline freedom is impossible.

Likewise, we see here a clear demand for the right to act. As Sir Oswald Mosley says, "The beginning of liberty is the end of economic chaos. Yet how can economic chaos be overcome without the power to act? Constitutional freedom must be preserved, but that freedom is expressed in the people's power to elect parliament and government, and thus choose the form of leadership which it desires. Beyond that it cannot go." Or to quote the official manifesto of the British Union: Fascism is a leadership of the nation. It is not dictatorship in the old sense of the word, which implies government against the will of the people. It is dictatorship in the modern sense of the word, which implies government armed by the people with complete power of action to overcome problems which must be solved if the nation is to live."

Carlyle's doctrine of leadership and authority does not involve either of the attitudes adopted towards class by the old parties. Equally repulsive to him are snobbery and class war. Lengthy quotations can scarcely be justified unless they are of exceptional value, but here we take the liberty of quoting a long passage because it as one of the greatest ever written in our language :

> "Two men I honour, and no third. First, the toilworn Craftsman that with earth-made implement laboriously conquers the Earth, and makes her man's. Venerable to me is the hard Hand; crooked, coarse; wherein notwithstanding lies a cunning virtue, indefeasibly royal, as of the Sceptre of this Planet. Venerable too is the rugged face, all weather-tanned, besoiled, with its rude intelligence; for it is the face of a Man living manlike. Oh, but the more venerable for thy rudeness, and even because we must pity as well as love thee! Hardly-entreated Brother! For us was thy back so bent, for us were thy straight limbs and fingers

> deformed: thou wert our Conscript, on whom the lot fell, and fighting our battles wert so marred. For in thee too lay a God-created Form, but it was not to be unfolded; encrusted must it stand with the thick adhesions and defacements of Labour; and thy body like thy soul, was not to know freedom. Yet toil on, toil on: thou art in thy duty, be out of it who may; thou toilest for the altogether indispensable, for daily bread.
>
> A second man I honour, and still more highly: Him who is seen toiling for the spiritually indispensable; not daily bread, but the Bread of Life. Is not he too in his duty; endeavouring towards inward Harmony; revealing this, by act or by word, through all his outward endeavours, be they high or low? Highest of all, when his outward and inward endeavour are one: when we can name him Artist; not earthly Craftsman only, but inspired Thinker, who with heaven-made Implement conquers Heaven for us! If the poor and humble toil that we have Food, must not the high and glorious toil for him in return, that he have Light, have Guidance, Freedom, Immortality? These two, in all their degrees, I honour: all else is chaff and dust, which let the wind blow whither it listeth."

The dignity of labour has never been more faithfully expressed than in these lines, which alone proclaim Carlyle as a great National Socialist thinker. Much has been written on the same subject by countless Socialist scribes, but not one of them treats the theme in this way. At the best labour is presented as a hardship, and, at the worst as a curse, their general attitude being that work is an expedient and inevitable injustice inflicted upon man who must redeem himself from disgrace by demanding the highest price for his services. But however high the price he obtains, he will be, in Socialist philosophy, only a "wage-slave". It is, therefore, interesting to read what Carlyle has to say concerning the motives for heroism and achievement. He writes:

> "It is a calumny on men to say that they are roused to heroic action by ease, hope of pleasure, recompense—a sugar plum of any kind in this world or the next. In the meanest mortal there is something nobler. The poor swearing soldier, hired to be shot, has his honour of a soldier different from drill regulations and the shilling a day. It is not to taste sweet things, but to do noble and true things, and vindicate himself under God's Heaven as a god-made Man, that the poorest son of Adam dimly longs. Show him the way of doing that, the dullest day-drudge kindles into a hero. They wrong man greatly who says

he is to be seduced by ease. Difficulty, abnegation, martyrdom, death, are the allurements that act on the heart of man. Kindle the inner genial life of him, you have a flame that burns up all lower considerations."

Such sentiments as these could never take their origin from financial democracy or its admirers. Carlyle, be it noted, is here discussing motives for heroism, not for mere work. He strikes at the root of the old Marxian dogma known as the Labour Theory of Value and annihilates it. He shows the clearest understanding of what Marx would never understand: that creative intellect and heroic action are quite incommensurable with the ordinary processes of labour; and that by no means can the noblest and therefore the most important achievements of man be brought within the category of mere mechanical effort.

Carlyle, it may be objected, is merely representing man as an unreasoning or unreasonable creature. If that be so, Carlyle is right.

In some societies heroism dwindles to the meanest limits. In the financial-democratic countries today it is even discounted and hated by the Jewish financiers because it would inform the national character with the pride demanding national independence; but that the heroic motive can be the rule rather than the exception has been demonstrated in Germany and Italy, where, although the whole object of the Fascist system is to improve beyond recognition the lot of the people, the vast majority of men are prepared to sacrifice everything, not for material gain, but for the principles which they hold sacred.

Our author shows in one very striking passage the true relationship between labour and Empire. When it is maintained that Thomas Carlyle was a mere Socialist, we have to think of the propaganda which International Socialism has for so many years conducted against Imperialism, and to invoke one of the most striking passages in Sartor Resartus:

"True, thou Gold-Hofrath,' cries the Professor elsewhere : 'too crowded indeed.' Meanwhile what portion of this inconsiderable terraqueous Globe have ye actually tilled and delved, till it grow no more? How thick stands your Population in the Pampas and Savannas of America; round ancient Carthage, and in the interior of Africa; on both slopes of the Altaic chain, in the central platform of Asia; in Spain, Greece, Turkey, Grim Tartary, the Curragh of Kildare? One man, in one year, as I have understood it, if you lend him the Earth, will feed himself and nine others. Alas, where now are the Hengists and Alarics of our still glowing, still expanding Europe; who, when their home is grown too narrow, will enlist, and, like Fire-pillars, guide onwards those superfluous masses of indomitable living Valour; equipped not now with the battle-axe and war-chariot, but with the steam engine and plough-share? Where are they?—Preserving their Game?

It is interesting to note an instance here of the attitude towards Aristocracy which Carlyle reiterates on almost every occasion. He was too deep a thinker and infinitely too honest to pretend that Aristocracy was unnecessary. Again and again it is made clear throughout the course of his writing that he can conceive of no people acting as a community save under the direction of a class of leaders. But what he expects from this class is also made very plain, and is most sharply contrasted with what the people of his day received and what the people of our own day are still, for a very short time, bound to receive. He wanted to build a real British Empire, and this desire is plainly written in his own words:

> "England, before long, this island of ours will hold but a small fraction of the English. In America, in New Holland, east and west to the very Antipodes, there will be a Saxondom covering great spaces of the Globe. And now, what is it that can keep all these together into virtually one nation, so that they do not fall out and fight, but live in peace and brother-like intercourse? This is justly regarded as the greatest practical problem, the thing all manner of sovereignties and governments are here to accomplish. What is it that will accomplish this? Acts of Parliament, administrative prime ministers cannot. America is parted from us so far as Parliament could part it. Call it not fantastic, for there is much reality in it. Here, I say, is an English king, whom no time or chance Parliament or combination of Parliaments can dethrone. This King, Shakespeare, does he not shine with crowned sovereignty over us all as the noblest, gentlest, yet strongest of rallying signs; indestructible?"

The inference is not, of course, that we would have Shakespeare as a Fascist Emperor, but that the strongest bonds must really have their strength in the spiritual culture of our people in whatsoever part of the Globe they be; and, in the last resort, this proposition means no more than that the conduct and fate of peoples are determined by the philosophies which they hold. To be thoroughly informed of the noblest philosophy is to do noble deeds; to be debased with a bastard corruption of negroid and Semitic cultures is for the white man to be ruined.

Carlyle knew that neither treaties nor conferences could produce world unity which he so desired. Its achievement could be made possible only by spiritual unity. As we have written on another occasion: "Where there is no collective spirit, there can be no collective security." But this source of spiritual power, this culture and philosophy, can but come from a true aristocracy based upon no such class conventions as those which exist in financial democracy. On the other hand, Carlyle rightly stressed the connexion between the ownership of land and the power to influence the culture of a nation. In *Past and Present* it is well said that "Land is the right basis of an aristocracy; whoever possesses the land, he, more emphatically than any other, is Governor, Viceking of the people on the land. It is in these days as it was in those of Henry Plantagenet and Abbot Samson, as it will in all days be. The Land is the Mother of us all; nourishes, shelters, gladdens, lovingly enriches us all: in how many ways, from our first wakening to our last sleep on her blessed mother-bosom, does she, as with blessed mother-arms, enfold us all."

Carlyle, however, did not fully foresee the effects of the Industrial Revolution. He could hardly visualize the day when everything should be ruined, and the agriculturist, the farmer, the landowner, reduced to a position of miserable impotence, laden with the chains of Jewish usury. He would not have thought that the landowner in this pitiable condition could play the role of a benevolent aristocrat; for to him aristocracy was power, and power meant responsibility and service. "A High Class," he writes, "without duties to do is like a tree planted on precipices; from the roots of which all the earth has been crumbling. Nature owns no man who is not a Martyr withal. What is the meaning of nobleness if this be noble? In a valiant suffering for others, not in a slothful making others suffer for us did nobleness ever lie."

By the hour one may read in Carlyle passages dealing with conditions of his time which would be equally applicable to the conditions of ours. One can scarce help wondering if anything has happened to Parliament in the last hundred years when one reads:

"Parliament will, with whatever effort, have to lift itself out of those deep ruts of do nothing routine; and learn to say, on all sides, something more edifying than Laissez-faire. If Parliament cannot learn it, what is to become of Parliament? The toiling millions of England ask of their English Parliament foremost of all, Canst thou govern us or not? Parliament with its privileges is strong; but Necessity and the Laws of Nature are stronger than it. If Parliament cannot do this thing,

Parliament we prophesy will do some other thing and things which, in the strangest and not the happiest way, will forward its being done—not much to the advantage of Parliament probably! Done one way or other the thing must be."

As Adolf Hitler said: "Etwas muss geschehen." Or as Oswald Mosley has observed: "The result of both systems of the two great organization parties of the State is in the end the same, stability confused with reaction and a resistance to change, together with progress confused with obstructive debate and committee irresponsibility, end alike in chaos. Both are instruments for preventing things being done and the first requisite of the modern age is that things should be done." This passage from The Greater Britain shows an agreement with Carlyle passing beyond conviction into method of expression.

Any passage at random may be chosen from our author to illustrate his hatred of the sordid materialism of the Manchester School:

"In these complicated times," he writes, "with cash payment as the sole nexus between man and man, the Toiling Classes of mankind declares, in their confused but most emphatic way, to the Untoiling, that they will be governed; that they must, under penalty of Chartisms, Thuggeries, Rick-burnings, and even blacker things than those .. . Cash Payment the sole nexus; and there are so many things which cash will not buy! Cash is a great miracle, yet it has not all power in Heaven, nor even on Earth."

In view of all that Carlyle wrote, and all that has been written about him, it would be vain and presumptuous in so short an article to attempt to make a complete analysis of his work. It would even be rash to select passages from his writings and to treat them as professions of mere political faith. It is for this reason that we have adopted the other and more direct method of selecting at random from his immense work passages which are not intended to be limited by the terms of mere political doctrine; but which in spirit and in reason are expressions of National Socialist thought of which any Fascist might well be proud.

If it be suggested that the selection has been impaired by partiality, the only answer is that no responsible person has ever accused Carlyle of inconsistency. The philosophy that we find on one page, we find on another, and so to the end of the volume. Instead of assuming that our initial proposition has been proved to the satisfaction of the reader, we should much prefer him to seek the proof for himself in the further study of Thomas Carlyle, whose hardness and purity of thought should set an example to those who hold the steel creed of an iron age, which, in the words of Mosley: "cuts through the verbiage of illusion to the achievement of a new reality".

William Morris - National Socialist
by Arthur Reade

THE attitude of English Socialists to William Morris has long caused surprise and disappointment among his admirers. Here was a man, among the greatest of the 19th century, who at the height of his powers neglected many of his former interests, to throw himself into the Socialist movement. No Englishman of equal calibre had ever joined its ranks. And yet he has, in a sense, remained always a stranger in the movement and is felt to be such by his fellow Socialists. His greatness has at times been uneasily recognised by them, lip-service has been paid to his work and achievements, but they have never given him their hearts, have never regarded him as one of them, and as their inspired leader. That position has been reserved for the German-Jew, Karl Marx.

This is a fact which throws considerable light on the embarrassment caused by Morris's presence among the Socialists. He was, indeed, at one with them in desiring to make an end of sordid poverty and its attendant evils, and in believing that Socialism, in some form or other, provided the way out. But his outlook on life and his vision of Socialism differed in many vital respects from those of the "comrades" and he felt in his bones that a society which commended itself to them would be a prison to himself. He struggled dutifully with Marx and conscientiously tried to absorb him. He even had his moments of enthusiasm for "Das Kapital." But in the long run something in him, stronger than his surface self, revolted. He wanted a revolution—yes, but this Marxist society was not the way of life that corresponded to his vision. It was altogether too mechanical for him, too abstract, too urban; too cosmopolitan, too un-English.

Between the outlook on life of Marx and of Morris there was, indeed, a great gulf fixed. Marx was a cosmopolitan Jew, Morris was a southern Englishman. Marx was a man of the study, Morris a man of the open air and the workshop. Marx hugged the city, Morris dreamed always of a countryside purged of "the snorting steam and piston stroke" and of a London "small, and white, and clean." Marx was a machine-enthusiast, Morris desired to revive the individual craftsmanship which had made England beautiful. Marx was a materialist, with visions of a mechanised social organisation, Morris was a poet, and as such, a bit of an anarchist. Marx preached Class-Hatred and civil war. The cry of Morris's heart was for Fellowship. "Fellowship is heaven, and lack of fellowship is hell: fellowship is life, and lack of fellowship is death! and the deeds that ye do upon the earth, it is for fellowship's sake that ye do them."

Morris, then, however hard he tried, was never at heart a Marxian. Cosmopolitanism, whether of international socialism or of international finance, was anathema to him. Not only as a dreamer of dreams was he born out of his due time, but also as a Socialist. As a Socialist he was a forerunner of something still in the womb of time. His spiritual affinities were with a movement which only arose and gathered way after his death. His real place is not among the Marxian but among the National Socialists.

For Morris was a man of strong passions and none throughout his life was stronger or more constant than his passion for England. How lovingly and understandingly he writes of her outer appearance.

"The land is a little land, too much shut up within the narrow seas, as it seems, to have much space for swelling to hugeness; there are no great wastes overwhelming in their dreariness, no great solitudes of forests, no terrible untrodden mountain walls: all is measured, mingled, varied, gliding easily one thing into another; little rivers, little plains swelling speedily-changing uplands, all beset with handsome orderly trees; little hills, little mountains, netted over with the walls of sheep-walks: neither prison nor palace, but a decent home."

The same affectionate appreciation informs the lovely descriptions of English scenery in the introductions, month by month, to the stories of "The Earthly Paradise" and is a perpetual accompaniment of that dream of an England renewed and awakened which is the theme of "News from Nowhere," and lends such colour and glow to "A Dream of John Ball." Morris's Socialism, indeed, was largely inspired by the longing to save or to recover the old English values, the glory of her architecture, the beauty of her landscape, the individual workmanship which made craftsmen even of her humblest folk, the character of her people "rustic and narrow-minded indeed, but serious, truthful, and of simple habits." In an out-of-the-way corner of the Upper Thames, he once told a Birmingham audience, he had just seen half-a-dozen "tiny village churches, everyone of which is a beautiful work of art. These are the works of the Thames-side country bumpkins, as you would call us—nothing grander than that. If the same sort of people were to design and build them now they could not make anything better than the ordinary plain little Nonconformist chapels that one sees scattered about new neighbourhoods. That is what they correspond with . . ." And of Westminster he wrote that "the authors of this great epic itself have left no names behind them. For indeed it is the work of no one man but of the people of South-Eastern England. It was the work of the inseparable will of a body of men, who worked, as they lived, because they could do no otherwise ..." To find in terms of modern life some equivalent of that achievement, that spirit of an earlier, happier England—this was the motive force behind Morris's Socialism.

His real place, then, is in a Socialism which has ceased to be cosmopolitan and has become National. And soaked as he is in the Middle Ages, he would have felt particular interest in all these aspects of National Socialism which call up to mind the mediaeval crafts' guilds. That the Corporate State should base citizenship not merely on a territorial foundation but on active membership of a great guild of workmen, would have seemed to him the highest common sense. He would have regretted, indeed, that the individual craftsman of the Middle Ages had been so largely superseded by the engineer and technician. But he would have felt that in recognising the importance of the organised workers as such, the Corporate State was inspired by the right idea. Too long had politics been divorced from the needs and desires of the common man and left in the specialised hands of those lawyers, rascally forestalled and regraters whose monopolies the angry populace in "A Dream of John Ball" is so eager to get rid of. In "News from Nowhere" the Houses of Parliament are merely an interesting relic. England is governed by and for the English and has ceased to be the pawn of the financial interests which today manipulate her party politics at Westminster.

Another feature of National Socialism which would have had Morris's whole-hearted approval is its insistence on the fundamental importance of agriculture. Morris, like the National Socialists of today, conceived of a happy community not in terms of large cities but of a society mainly agricultural. The land is for him a passion. "The earth and the growth of it and the life of it! If I could but say or show how I love it!"

But not merely as something to write poems about. Also as something to cultivate and to nurture a strong race. One of the loveliest sights in the world for Morris was "the green-growing acres with increase begun" and in one of his letters he speaks of August, with its golden harvest fields, as the best of all months for seeing the English countryside. "News from Nowhere" has a delightful vignette of the haymakers at work in the Thames Valley, all gaily clad so that the meadow looked like a gigantic tulip bed. "All hands were working deliberately but well and steadily, though they were as noisy with merry talk as a grove of autumn starlings." The country had long ceased to be looked down upon, to be neglected, to be dull. Elsewhere, he writes, "I want the town to be impregnated with the beauty of the country, and the country with the intelligence and vivid life of the town."

Morris, indeed, would have subscribed enthusiastically to the whole doctrine that goes under the name of economic autarchy. He understood the romance and the usefulness of trade, and pictures, below the old London Bridge, the green waves lapping.

> "Some few keels that bear Levantine staves,
> Cut from the yew wood on the burnt-up hill,
> And pointed jars that Greek hands toiled to fill,
> And treasured scanty spice from some far sea,
> Florence gold cloth, and Ypres tapestry,
> And cloth of Bruges, and hogsheads of Guienne."

Certain beautiful and rare things must necessarily be procured through trade. But for the modern economic doctrine of living by one's exports, of sacrificing everything to "a favourable trade balance," he had nothing but contempt. The foundation and secret of a happy life lay for him in producing things from one's own soil. A classical expression of this feeling is to be found in his description of the life of the men of Burgdale in that noble romance "The Roots of the Mountains." In "News from Nowhere" England has emancipated herself from her dependence on an immense foreign trade and found happiness and substantial plenty from her own resources.

Yet another link between National Socialism and Morris is to be found in the former's philosophy of *Kraft durch Freude* (Strength Through Joy). This coincides closely with Morris's teaching about joy in work. Much of ordinary Socialist propaganda is concerned to represent work as a curse. This is miles away from Morris. "I tried to think what would happen to me," he writes, "if I were forbidden my ordinary daily work; and I knew that I should die of despair and weariness." But he held that "no work which cannot be done with pleasure in the doing is worth doing," and he strove through his Socialism to ensure that all his fellow-workers should also be in a position to choose the work they liked and to love it as he did. Of the Thames-side country bumpkins already alluded to, he wrote, "Time was when everybody that made anything made a work of art besides a useful piece of goods, and it gave them 'pleasure to make it. Whatever I doubt, I have no doubt of that." And referring to the present day, he says : "In a properly ordered state of society, every man willing to work should be ensured : First, honourable and fitting work; Second, a healthy and beautiful house; Third, full leisure for rest of mind and body." How far we are from that today! Looking out of a window at Hammersmith, he hears the "yells and shrieks and all the degradation cast on the glorious tongue of Shakespeare and Milton" and sees "the brutal, reckless figures and faces go past." "I know by my own feelings and desires what these men want, what would have saved them from this lowest depth of savagery: employment which would foster their self-respect and win the praise and sympathy of their fellows, and dwellings which they could come to with pleasure, surroundings which would soothe and elevate them; reasonable labour, reasonable rest." He disbelieves in excessive specialisation—a man should be able to turn his hand to many different things. And pleasure is to be had in strain and effort as well as in the more delicate and refined work. "News from Nowhere" contains a spirited description of a group of men energetically road-mending and of their pleasure in it, and a word of regret that rough work is getting rather scarce in these Utopian times.

Another point of contact between Morris and National Socialism is his passionate desire that a people should get down to its own roots. From first to last he was a great North European. He might have quarrelled with Hitler's insistence on Race, as being excessive, but he loathed the cosmopolitanism which produced that insistence and was deeply Nordic at heart. Though loving all the elements which go to the formation of the English character and story, he yet had a special affection for those which are Northern. Thus, while as a storyteller he did full justice to the classical and Celtic roots from which we also draw our blood and strength, re-telling their sagas with affectionate enthusiasm, yet it is round the Northern saga that his mightiest enthusiasms surge, and especially that Icelandic saga of which he wrote so starkly and so movingly in "Poems by the Way." Its unknown writers had found "the spell, whereby the mist of fear was melted" and to them Morris turned in the stresses of his own life, and could say in retrospect, "Well ye have helped me at my need." That men should not know these stories caused him physical pain and in re-telling them in his "Sigurd the Volsung" he gave out unstintingly the full measure of his strength. Twice he visited Iceland and came to regard it as a kind of Holy Land of our race. Our enfeebled England of today might breathe with advantage that inspiring tonic air.

Even from so brief a glance as this, it is evident that Morris's affinities with National Socialism are of the most striking character. His probable criticisms it is not difficult to imagine. He was a great poet and in the poet there is always something of the anarchist. The least attractive thing to him about National Socialism would be the great stress it usually lays upon the State. In doing so National Socialists may well be right; it is at least certain that during a period of great crisis and transition, when new forms are being created and tried out, a strong unified command is essential to survival. But there always exists the danger that a highly-centralised organisation, because it is a necessary means to social health in times of stress, may linger on and become an end in itself, in days when greater freedom is required. National Socialism can deal with that danger if and when it arises. Meanwhile, it is no bad thing to be reminded by so robust a forerunner as William Morris that, other things being equal, National Socialism, when once the new forms it has created have been soundly established and consolidated, should aim at less State interference rather than more.

The Jewish Myth
by "Scepticus"

AT the Annual Meeting of the British Association at Nottingham in September, 1936, Mr. H. G. Wells spoke the historical truth in regard to the part played by the Jews in religious thought, which he claimed had been very much exaggerated. When Mr. Wells made his speech, Jews from every station of life came out to reply, and got many Gentile public figures to repudiate the views of Mr. Wells. The chief Jewish argument in their replies was—as it has been from the beginning—that Hebrew prophets have taught monotheism to mankind.

The great problem is whether this Hebrew contention can be established by the lights of cuneiform documents and classical authors, both coinciding with the period of Hebrew origins and the Jewish Kingdom in Palestine.

It is extraordinary that all the sources mentioned above prove the exact opposite of those contentions.

The Egyptian documents of the Middle Empire (1750-1350 *b.c.)* under the two Amenhoteps, show beyond doubt that about 1400 *b.c.* Akhenaten and his Court made a religious revolution in introducing monotheism as the State religion. The facts are carefully described in the Cambridge Ancient History.

The evidence of the Latin historian Justinus that the origin of the Jews was from Damascus, is now more than confirmed by the Tell-Amarna letters. This correspondence shows that for many centuries Canaan was a mere Egyptian border province the possession of which was frequently contested by the Hittites. The language of the correspondence was Babylonian.

These Tell-Amarna letters are further illuminated by the Hittite archives of Boghaz-Keuy. Both mention a class of people named *Habiru,* a class of slaves. Scholars of Jewish extraction in every country deny that the *Habiru* have anything to do with the Hebrews. There are interesting details in the Tell-Amarna letters. Six letters addressed to the Pharaoh of Egypt are from one *Abdi-hiba*, the governor of Urusalim (Jerusalem). I believe this Abdi-hiba is the Egyptian transcription of the name Abraham itself, in any case a native of Syria, whereas the Old Testament brings Abraham from the Ur of the Chaldees. Abdi-hiba is hard pressed by the Habiru (about 1400 b.c.). In letter after letter he requests military aid from Egypt. "To the King, my lord, my Sun. Abdi-hiba, thy servant, at the feet of the king, my lord, seven and seven times I fall down ... It is a calumny, what they allege against me. Behold, I am no prince . . . Behold, neither my father nor my mother established me in this place; the arm of the mighty king has caused me to enter the house of my father."

In another letter for help he writes to the Pharaoh, "the Habiru are capturing the fortresses of the king ... all have perished. May the king, my lord, send help to his country."

The Old Testament does not know any of these or subsequent facts, nothing of the great world war fought between Rameses II (1292-1225 b.c.) and the Hittites of Kadesh, where all the organised states of the day had joined one or the other of two belligerents.

There is not a word about King David or Solomon from any source, except the oral tradition of the Old Testament written down many centuries later, probably during the captivity in Babylon, that is to say after 585 b.c. The fact that there is no mention of them in any source, does not necessarily preclude the possibility of their existence, and the approximate truth of the story; the more so, as the country most interested in Syria and Palestine, Assyria, was then in eclipse, that is about 1000 b.c.

The following cuneiform evidence raises the questions of the origins of Jahur-Jehovah. The Old Testament tradition of the Jewish origin of the name is well known. But Aramaic inscriptions found at Zinjirli (middle Euphrates valley) show clearly that at the time of the invasion by Tiglat-Pileser III (740 b.c.) of the land of Sam'al, there was a small independent kingdom of Y'di which is indeed Yaudi. This dynasty of Y'di was apparently founded in the 8th century b.c. by K-r-L; who was succeeded by Parra I. who has left an inscription to his god Hadad. Therefore the King Azrian of Yaudi, who was identified with Azariah of Judah (2 Kings, xv.) up to the discovery of this Aramaic inscription, turns out to belong to a middle Euphratean Dynasty. This revelation also has created a great disturbance in the Old Testament story. Throughout the period of the military power of Assyria, from Assurnatsirpal II (884-860 b.c.) down to the end of Assyria (612 b.c.), one king of Samaria and one of Judah are mentioned by the Assyrians. It is strange that Israel and Canaan are not mentioned. They were small principalities always tributary to Assyria, as well as to the nearer kingdom of Damascus. During his 35 years of power Shabuanassar III (859-824 b.c.) invaded Syria and Palestine fourteen times. He mentions at least five invasions during which he carried off people of Palestine into Assyria. Tiglat-Pileser IV (745-728 b.c.), Sargon II (722-705 b.c.), Sanherib (705-682 b.c.), Azarhadon, etc., all in turn invaded and ravaged Syria and Palestine, each of them several times, and carried off people to Assyria and Babylonia. Like Amenhotep IV of Egypt, Zoroaster had been singing hymns to the Sun and the Ahuramazda, the purest form of monotheism since the beginning of the 8th Century b.c.

The one god Ahuramazda, the source of goodness and purity, survived even after—and probably on account of—the martyrdom of Zoroaster himself. The proof of it is that the Achaemenians (from 548 b.c. onwards) adopted Ahuramazda as their one god. Now it can be proved that Zoroaster lived in the first half of the 8th Century b.c. The peoples of Syria and Palestine scattered all over the Assyrian Empire through the deportations would not be altogether unaware of the monotheistic doctrine of Zoroaster.

The Old Testament says that Nabu-kudur-utsuri (Nabukednezer) of the Old Testament), the King of Babylon, carried the Jewish people into captivity (about 555 b.c.). There is no record of it in the Babylonian texts. But assuming that it is true, as most likely it is, the Jewish captives in Babylon, after the destruction of the temple in Jerusalem in particular, would naturally be inclined to some deeper thought. The Zoroastrian religion must have been quite prevalent there. There is a proof that Western Asia was deeply stirred by the utter downfall of Assyria (612-606 b.c.) and the rise of Aryan races, all more or less worshippers of Zoroaster. The one-god idea must have penetrated even among such a conservative people as the Babylonians. Nabunaid (553- 538 b.c.) the last king of Babylon, conscious of the rising tide, tried to forestall the danger. Under one pretext or another he collected into the capital all the idols of the different Babylonian cities, and the images of local gods. That action caused immense discontent among the local priests and the vast numbers of their hangers on. This is probably one of the reasons why the Babylonian army did not resist when Cyrus quietly entered the city (538 b.c.) and ended the Babylonian Empire.

The Old Testament tradition says that Cyrus released the Jewish captives. I think that the easy-going Persian did not bother at all about the people in the city, so long as he received the tribute. My view is that the Jewish monotheism was brought to Palestine by the captives of Babylon. A critical survey of Ezra 1. and other chapters in the Chronicles are susceptible to such an interpretation. A racial consciousness grew among the Jews—if ever before the great dispersion in 71 a.d. —as a consequence of the captivity in Babylon. The experience had proved that too many gods had not saved mankind. There was more probability of redemption by the worship of one almighty god.

It has greatly puzzled scholars that throughout the Hellenistic period, the common medium of communication among the Jews was Greek. Of course there were the Sanhedrin and the priesthoods. The main speech among the Semitic natives seems to have been a vernacular of the Aramaic. It cannot be ascertained whether the Jewish priests spoke Hebrew between themselves.

Without any doubt Cicero is the most intelligent and fair statesman of the Roman Republic. In a world of utter corruption and license, he is alone with Cato, against whom no charge of bribery or misconduct has been alleged. His writings prove the range of his intellectual powers and reasoning. Amongst hundreds of consuls and praetors, he is the only consul who returned from Cilicia with an honourable record. Cicero is an exalted political thinker, fair and honest. He is very objective in regard to foreign nations. He wrote of the levity of the Greeks, of the slavishness of the Lydians, but never called any one of them the enemies of Borne. It is Jews alone that time and again he calls "our enemies." *Sequitur auri ilia invidia Iudaici.*

The next thing is the charge about the Jewish gold . . . *Cum aurum Iudaeorum nomine quotannis ex Italia et ex omnibus nostris provinciis Hierosolymam exportari soleret.*—As to gold being exported to Jerusalem by Jews from Italy and from all our provinces. . . . *Huic autem barbarae superstitioni resistere severibatis, multitudineum Iudaeorum flag-rantem non numquam in contionibus prae re publica contemnere gravitatis summae fuit.*—But to resist this barbarous superstition were an act of dignity, to condemn the multitude of Jews an act of greatest wisdom, when often they were most unruly in the assemblies, held in defence of the interests of the Republic . . . *Non enim credo religionem et Iudaeorum et hostium impedimenta.*—The religious creed of the Jews, our enemies, was not an obstacle . . . etc., etc.

This oration of Cicero is probably one of the most beautiful and patriotic pieces in Latin; for the last fifty years, however, there has been no school edition of it for the public schools and universities in this country, for obvious reasons. Nor has there been any edition of *The Histories,* by Tacitus, for the same reason. Tacitus (Annalium. il.85) mentions that under Emperor Tiberius the senate issued a decree forbidding the Egyptian and Jewish worship and expelling 4,000 Jewish freedmen from Rome to Sardinia, and the remainder to leave Rome immediately.

Tacitus actually states in one passage that at the most successful period of the Jewish Kingdom (the Century b.c. and until the destruction of Jerusalem by Titus in 70 a.d.) the Jews worshipped an ass’s head in their temple. (Tacitus: Historiarum V. 2-5).

Horace and Juvenal have many other things to say about them. Constantine, so-called the Great, committed the horror of allowing the canonisation of the Old Testament at the first Church Council of Nicaea in 325 a.d. For about a generation or two Jews became very popular throughout Christendom as the sons of prophets. But hardly a century passed (i.e. from early fifth century) before masses of them were ordered to leave Constantinople and Alexandria.

There can be little doubt that, with a view to avenging themselves on ‘Christendom, the Jews played a considerable part in organising the movement of Islam. Yet it is most curious that in spite of the services rendered by Jews, the first Caliphs wrecked fearful fanaticism upon them. As “peoples of the Book” Arabs never forced Christians to adopt Islam, except a formal invitation. But until the Abbasid Caliphs (850 a.d.) Islam did not recognise Jews as monotheistic. Whole communities of Jews in the Levant parts were forced to conversion, and the males driven into the front ranks of the armies of Islam.

The Muslim World and Palestine by A. Yusuf Ali

POST-WAR British policy in Palestine has been a running sore in the relations between Great Britain and the Muslim world. The misunderstandings which it created were bad enough in the 1920s—in the 1930s the heat which they have generated has been so tremendous that there is the danger of an explosion. And in this year of grace 1938, the world situation has deteriorated so rapidly that no one can afford to ignore Palestine as an important factor for the future peace of the world. The British authorities have in a vague way realised their impossible situation and have within two years sent out two Commissions to help them to solve the problem. What they have not realised is the strength of Muslim feeling and the unassailable grounds on which that feeling is based.

It is not true that only the Arab countries are interested in the question. Every week the newspapers from India bring news of meetings at various centres in the country expressing sympathy with the Arabs and asking Great Britain to change her policy in Palestine.

Not only the Muslims, but the Hindus also, are interested in the question. More than one Palestine Day has been observed, on which strong speeches have been delivered. Hijrat (voluntary exile) and non-co-operation with Government have been suggested as means for putting pressure on the authorities. The Java Muslims under Dutch sovereignty have shown the same keen interest, and have caused a great deal of embarrassment to their Government. In the French Muslim colonies the Palestine feeling adds materially to the very complicated problems which French colonial policy has to face. And it is only natural that in Arab countries themselves the feeling of sympathy with their Arab brethren and of indignation against the repression and injustice being practised in Palestine should find strong expression.

Prince Saiful Islam of Yemen, with his Coronation Delegation in 1937, publicly expressed his deep feeling and that of his people in meetings in London. Speaking at a reception attended by various members of the diplomatic corps, he said: "All the Muslims in the world sympathise with the Arabs of Palestine and will not rest until the Palestine question is solved without prejudice to the civil rights of the Arabs." And Yemen has not been silent since, but has made various efforts to suggest a solution.

Iraq has been even more insistent. The present Prime Minister of Iraq has made pronouncements which have been criticised in some quarters as "blazing indiscretions." If they were indiscretions, they were at least inspired by a genuine anxiety that British opinion should not be misled into further mistakes in Palestine. It is believed that his recent visit (in autumn, 1938) to London was mainly with the object of presenting some reasonable solution of the Palestine question, and was in response to the very strong feeling on the question that exists among his own people at Baghdad. Transjordania, as a neighbour and in some respects part of the same geographical area, is, of course, intimately interested. King Abdul Aziz Ibn-Saud, of Saudi Arabia, has so far maintained a diplomatic silence, but his subjects, the ardent Ikwan, are perhaps among the most important of the Arab groups which are watching events in Palestine with more than platonic interest.

Syria is in the birth-throes of its new liberty as a sovereign Arab State, and the Arab view of Palestine is nowhere a more live issue than in Damascus. Historically and geographically Palestine is a part of Syria and the Palestine rebellion has the heartiest sympathy and support in the nascent Syrian republic. The Grand Mufti of Jerusalem is a refugee in one of the constituent States of Syria—Damascus has been and is one of the most important centres for the support of the Palestine Arab cause. More than one international Muslim congress has been held in Bludan (near Damascus). The latest of such congresses was held in Cairo in October, 1938. It was attended by Muslim members of Legislatures from various countries. It pledged itself to the defence of Palestine, the establishment of a national Government in the country, and the abandonment of the impracticable idea of a Jewish National Home in Palestine. An international meeting of women supporters of the Arab cause in Palestine was held in Cairo under the presidency of Mme. Sharawy, immediately after the parliamentary congress. The Egyptians, both the people and their religious and parliamentary leaders, are wholeheartedly in the cause. And Egypt is the intellectual focus of the Arabic-speaking world.

Thus we have practically the unanimous voice of the Muslim world in resisting the Jewish ambitions in Palestine. The Christians in Arab countries are also entirely at one with their Muslim brethren in this matter. It is no exaggeration to say that the whole of the Near East is aflame on this question, and the whole of the Muslim world is in sympathy and cooperation. These States are gradually growing in power and importance. Their ambition is to form a compact *bloc,* and a number of treaties have been negotiated in furtherance of this aim. Iran and Turkey have joined in some of these treaties. Is it worthwhile alienating such important elements in the population of Western Asia and Northern Africa in order to carry out the Balfour Declaration, which was itself inconsistent with promises made to the Arabs? Indeed, if Jewish demands are to be met, they would infringe an essential part of the Balfour Declaration itself, for Mr. Balfour's letter to Lord Rothschild, published on the 2nd November, 1917, contained the words italicised below :—

> "*We view with favour the establishment in Palestine of a National Home for the Jewish people, and will use our best endeavours to facilitate this object,* it being clearly understood that nothing shall be done which may 'prejudice the civil and religious rights of existing non-Jewish communities in Palestine."

The Declaration was ambiguous and inconsistent with British good faith to the Arabs. It has been found unworkable in practice, and has done much harm to British prestige in the Muslim world. It is a running sore in world politics at the present moment, and is likely to be a fruitful cause of much disturbance and unsettlement in the future. The enemies of England are finding there a promising field for their propaganda, and are not likely to miss their opportunities in a time of crisis or danger. Surely, intelligent and well-instructed opinion would strongly pronounce against such a farcical policy.

So far we have considered only questions of policy. Let us examine the matter as a question of justice. Jerusalem and the Holy Land are not only sacred to the Jews; they are even more sacred to the Christians and Muslims. The central event in the foundation of Christianity was enacted in that land. The *Urasjid al Aqsa* is expressly mentioned as a holy place in the Quran (xvii. 1, 5, and 7). For 1,868 years, ever since the destruction of the Temple by Titus in 70 *a.d.,* the Jews have been driven out of the country. For 2,500 years (since the Babylonian captivity) Jews have held no supreme power in the country. For the six centuries or so (from the time of Joshua, 1254 b.c., to Nebuchadnezzar's capture of Jerusalem, 587 *b.c.)* they tried to rule a mixed population, but were divided among themselves. Their real power barely lasted two generations, viz.: in the reigns of David and Solomon (1055 to

977 *b.c.)*. At no time did they form a majority in the population, which consisted of Philistines (after whom Palestine is called) and various Arab tribes, such as Edomites, Amalekites, Moabites, etc. The Jews have been only in the land by fits and starts, and only as a minority.

Is it just, in these circumstances, to speak of Palestine as a land of the Jews? It is more correctly claimed as a portion of the Jazirat-ut Arab, the Arab Island nearly enclosed by the Mediterranean, the Red Sea, the Arabian Sea, the Persian Gulf, and the Euphrates-Tigris valley. Economically, Arabia, if it ever comes into its own, can only support itself with the stretches of fertile coast-lands which enclose its sandy deserts. Juristically, the Mandate which Britain holds over Palestine does not make Palestine British territory, or authorise Britain to dispose of the land as she pleases. She is a trustee for an "independent nation," and her function is to "render administrative advice and assistance," not to give away part of its territory to aliens, or keep it for itself. The Covenant of the League of Nations (Art. 22) says with reference to Palestine and Syria: "Certain communities formerly belonging to the Turkish Empire have reached a stage of development where their existence as independent nations can be provisionally recognised, subject to the rendering of administrative advice and assistance by a mandatory until such time as they are able to stand alone. The wishes of these communities must be a principal consideration in the selection of the mandatory."

The unanimous wish of the majority of the original population of Palestine, i.e., nearly all but the alien element recently introduced, is that they should be declared a sovereign independent nation. They have undergone enormous sacrifices and shed their blood freely in fighting for that aim. The only honourable course, therefore, that remains for Britain is:—

To abandon the mandate;

To hand over the territory to the people as a sovereign nation, with a constitution framed by the people themselves;

To forbid any future Jewish immigration;

To make a treaty with the new State for the reasonable protection of the Jewish minority who elect to remain loyal members of the State and obey its laws, with such safeguards for local autonomy as may be agreed upon, on the principle that *factum vale quod fieri non debuit*;

To allow free choice of withdrawal to such as do not wish to be incorporated in the State.

Some such arrangement will make for future peace and development and at last do justice to the harassed Arabs. This would be among the last of the flagrant acts of injustice committed by the Versailles Treaty to be remedied on principles of equity, good conscience, and a reasonable concession to the actual facts of the situation.

Fascism and the Dialectic
by A. Raven Thomson

THE uninterrupted progress of Fascism in Europe would seem to indicate the existence of a new historical process, which cannot be denied, but marches on to its inevitable conclusion. Marxists, who thought they had inherited from the prophet Karl, a perfect explanation of historical progress are now at a complete loss to explain this unexpected setback, which plays havoc with their strategic plan at the very moment when victory seemed within the grasp of the proletariat. It is all very well to call Fascism "the organised expression of the determination of the capitalists to stick at nothing in order to stay in power," as does Mr. John Strachey; but this does not explain the high-handed manner in which Fascist leaders treat the biggest of capitalists, nor their complete subordination of financial liberty to the national welfare.

Let us examine the Marxist system, "The Materialist Interpretation of History," to see where it has gone wrong. First of all we have to get back to Hegel, for as Lenin commented, "Marx is unintelligible without Hegel." Now Hegel was certainly not a materialist; quite the contrary, he was an idealist. He believed that the universe was all spirit, or more correctly, all "idea." This did not appeal to the Jew, Karl Marx; but in his explanation of phenomena Hegel invented a system called "The Dialectic" which had an immense attraction for the subtle mind of Marx.

Hegel's concept of the "Universe was a stupendous effort of the human intellect, perhaps the greatest mental achievement of mankind. He saw an awesome spectacle of an all-embracing "idea" engaged in a never-ending process of self-knowledge. In this process all phenomena, including the existence of mankind itself, were pieces in a vast and complicated "dialectic," or argument, by which the "idea" disputed with itself in pursuit of ultimate truth, or more correctly, "self-knowledge." He conceived the process to be the repeated postulation of some "thesis," or aspect of the truth, much as a scientist postulates a theory to explain chemical or physical facts. Then as this thesis did not, in fact, embrace the full truth, it would extort an "anti-thesis," or opposite concept, which would then engage in a "dialectic" struggle with the incomplete assumption of the "thesis." Much as the opponents of a scientific theory will marshal the arguments against it.

Eventually from this dialectic would emerge a "synthesis," including aspects of both thesis and anti-thesis in a closer appreciation of the truth. As this synthesis would then form a new, but still incomplete, thesis, it would provoke a further dialectic struggle, a further synthesis, and so forth, in a progressive pursuit of ultimate knowledge. Again the parallel with the progress of scientific research is close. Very naturally Hegel held man, and especially the organised, civilised state in the highest esteem, as the most advanced instrument in the dialectic perfection of the idea. This is the origin of the rather misconceived opinion that Hegel advocated worship of the State. Actually Hegel was a Pantheist; perhaps the most intense Monotheist ever known to mankind.

Marx And The Dialectic

Marx had little of the intellectual capacity of Hegel, whose system is outlined only in the crudest form above, but he fastened on to the dialectic process as an explanation of and justification for the Class War. Sharing Hegel's esteem for man and the organised state, Marx was particularly interested in the development of society under the dialectic process. Seeing society as an instrument of production, not like Hegel as an instrument of knowledge, he regarded the "workers" as the only section of society entitled to respect, and condemned the imperfection of a society that gave power and prestige to parasites and nonproducers.

The Marxist "Materialist Interpretation of History" is based upon the dialectic struggle between classes of society with the final objective of the perfection of the classless society in which all shall "work," that is, all be engaged in the process of production. Although this Marxist scheme falls far short of the sublime universal concept of Hegelian philosophy, yet it cannot fail to claim the sympathetic consideration of all Realists who reject both Idealism and Materialism as complete philosophies of existence. We may not share the Marxian prejudice in favour of material producers, and may still keep an honoured place for the seekers after Truth, whether through Art, Science or Religion, but we do revolt against the domination of society by any sectional class, particularly if that class contributes neither to knowledge of Truth nor production of Wealth.

Unfolding Civilisation

Whatever may be our view of the ultimate truth of Hegelian philosophy, it cannot be denied that the Hegelian "Triad" of thesis, anti-thesis and synthesis does form a fundamental rhythm of existence both in nature and in society. From proton and electron combining to form an atom to man and wife combining to form a family the same fundamental triadic base is to be found. In society the same law holds good in a continued dynamic process, which Marx held, no doubt rightly, would end in the perfected classless society. Let us trace this process through the unfolding of European civilisation.

Modern Europe has its remote origin in the impact of barbarian hordes upon the Roman Empire. What more perfect example of the dialectic process could be given? The thesis of Roman civilisation, artificial, materialist and decadent, was challenged by its anti-thesis, German barbarism, natural, idealist and virile. The result was an almost perfect synthesis, after a bitter dialectic struggle of conquest, reconquest, enslavement and vandalism, when the feudal system rose on the ruins of Rome, led by barbarian leaders who, nevertheless, still bore the traditional titles of Imperial Rome, dux (duke) comes (count), imperator (emperor) and so forth, ruling over villeins, but recently released from service to the Roman villas.

This feudal system rested entirely upon military power of protection by the sword in return for military service to the overlord. Very naturally in a dialectic process (completely ignored by Marx) military power provoked its complete anti-thesis-spiritual power. The power of the feudal baron was challenged by the power of the priest, and the Middle Ages rang with the great struggle of Church and State; culminating in the rivalry of Pope and Emperor that ended at Canossa with the triumph of the Papacy, and the amazing synthesis of military and spiritual power in the Crusades.

Papal supremacy, however, centralised upon Italy, became intolerable to the provincial nobility, who eventually broke the power of Rome in the Reformation and founded the independent states of Europe, breaking up the previous unity of Christendom. Another synthesis followed when nobles and clergy united in service to absolute monarchy. It matters little whether this was achieved by the ruthless methods of Henry VIII, or the finesse of Louis XIV, who made a Cardinal his leading minister of state: in Protestant and Catholic nations alike, the synthesis of monarchy ended the dialectic struggle of temporal and spiritual power.

Monarchy was, however, but the shield and justification for privilege of birth and of clergy, that aristocratic privilege which is miscalled "feudal" by Karl Marx. It is now at last that we emerge into the short period of history that alone interests the Marxists, the period when materialist motives begin to dominate over idealist motives, and class domination begins to be felt. Inevitably the common people resented and revolted against aristocratic pretensions, and the Great Rebellion, the French Revolution, the "mad year" of 1848, were merely incidents in a vast dialectic struggle which ended in the overthrow of aristocracy. Yet the remorseless logic of synthesis only ended one privilege to begin another, even worse than before. Purse-proud burghers replaced landed aristocracy. Privilege of birth gave way to privilege of wealth. Aristocracy gave place to plutocracy.

Capitalism

So came Capitalism, and the new dialectic of the class war between the privileged owners of property and the dispossessed proletariat of worker and peasant wielding their symbolic hammer and sickle. Like the feudal landowner the industrial capitalist relied upon sheer Might to maintain his position, and like the feudal landowner he was met by an appeal to Right from his workers, who opposed their negative resistance to his positive power. Trade Unions united the workers and developed their right to strike and withhold their labour as a powerful defensive weapon. Organisation was an essential part of this operation, and vast Trade Union movements took form in all the nations of the Western World.

The industrial capitalists replied by building their own vast trusts and combines, which soon reached out far beyond national boundaries into international federations linked by the ultimate capitalist over-lords of international finance. Meanwhile the workers too were extending their Trade Unions into ever larger organisations, seeking their international affiliations, and eventually looking to Moscow and Stalin for a lead in world revolution. So grew up the rival organisations of International Finance and International Socialism arrayed for what the Marxists fondly hoped would be the final struggle for the social millennium. A strange parallel, indeed, to the international organisation of Feudal Europe under Emperor and Pope for what many millions in those days imagined was to be a religious millennium.

Why has this millennium been intolerably withheld? The powers of production have been immensely extended by the scientific invention and technical advancement of recent years, and yet the standard of life of the masses of the people remains low and social conditions deplorable. Meanwhile, greater efficiency of production merely involves the creation of a huge army of unemployed. How is this to be explained? Why does the social revolution hang fire?

Privilege Of Power

The explanation is that organisation for power brings its own corruption. The development of gigantic Trade Union organisations vests the leaders of these organisations with immense power. They then become reluctant to risk their organisations in the culmination of the Class War to create a Classless State, in which such organisations will lose their main justification. Trade Union bosses commanding millions of men, just as much as monopoly capitalists commanding millions of money, have a vested interest in the maintenance of a system which endows them with great personal power.

So we have a new and corrupt synthesis. Financiers and Trade Union officials make truce, and later even enter into alliance to defend the system which is so beneficial to both. The first betrayal came when the Trade Union leader, Ben Turner, met the international Jewish financier, Alfred Mond (later Lord Melchett) and signed the notorious Mond-Turner agreement repudiating the strike weapon. The second and more serious betrayal has come more recently when the bosses of Trade Unionism and the financiers of World Capitalism combined to "defend democracy" and "preserve liberty." Internationalism sought first as a means of extended organisation for the Class War becomes an end in itself, something for which workers must be prepared to sacrifice wages, conditions and life itself. So come the pleas for Abyssinia and Czechoslovakia, China and Spain, while unemployment and misery mount at home.

What is all this but the old familiar struggle to preserve privilege—this time the privilege of power. Such is the abject conclusion of the Marxist Class War in the Western World. Privilege of birth gave place to privilege of wealth: both now bow to the privilege of power possessed by the bosses of men and of money.

The Classless Revolution

The dialectic process does not end there, however. One may no more cry "Halt" to history than to the tide. The thesis of monopoly privilege most inevitably provoke its anti-thesis, and this anti-thesis is the mass popular movement of all classes who suffer under financial and Trade

Union tyranny. At last the hope of a real "classless" state emerges, for the antithesis of "boss rule" is the "classless" revolution. All class privilege has now been liquidated. A few men alone possess the power vested in them by millions of workers or millions of shares, and today exercise that power to maintain the system that affords it. Against these men rises the tide of the Classless Revolution.

It is scarcely surprising that this new revolutionary force should take a national form. Patriotism alone has always been the emotion that has united all classes of the community in common action. So it is to Patriotism that all classes turn to free themselves from a tyranny exercised either by aliens themselves (Jews for the most part) or by men who have become wedded to an international outlook.

So it is that Fascism plays its part in the dialectical development of society. The Revolutionary Movement of the Twentieth Century is as truly a part of the historic process, as ever was the democratic movement of the eighteenth or the proletarian movement of the nineteenth. Indeed, the next synthesis is already making its presence felt. Irresponsible exercise of power has provoked popular revolt. It might be expected that this revolt would take an anarchic form in indignant repudiation of personal power. Yet, in response to the inevitable law of synthesis, popular revolt grasps at power as its only means of defeating tyranny. The principle of Fascism is the responsible exercise of power by the popular national leader entrusted by the people with the authority to act in their name. Irresponsible power challenged by national revolt creates the true synthesis of national authority responsible for the use of its power to the nation.

The End Of The Struggle?

It only remains to discuss whether the Classless Revolution of Fascism ends the social process and perfects the classless state. This must largely remain a matter for the future. It may be hoped that the dialectic may now pass beyond the nation to the perfection of the world order, or rise above the political to the cultural sphere. In any case it would seem logical to expect that a classless revolution has a much better chance of creating a Classless State, than a deliberate class revolution like Communism, which has produced a State in Soviet Russia still fiercely concerned with class rivalry and rapidly creating its own bureaucratic tyranny of a much purged Communist minority.

It is also significant that every Fascist State has been intensely concerned to establish an organic structure of society, and subordinate all artificial class distinctions to national service. This would certainly seem to indicate that the Classless Revolution leads to the foundation of the Classless State, and thus to the ending of the struggle for class privilege, which Marx condemned. It may well be that National Revolution will achieve, what the International Revolution of Marxism has failed to establish.

In any case no Fascist seeks a Judaic "millennium" in which struggle shall cease and stagnation ensue. Enough for us that we have to deal with the evils of our time, and partake in the historic process which will yet bring regeneration to an age sunk in sordid materialism. Class struggle is a symptom of material selfishness. Mediaeval Europe knew other aims and higher ideals. Let us end the struggle of class that Western Man may turn his eyes to nobler things. We hail those future struggles, those greater conflicts yet to come.

The Disinherited of the Soil
by Francis Mcevoy

THERE are so many of us who, like you, peasant folk of Britain, were born and bred in the open country, and who, before they were driven by the blighting tyranny of modern capitalism to seek their livelihood in the sterile cities, knew the joy of waking each morning in pure air to the song of the birds, or the voice of the wind in the trees, to the glow of the sun, the sting of the frost, or the soft patter of rain on the grass. We loved Nature in all her moods and in all her seasons, for we were part of her. We lived lives of the greatest simplicity, and therefore of the deepest content. The best of all God's gifts to humanity, rugged health and peace of mind, were ours, for we broke no law, human or divine. We asked so little of life—only to work for a modest return, and thereby gain enough to live on the land of our fathers.

But the black days came upon the farmlands. We were destroyed by the system which crowds the people of Britain into offices and factories, and leaves farming to the foreigner. British manufactured products for imported foodstuffs.

No matter how much such a system harms the people, physically, intellectually, morally, or exposes them to the danger of famine in time of war, it is a "paying proposition" —for some.

And so we came to the great cities, to economic servitude. We became clerks, factory workers, chain-store assistants, lost the tan on our faces, and led the anxious soulless life of the wage slave. We were told that we should be thankful, and if need be fight, for the blessings showered upon us by democracy. A democracy which incarnates greed, materialism, triviality, and the commercial exploitation of every human need and instinct. A stultification of humanity hitherto unknown in history, outside of Soviet Russia. Long live the "little man," standardised like a mass-produced motor car, the swarm of "Babbitts" from the service flats and the suburbs, propagandised, exploited, and brutified, in "this England of ours"!

It is true that all have not yet left the land, but how much longer can the sorely tried remnant continue the fight against an economic order which is basically hostile, which wages the civil war of factory upon farm? Yeomen, peasants of England, our land is the slave of Export Capitalism, which places its entire emphasis upon the towns, industrialising and urbanising. What can it offer you but temporary palliatives to still the outcry of your dwindling numbers, and to gain the tribute of your deluded votes? You have been told that something will be done for you; an assurance of probably as much value as the "homes fit for heroes" slogan of contemptible memory. When you have proved its futility, then, in the name of your British manhood and traditions, let it be for the last time. British Union has a policy which will save you and Britain, and enable all who wish it, and they will be legion, to return to the land of their fathers. You have doubtless heard and read much to our discredit, but have you never thought that there might be a reason for this—that we might be challenging interests which are not yours, nor ours, nor those of the mass of the people? Is all this campaign of disparagement so very disinterested, do you think? Are you going to be told any longer just what you may, or may not, like, have your political opinions willy-nilly limited to the humbug of the "Old Gangs"? Judge our policy for yourselves, as it affects you, without any perfidious promptings from the penny press.

You will find that we are ardent nationalists, wholly devoted to the welfare of the soil of Britain. Industry, too, will prosper, for it will be assisted by the money which now finances the foreigner, but not at the expense of agriculture. There will be a just and healthy balance, in place of the lop-sided antisocial economy of today.

We exiles from the countryside love the soil as greatly as any of you. It is false to say that we aim at tyranny. We could not, even if we wished, tyrannise over the people of Britain.

The death of the countryside portends the death of the nation, for from the soil springs all life, physical and spiritual. You, who instinctively understand these truths, must know that we are not misguided, who emblazon them upon our banners.

Corporate Economics by A. Raven Thomson

A GREAT problem has been created for the modern world by the collapse of the present economic system. We can no longer tolerate a system which condemns most of us to poverty in the midst of the greatest plenty mankind has ever known, which deprives millions of people of the right to earn their own living, and brings ever nearer the danger of war in the international struggle for contracting world markets. What is the cause of this universal breakdown? Where have we gone wrong?

Before we can fully appreciate the cause of the trouble, we must consider the threefold nature of organized society as follows: —

- A Central Government vested with authority to plan and direct the national life.
- A Number of Social Groups with various purposes and interests.
- A Mass of Individuals endowed with powers of initiative and enterprise.

The classical economic theory of the nineteenth century concerned itself almost entirely with the third and least organized aspect of society, resenting either state or group interference with economic affairs. In earlier times of comparative scarcity there may have been some justification for this view, as the initiative and enterprise of the individual was then of vital importance in developing latent powers of production and advancing technical invention. Obviously the individual would develop his powers of initiative and enterprise to the best effect, if granted the largest possible measure of economic liberty, and this is precisely what the economists of the Manchester School demanded, when they advocated "laissez faire" and free trade.

Whatever the advantages of economic liberty in solving the problem of scarcity, however, it has become a positive menace to social welfare in a dawning age of plenty. There is no need to condemn classical economic theory as such, but we must realise that there can be no absolute "laws" of economics independent of social organization. No doubt the individualist system was very necessary in an age of scarcity, and we have to thank the Manchester School for solving the problem of production, but the time has now come for a new economic system in keeping with the needs of a new age. Individual enterprise encouraged by complete liberty of exploitation has put an end to scarcity, but is completely incapable of distributing the plenty it has created to the people as a whole. Production is in its very nature an individual or at most a group process: distribution, on the other hand, is based upon the needs of the whole community, and obviously cannot succeed without a large measure of conscious social planning.

Socialism and the Class War

As individualism has now passed its period of usefulness and has become an actual danger to economic progress, the time has come to turn the focus of economic interest to the social group, if not to the nation as a whole. Hitherto those who have most vigorously attacked the present system, and have adopted such collective terms as "Socialist" or "Communist," have never really risen above group considerations. Despite their grandiloquent claim to "nationalize" the means of production, the very basis of Socialist and Communist appeal lies in the exaggeration of class differentiation and insistence upon the "class war." Clearly such a class-conscious doctrine belongs to the realm of the social group, and fails to rise to any appreciation of the whole community as a living organic entity. Indeed the stress laid by the Socialist upon internationalism, and his denial of patriotism, confirm his inability to grasp the full implications of social organization, which should rise far above class considerations to a realization of national purpose. The ultimate "reductio ad absurdum" is reached, when the Soviet regime in Russia claims that it is the "dictatorship of the proletariat" for this would imply the permanent and conscious ascendancy of a group over the national life.

Actually the class war becomes a sheer absurdity in an age of plenty, for what object can there be in a struggle between the classes when there is plenty for all? The class war is nothing more nor less than a grisly relic of the age of scarcity, which is only able to linger on into the present era owing to the inefficiency of our present economic system. Solve the problem of distribution and the class war is at an end. In any case the separation of society into warring classes is very largely an artificial invention of Karl Marx, for the differentiation of owning and exploited classes is becoming more and more difficult, as modern life becomes more and more complex. Karl Marx had no conception of the great stock companies which spread ownership over huge numbers of people who normally earn their own living in industry; nor did he anticipate the great numbers of organizers and engineers, experts and technicians, who would be interposed between employers and workers by the development of modern industry.

Even if we accept the division of society into employers and workers, however, it does not necessarily follow that their interests are opposed. It is true that both employers and workers consider themselves as opposing armies with conflicting interests, but this arises from an inability to grasp the benefit of collective organization for both parties. In the case of every single business enterprise it is obvious that the interests of employer and workers are opposed, and that if the workers demand too high wages there will be no profit left over for the employer, while if the employer can force wages down he will enjoy a higher profit. It does not follow, however, that employers and workers as a whole can, therefore, benefit their own class at the other's expense. Actually in an age of plenty, as at present, the interests of workers and employers go hand in hand. Obviously the need of modern industry is for large and expanding markets. The attempt to find these in illusory international trade has failed dismally of recent years, with the result that now industrialists are turning more and more to the home market. Clearly the purchasing power of the home market, however, will be determined very largely by wage-rates, so that it has actually become in the interest of the employer that the workers should receive higher wages in order that they may be able to buy the products of modern industry. Surely the Socialist workers will not extend their belief in the class war to the point of refusing higher wages, because they will benefit the employers!

The Corporate Concept

We see then that the present economic system has failed because it placed too much emphasis upon the interests of the individual, but that the Socialist and Communist doctrine is equally at fault because it exalts the social group at the expense of the community as a whole. Fascism turns to the third alternative, and insists upon treating the community as a single organized corporate state, controlled and planned by a central government empowered with sufficient authority over individual and group to protect the general welfare of the whole, and advance the national purpose. This is the corporate concept of the nation as an organism of a higher order, but essentially similar to the human body, with its organs and functions serving a collective purpose. It is the essential basis of the organization of the Fascist regime in Italy which regulates the relations of Italian employers and workers along lines of common interest according to the rules of the famous Charter of Labour.

Such a system, based upon an entirely new concept of economic purpose, will require an equally new science of economic adjustment to social needs. It is my belief that this new economic science will be worked out in this country, which has been for so long the commercial centre of the world. It would be idle to ignore the fact that both Italy and Germany, the first countries to adopt a Fascist political constitution, have had the greatest difficulty in developing the economic side of their regime, although they have both responded far better than democratic countries to the strain of world depression. We must remember that although democracy and liberal principles came first to France and the Continent, it was in Britain that the economic implications of Liberalism were worked out by the Manchester School of individualists. As it was Britain that gave this dangerous, almost disastrous, economic theory to the world, it will clearly be the duty of Britain to apply the new principles of Fascism to the economic sphere, and produce the commercial structure of the future that will replace the discredited remnants of Liberal Free Trade.

Corporate Principles

It can be no part of the present discussion to lay down the basis of such a science, but certain principles of corporate economics immediately suggest themselves in contra-distinction to present individualism. In place of the "economic man" whose personal self-seeking was the essential basis of the old school, we shall have the "economic community" for whom the individual will engage in patriotic service. In place of classes of men combining together to protect their common "interests," we shall have occupational groups combining together in functional service to the community as a whole. In place of the competition of individuals struggling for a living, each against all and the devil take the hindmost, we shall have the co-operation of individuals for their common benefit.

How shall these principles be put into effect? First of all undoubtedly by the exercise of authority. Discipline and control must be introduced into the chaos of present economic affairs. The horrors of the present system, which feed the fires of the class war, and give the Socialist agitator grounds for his attack upon "capitalism", arise very largely from the undue exercise of economic power by the powerful individual who has amassed sufficient property or capital to exert an appreciable influence upon commercial affairs and thus advance his interests by unfair methods. Under Fascism no individual will be permitted to use his property in this sense as a means of exerting power for his own benefit. "Power" is the monopoly of Government.

Here we have the complete answer to the Socialist who demands the abolition of private capital and the nationalization of the means of production. It is true that the private capitalist has in the past abused his control over capital to advance his own interests, but that does not justify the abolition of private property, but rather the control of its use to prevent anti-social action. The truth is that the Socialist is no more than a disgruntled bourgeois, who envies the capitalist his wealth and power. By implication he accepts the bourgeois principle that the owner may do what he likes with his own, and hence can find no alternative for capitalist exploitation than wholesale confiscation, which overwhelms the good capitalist with the bad. Fascism recognises that capital and money have endowed individuals with power which they have abused in the past, and demands from the electorate sufficient authority and means of action to deal with the most powerful vested interest in the land. As Oswald Mosley has put it perfectly clearly, "Under Capitalism Capital uses the Nation for its own ends: Under Fascism the Nation uses Capital for its own ends."

It is clearly impracticable that Government, however powerful and efficient, should attempt the detailed planning of the economic affairs of the whole nation. This would be a denial of all group organization, which is an essential part of the healthy body politic, and would tend to perpetuate and aggravate the present menace of bureaucracy which is rapidly socializing this Country. Socialists and Conservatives alike compete in increasing the power and influence of Whitehall, which is rapidly becoming the "New Despotism" that Lord Chief Justice Hewart has foretold. Under Fascism a great deal of this bureaucratic control will be devolved once more along new lines of functional organization to Corporations controlling the principal industries and groups of industries in the country. Corporations of Agriculture, Fishing, Transport, Mining and Medicine will take the place of Ministries at Whitehall, and will be staffed by men who have worked up through their industry and profession and will be much better fitted to control it than any permanent government official. These new institutions of industrial self-government will replace local self-government which is becoming rapidly out of date in face of the rapidity of modern communications and the wider planning of public utilities. By this means group organization will be transformed from the more rigid structural basis of the past to the more flexible functional basis of the future.

A very large measure of self-government will be granted to the Corporations to settle all internal matters concerning the industries which they control, and employers, workers and consumers will all be represented upon the council of the Corporation. The employers will be represented through their employers' federation, and the workers through their trade union, while Government will appoint consumers' representatives to watch over the interests of the general public and those of other Corporations which are particularly interested in the product. The Corporation will be required to lay down standards of wages and conditions of work for the industry as between employers and workers, and also prices and terms of competition as between employers and consumers. All agreements made will be legally binding upon the entire industry and any employer or worker who breaks what is in effect a by-law of the Corporation will be guilty of an offence for which he can be brought before a court of law. Actually employers' federation and trade union will be expected to maintain discipline among their members, who will compose 100% of the industry in question. With such adequate means of arbitration, strike and lock-out alike will, of course, be prohibited, but employers, workers or consumers may appeal to the Minister of Corporations sitting in council with representatives of all industrial corporations for a just decision in keeping with general industrial practice and the national welfare. It will be seen that by this devolution of authority and self-government to the Corporations the central Legislature will be relieved of a large measure of detailed legislation which at present hampers the work of Parliament.

Use of Corporate Organization

So far the new economics may seem an interesting new conception, but of doubtful practical value to compensate for their considerable complexity. Such a system is not, however, devised merely as an intellectual exercise, but has immense advantages just where the present system is particularly weak. For example, let us take the worst problem of all, that of poverty in the midst of plenty, arising from what the Conservatives used to call "over-production," but which may be much better described as "under-consumption". Obviously this defect in the present system can only be rectified by bringing about a much higher standard of life, when the people are able to consume the immense production of modern science and technique. Unfortunately the individualist system forces down purchasing power either in the form of wages or profits during a period of plenty, because of the intense competition to sell goods on an already overstocked market, which compels manufacturers to lower prices in a cut-throat endeavour to capture the market. Under Fascism, however, prices and terms of competition will be controlled, and no manufacturer will be permitted to sweat his workers against the regulations of his Corporation in order to steal a march on his competitors. Not only will the decline in purchasing power be checked by this means, but the whole wage system can be permanently raised by concerted action over the whole field of industry. Obviously such action is perfectly sound and has been advocated by several public men of recent years, but unfortunately it cannot be effected under the present individualist system, for if any single employer were foolish enough to attempt to raise the wages of his workers in the cause of national recovery, he would soon find plenty of unpatriotic competitors who would cut theirs and drive him off the market. It is only under the discipline and control of the organized Fascist regime that such a policy can be carried through with success.

By the same means the great scourge of unemployment can also be cured, for it is obvious that this is purely the result of the complete lack of organization in our present national economy. There must be at any one time in this country a certain amount of work, calculated in man-hours, which requires to be done, and a certain number of workers willing and anxious to do this work. The work can certainly be spread over the total number of workers by a readjustment of the hours of work, as is at present being done in Italy, where the 40-hour week is now being introduced. Actually Fascist Government in this country would rather seek a more beneficial solution along the lines of raising the standard of life of the people rather than shortening the hours of work, but in any case the problem of unemployment becomes completely and permanently soluble in the organization of a planned corporate state.

The Function of Finance

One of the major defects of the present system has been its failure to imbue the various occupations and professions of society with a sense of their functional purpose of service to the whole. This has led to the worst results in the realm of finance, where money power has been disgracefully exploited by bankers and financiers for their own benefit. Indeed it is no exaggeration to say that this country, in common with many others, is dominated by a dictatorship of high finance, which is far more interested in the lucrative returns of the foreign bond market than in the well-being of the British people. The first and most urgent task of Fascist Government will be to break down this present dictatorship of international finance, and replace it by an authoritative regime empowered by the nation to enforce a functional and social purpose upon even the most powerful interests in the country.

The function of money, which is too often forgotten at the present time, is to facilitate the exchange of goods and services. The fact that we are finding it so difficult to exchange our goods and services today is a clear indication of the failure of finance to carry out its primary duty to the community. However skilful and ingenious our technicians and inventors may be, the standard of life of the people cannot be raised to a higher level unless sufficient currency and other means of exchange are put into circulation. Otherwise the only result of invention and rationalization of industry will be to throw more and more men out of work. At the present time we suffer from a very serious restriction of money, which is carried out by the banks in pursuit of their policy of deflation. The reason for this policy is twofold. First there is a certain innate conservatism which still clings to the gold standard of currency as a last relic of the age of barter. Secondly, financiers realise that a restriction in the amount of the article in which they trade renders it more valuable and themselves more powerful. For these two reasons the quantity of money in circulation is not adapted, as it should be, to the volume of potential production in the country, but is restricted to a proportion of the supplies of a certain precious metal, gold, in the vaults of the Central Bank. Clearly the available supplies of this metal are entirely irrelevant to the problem of distribution which finance must solve, and in fact the quantity of gold in the whole world is pitifully inadequate to finance the immense powers of production of modern industry. Yet instead of expanding currency and credit to meet the needs of industrial development, our financial masters are endeavouring to return to the gold standard by restricting production to the limits set by world gold supplies. No doubt by these means international financiers are maintaining and extending their control over world affairs, but only at the expense of condemning the greater part of the world to poverty in the midst of plenty.

Fascist Government will insist upon a reversal of this unnatural domination of finance over industry. It must be made perfectly clear that finance has a function of service to industry, and is in no way suited for that government of industry which it has usurped. Not only must the encouragement of foreign production in competition with our own through the foreign flotations of the City of London be brought to an end, but our financiers and bankers must be compelled to face the problem of distribution which they have so consistently neglected in the past. We have already pointed out that the future of our trade lies in the revival of the home market, and finance must now turn its attention to means of bringing about this revival by raising the purchasing power of the people.

This involves a tremendous and revolutionary break with all the most sacred traditions of banking business, for the essential feature of the problem is that it involves the financing of consumption. Hitherto bankers have confined their operations entirely to the financing of production in the commercial sphere, for instalment-payment business does not really finance consumption, as it merely mortgages future purchasing power for the sake of immediate sales. We must find some method of financing a higher scale of wages and salaries in order to release the powers of production. At present, of course, in an individualist system engaged in intense competition any such proceeding is impossible, and any employer who went to his bank and asked for an overdraft to pay higher wages would be rightly condemned as a lunatic, for he could give no guarantee that his competitors would do the same or would not lower their wages to capture the market from him. Lord Beaverbrook who has frequently advocated higher wage rates has never been able to overcome this essential difficulty.

Corporate economics, however, offer an immediate solution, for the very purpose of the Corporations is to control and regulate wage rates and conditions of labour, so that if the Fascist Government undertook a policy of higher wages, there would be no question of unpatriotic or alien-controlled firms hanging back to take advantage of their competitors; all would be compelled to conform to the same standards. If the employer then went to his bank and asked for an overdraft to carry through his part of the programme, the banker would have no difficulty in obliging him, for he would know that the increased purchasing power of the whole community would result in increased orders and greater prosperity for the particular firm with which he was doing business. It is by this means that Fascism would raise the standard of life of the people, and place that larger volume of currency and credit in circulation which is necessary to finance the increased productive power of industry.

Clearly this policy of monetary expansion must involve a complete break with the gold standard, and more conservative critics may fear for the stability of the currency in consequence. Fascism, however, points out that money is in reality a claim for goods and services, and that no person in his normal senses really goes to a bank and demands gold bullion for his currency notes: he is perfectly satisfied if he can exchange his money for those goods and services of which he stands in need. Now there are obviously plenty of goods and services available in this country at the present time: warehouses stocked with goods, in fact, and over two million of our fellow countrymen and women offering their services in vain. As long as we do not issue notes that are not covered by available goods and services there can be no danger of inflation; so Fascism will base the currency upon the broad basis of the whole productive resources of the nation, instead of upon the narrow insecure foundation of gold in the Bank of England.

Empire Autarchy

The only valid criticism of this policy of corporate organisation of industry, raising, as it does, the standard of life of the whole people, lies in the argument that this country depends upon its foreign trade to a very large extent, and cannot therefore afford a higher standard of life than its competitors upon the markets of the world. This argument can, in fact, be refuted, however, by reference to the example of Henry Ford, who produced the world's cheapest motor car while paying the highest wages. He was enabled to do this by the huge home market in America, which enabled him to introduce mass-production methods, and compete favourably upon the markets of countries with a much lower standard of life. Actually we are losing our markets overseas, not because our goods are dearer than those of our competitors, so much as because these markets are being closed to us by insurmountable tariff barriers, behind which native industries are being rapidly developed. However cheap our goods may become, we cannot expect other countries to ruin their own industries and put their own people out of work in order to buy them. In any case oriental peoples, like the Japanese, can outbid us hopelessly when the question of wage rates is taken into account.

The export trade is not in any case essential to the well-being of a country, as it implies sending goods out of the country for foreigners to consume, instead of retaining them at home to swell the standard of life of the home population. Only the financial magnates of the City of London stand to benefit in the long run from an excess of exports, since it is upon the basis of this surplus that they float the great foreign loans, from which they draw such munificent commissions. Exports are only really justified to pay for essential imports, and the imports of this country could be very largely reduced by the exclusion of all imported goods which we can produce at home. It is a scandalous fact that large quantities of manufactured articles are imported into this country, which could be perfectly well produced here, and there is no excuse for our neglect of home agriculture merely because our resources are not sufficient to feed our entire population; we should produce at least the maximum of home grown produce before going abroad for the remainder.

Even after we have produced the maximum variety of goods in this country, it would be idle to deny that we cannot make ourselves entirely self-sufficient, but on the other hand there are very few products which we require that cannot be found somewhere within the British Empire. Fascism is no narrow Little England policy, but has a great imperial plan of autarchic development to offer to the Empire as a whole. A much larger share of the expanding home market will be offered to the dominions than was offered at Ottawa, for foreign competition will be entirely excluded. There can be no doubt whatever that the Empire as a whole will be perfectly willing to co-operate in such an economic system, which will form a completely self-sufficient Empire insulated from the effects of world crises and world depressions, and enabled to build up a higher standard of life than has yet been known.

Finally, we must imagine the corporate principles of Fascism applied to international trade. No longer will the importer be permitted to buy in any market he thinks fit, but he will be obliged to work through a Foreign Trade Board, which will use the purchasing power of the nation, as a means of gaining export markets. From the very start Fascism will adopt the policy that Britain buys from those who buy from Britain, and if any foreign country desires to sell us goods that we lack, she will be required to accept our goods in return. As other countries adopt similar methods, we shall eventually arrive at a general system of organized barter from country to country, which is the only practical means of planned international trading, free from the machinations of international finance and the bonds of international usury.

Corporate World Order

It must not be assumed that Fascism is entirely self-centred in the national sense. Certainly it is an essential feature of Fascist philosophy to put one's own country first, but it would be rash to assume on that account that Fascism implies national rivalry and may lead to war on economic grounds. On the contrary, a very serious danger of the present system is that the ever-increasing struggle for world markets may lead to war. Indeed in the Far East wars for markets have already taken place, and it is only with difficulty that the European powers have avoided being drawn into the struggle. Actually the corporate system of economic planning will minimize the danger of war, for it will bring the economic causes of war under conscious human control. No longer will it be a question of each country's dumping a maximum of exports upon its neighbours, but of authoritative governments in full corporate control of their national economic affairs meeting together to share and exchange the essential raw materials required for their industrial development. As there is no scarcity of these raw products, and as in fact their production has been drastically curtailed to prevent flooding the market, there should be no difficulty whatever in arriving at an amicable solution of this comparatively simple problem, when once the nations have abandoned the ridiculous idea that they can benefit themselves by ruining one another. Rivalry there certainly will be in the world of the future, but rivalry in achievement, not in competition. It is only along the lines of the corporate organization of society and of economic life that we can attain peace and prosperity in an ordered world. Let us play our part by putting our own national affairs in order and encouraging other nations to do the same.

The Nazi Movement in Perspective by James Drennan

THE Italian Fascists have never attempted to give the prodigious racial background to Italian nationalism which Herr Hitler has produced as the intellectual inspiration of the "Dritte Reich." If any people had a temptation to base modern policy on the claims of past history, it might have been the masters of Rome, but Signor Mussolini appears to aim at an ultimate Pan-European association based on the concepts of Fascism rather than at a literal revival of Roman territorial glories. Herr Hitler, on the other hand, has elaborated an ideal of German (or Aryan) racial exclusivity, which has deep roots in German history. However, this German concept, if properly understood, need in no way conflict with the Italian understanding of Fascism as a creed destined to form the spiritual basis of the regeneration of the West. Neither should it conflict with the lofty conception of British Empire, which inspires Fascism in Britain, for at no point does any clash of interest arise. On the contrary, all the diverse contributions to the theory of World Fascism can be complementary rather than disruptive.

In order to arrive at an understanding of the adoption by the Nazis of the racial interpretation of history, first formulated during the last century by such non-German writers as the Frenchman Gobineau and the Englishman Houston Stewart Chamberlain, and adapted by the Nazi leaders as the basis of a revolutionary ideal accepted by the German masses and as the motive-force of the present state policy of the German Reich, it is necessary to consider certain conditions and trends of German history over the whole period of the last thousand years. Only by such a study can we arrive at the bases of belief of the modern German people, and understand the direction in which the masters of Germany are likely to lead a people devotedly convinced of the validity of their belief.

It was the Germanic tribes who, in the eighth century, really succeeded to the imperial conceptions of ancient Rome. The Empire of Charlemagne—styled Emperor of the West—was ethnically more German than French, and it was only after his death that the Franco-

Gaullist elements came to be distinguished from the Germans, when the heirs to the different parts of his dominions took the oath, respectively in French and German dialects. As late as the thirteenth century the Hohenstaufen Emperors continued to regard the whole of Italy and a large part of what is now France as provinces of the German Empire. It is worth remarking, that while at this date, Germany hardly extended east of the Elbe, the Netherlands, Burgundy and parts of Savoy and Franche-Comte were in differing degrees and at different times, included within the Imperial dominions.

It is one of the faults of the teaching of history in this country that we are seldom enabled to see our own history in perspective and in relation to that of the rest of Europe. For the four centuries between the accession of Louis the German in 825 and the death of Frederick II in 1250—roughly the period in our own history between the reigns of Alfred the Great and Henry III—the history of Europe was very largely the history of Germany. At a period when our own history was exceedingly provincial—when its events were as remote from those of the main current of European history as, for instance, the individual history of modern Norway is from that of present-day Europe—Germany was the scene of the great struggles which saw the birth of mediaeval European culture, and her Emperors, like Henry the Fowler, Otto the Great and Frederick Barbarossa became the arbiters of Western Europe, and the masters of events from Jutland to Sicily, from Burgundy to Hungary. It is necessary to appreciate the significance of this period on the minds of modern Germans, in order to understand their extraordinary pride in their history, and their sense of frustration and confinement in the territorial conditions of post-War Europe.

Otto the Great—who died in 973, nearly a thousand years ago—has, in the last few years, become the supreme figure of the Nazi Pantheon, and his portrait figures in German bookshops almost as frequently as those of Hitler and Goring. The whole process of Germany history is, in fact, an example of the phenomenon of "arrested development," and the peculiar manifestations which we associate with contemporary German national psychology derive from the "frustration complex" which is its inevitable derivative. The very scope and swing of the Hohenstaufen power was the undoing of the German people. The splendid Emperors of this line were fascinated by the dream of the Charlemagnian Pan-European Empire, and for more than a century they wasted the strength of the Germans on the pursuit of their Italian ambitions. The earlier policy of Otto the Great had been to consolidate a great German state. The Hohenstaufens were attracted by the Pan-European conceptions to which the Hapsburgs became heirs. And the ruin of the Hohenstaufens left Germany weakened and without central force, at the moment when England and France were on the verge of developing towards that national statehood which was ultimately achieved under the Tudors and the Valois. The errors of the Hohenstaufen policies appear even more tragic from a German point of view, when it is remembered that the great "Drang nach Osten" of the Germans across the Elbe and round the shores of the Baltic was being undertaken by the Teutonic Knights during the reign of Frederick the Second, and that this drive was ultimately aborted in its wider possibilities by the slacking of impetus from the German centre.

There are almost exactly three centuries between the death of Frederick II in 1250 and the death of Martin Luther in 1546, and although this is rather an arbitrary division to make, it is permissible for the purposes of generalisation. This period of three centuries saw a complete transformation, both in the prospects and character of the German people. There are three main historical currents which had a fundamental influence on the subsequent development of German historical life.

First, both the German and the North Italian cities lost that economic supremacy which they had enjoyed during the Middle Ages, when they had grown up along the main East to West route of the trade between Europe and the Byzantine-Saracenic East. The capture of Constantinople by the Turks largely destroyed the prosperity of all the regions along this route, and the discovery of America and the opening of the Cape route transferred the centre of economic power to the countries along the Atlantic littoral—Spain and Portugal, England, France and Holland. It is, in fact, no exaggeration to state that both the Reformation in Germany, and the Thirty Years' War in the Seventeenth Century, had their roots in the terrific process of economic dislocation which must have followed this shifting of main trade centres.

The second great historical current of this period was the rise of the Hapsburgs, in the shoes of the Hohenstaufens. The Hapsburgs were German princes with wide personal dominions in German lands, but their very position in Austria— Østermark Mark —on the Eastern Marches of Germany made them essentially non-German in their interests. The traditional policy of the Hapsburgs explains, easily enough, the extraordinary hatred which the Pan-Germans, and particularly the Nazis, have for the whole "Austrian theory." The Hapsburgs—like the earlier Hohenstaufens—regarded themselves as the heirs of the Roman Empire, and they laid claim to world dominion, or at least, in practical politics, to a Pan-European supremacy. This amazing House was, at different periods in its history, an Italian power, a Spanish and South American power, a Slav power, a power with aspirations in Asia—and even in Africa—but it was never a power which consciously allowed purely German interests to predominate.[1] The Hapsburgs fulfilled a great role, during the four centuries following the conquest of Constantinople by the Turks. They checked the military progress of the Turks westward, and they succeeded the Byzantine Emperors as the principal civilising agents over all South-Eastern Europe. But their role was as valuable to Europe as it was disastrous to the conception of German nationality. Their preoccupation with the Mediterranean postponed indefinitely any process of unification in Germany, and their dynastic policy led in practice, to what amounted to the partition of the German-speaking lands.

The third important influence on the development of German history was the partition of the German-speaking lands, and the transformation of the whole racial character of the populations calling themselves German, which was in process during the period 1250-1550. This phenomenon was of supreme significance, particularly when it is remembered that it was during the same period that nations like the English, French and Spanish, and even the Hungarians, Czechs and Poles emerged and were consolidated, and Europe began to take on the forms with which we are at present familiar.

In the time of Charlemagne the differences between Teutons and Franks were not very clearly defined. England, under the Saxon hegemony, was very largely a German Kingdom, and the same may be said of Northern Italy under the Lombards. There first of all took place an absorption of German elements in England, Eastern France and Northern Italy. This process had really been completed long before the death of Frederick II in 1250. During the following three hundred years the Western frontiers of Germany were pushed back towards the Rhine. Regions like Burgundy and Franche-Comté were becoming more French and less German. The Netherlands became definitely non-German. Switzerland took form, and considerable German populations became attached to the Swiss idea. The important German marches in Austria became an integral part of the largely non-German Hapsburg Empire. The results of these detachments are still

1 Except possibly during the brief reign of the Emperor Joseph II.

significant in modern European history. They explain the Austrian question. They explain the Alsace-Lorraine question—the feud over a region which has never quite ceased to be German and which has never become wholly French. They explain also the attempted revival by the Nazis of Pan-German consciousness, not only in Austria and Czechoslovakia, but also to a lesser extent in Holland and Denmark, in Switzerland and Belgium.

But at the same time as the German linguistic frontiers were being pushed back towards the Rhine, and while populations of the most authentic German blood were becoming transformed into Swiss, French and Dutch, the German language and German culture was spreading rapidly towards the East, and the primitive non-German populations of North-Eastern Europe were learning to think of themselves as Germans. The German colonisation to the eastward was the work of the Teutonic Knights who conquered and proselytised the Slav and Finnish tribes east of the Elbe, and later beyond the Oder, and of the German Hanseatic towns who were engaged in founding trading centres all along the coast of the Baltic. Ultimately, the German progress in this direction was checked by the military power of Poland, and by the rivalry of the Scandinavian states, and, of course, later, by the emergence of Russia as a great power at the beginning of the eighteenth century. But it was a great achievement, particularly when it is borne in mind that this drive was pushed to its conclusion between the thirteenth and fifteenth centuries, when the central German inspiration was weak, and, at many times, non-existent. The role of the Hanseatic towns and of the Teutonic Knights in the Baltic corresponded very much to that of the Italian Republics and of the Latin Knightly Orders in the Mediterranean, who managed to maintain an aggressive Italian policy in the East at a time when no central Italian power existed.

In the half-failure of the mediaeval "Drang nach Osten" is to be discovered the second element of the "frustration-complex," which underlies the modern German's interpretation of his country's history. The Nazis—particularly of what one might call the "Prussian school" to which General Goring and Herr Rosenberg belong—look constantly to a revival of German penetration and colonisation of the Baltic lands, as compensation for the confinement of German aspirations in the West.

The most important result of the mediaeval "Drang nach Osten" was the foundation of the Prussian state. The autochthonous population of Prussia was largely of Slav and Finnish origin—the most primitive stocks of Northern Europe—mixed with the warlike and needy elements who had migrated eastward from the older seats of German culture. The Prussians were hammered out as a people, as a result of two centuries of the most bloodthirsty warfare of the Middle Ages.

The Reformation in Germany—which occupies the history of the greater part of the sixteenth and seventeenth centuries—may in certain aspects be regarded as a largely unconscious movement of frustrated German nationalism against Pan-German—Roman Catholic conceptions of the Hapsburgs. The Reformation culminated in the Thirty Years War which ruined Germany for nearly a century afterwards, and which seriously crippled Hapsburg power. The recovery of Turkish power which was demonstrated in the Siege of Vienna in 1683 was one result of the weakening of the Hapsburgs, and the Thirty Years' War probably had the result of prolonging Turkish rule in South-Eastern Europe for more than two centuries.

The rise of the French Monarchy was a serious and enduring menace to the consolidation of any kind of German unity. Francis I worked with the Turks against the Hapsburgs, and it was the Valois who first began to play for a Polish barricade against Germany in the East. In the following century, it was Richelieu who really moved the German pawns during the Thirty Years' War. The result of his policy was to leave Germany at the mercy of the Bourbon Monarchy for a century, until the emergence of Prussia under Frederick the Great introduced an entirely new force into German politics.

With the appearance of Frederick the Great we approach the modern phase of German history—and that struggle between Hohenzollern and Hapsburg, between Protestant, half-German Prussia aspiring to be German, and German Austria, aspiring to be non-German, and—within dynastic limits—Pan-European, which was one of the principal, if indirect, causes of the last war. The Reformation had been within certain German limits, a Pan-German movement, and it may be considered also to have represented a reaction against the state of economic backwardness into which Germany had fallen as a result of the shifting of trade-routes during the fifteenth century. Wallenstein, unquestionably the greatest German of his century, had wide, if vague ideas of Pan-German unity, and he met his death as a result of intriguing with the North German princes against the interests of the House of Hapsburg. Frederick the Great seriously challenged the Hapsburg hegemony in Central Europe, and he took advantage of the weakness of France in the pre-Revolutionary period to break down the Polish barricade against Prussia in the East. The

Napoleonic Wars were scarcely more than a disagreeable interlude in the rivalry between the two Germanic powers. Their results were to strengthen the Prussian position substantially, for they weakened the independent princely houses in Germany, and allowed Prussia during the first half of the nineteenth century to force the minor states into customs unions. Frederick the Great had conquered Silesia. The enforced participation of his successors in the Continental blockade during the Napoleonic Wars laid the foundation of German manufacturing industries which were set up to supply the gap left by the exclusion of British goods. The customs unions united with Prussia the old Hanseatic cities, and a modernised North Germany confronted an Austrian Empire which was really a survival of the Renaissance.

In 1866 Austria had been pushed out of the German Confederation and had ceased to be a German power. About the same time she had been thrust out of Italy, which she had really dominated until after the first half of the nineteenth century, and she now ceased to be an Italian power. But here can be observed the amazing political flexibility of the Hapsburg dynasty. Austria, during the latter half of the nineteenth century, rapidly tended to become a Slav power, ruling over a minority of German subjects who happened to live in Austria and Bohemia. It is possible that Austria might have survived as a Magyar-Slav Confederation had Francis Joseph died sooner and had Francis Ferdinand lived longer. But the old Emperor, as he told King Edward, "could never forget that he was a German Prince."

During the twenty years preceding the war there grew up a powerful Pan-German movement in Austria, led by Karl Leuger—the popular Burgomaster of Vienna—which really desired to see the end of the Hapsburg Empire and Monarchy, and the union of the German parts of the Empire within Greater Germany. Had either the Pan-German solution or the "Federal" (Slavist) solution of the Archduke Francis Ferdinand been achieved, the history of Europe might have received rather a different impulsion. But the Hohenzolierns had, in fact, succeeded to the role of the Hohenstaufen and the Hapsburgs. The latter had practically been manoeuvred into the position of vassal princes, and with the development of the policy of the Triple Alliance the Hohenzollerns merely gave a new force and a new directive to the Pan-European policy of the Holy Roman Emperors.

Adolf Hitler grew up in the atmosphere of the Pan-German propaganda of pre-war Vienna, and in his writings after the war he bitterly denounces what he regards as the anti-German and purely dynastic and capitalist-monopolist policies which he attributed to the Hohenzollerns. He was also opposed to the policy of colonial expansion which the Hohenzollerns initiated, and to which older Nationalist politicians like Hugenburg and Schacht still adhere. It is necessary, therefore to bear in mind these two important tendencies which govern National Socialist policy in action. First, Nazi policy is essentially national in that it is a reaction from the disastrous Pan-European policy of the Hapsburgs and Hohenzollerns. In the spirit of Bismarck, who proclaimed that "the whole Eastern Question is not worth the bones of a single Pomeranian grenadier," it repudiates any ambition to bring non-German territories under German rule. On the other hand it offers a challenge to the established State-system of Europe when it emphasises the necessity of bringing all territories inhabited by German-speaking populations within the structure of the "Drittes Reich."

Regarded superficially, the Pan-German reclamations of the Nazi idealists appear to be incompatible with the continued peace of Europe. But what Herr Hitler appears to be driving at, fundamentally, is the recognition of the fact that Germany has to be considered not only as an equal among the Great Powers, but that these Powers have also to allow for a legitimate expansion of Germany, and, if necessary, to find the avenues into which she may expand. There is nothing particularly immoral about an ambitious German territorial policy. During the last fifteen years we have found ourselves tolerating the exclusive and intransigent Continental policy of the French democracy, and the League of Nations has been largely used to favour the development of a new Slav group in Eastern Europe. It is necessary to remember that European frontiers have always been extremely fluid, and there is no historical justification for regarding them as particularly permanent in character at the present moment of European history.

In Eastern Europe the Slav group—Poland, the Czechs and the Balkan Slavs, as distinct from the Russians—must be considered to be a fairly permanent element in European history. Both Poland and Bohemia were really older states than Prussia. On the other hand Russia is a comparatively recent phenomenon, which only emerged as a European power at the beginning of the eighteenth century. It was the work of two great rulers—Peter the Great and Catherine the Great. The last war saw the work of Catherine undone, and the Russian frontier thrust back behind the Pripet marshes. The Bolsheviks have done much to undermine both the cultural and national basis of the former Russian Empire. Stable institutions and ideas have been destroyed, and the many peoples who make up the Soviet Union are developing disintegrative tendencies at a rate which is not generally realised. Russia is becoming a political No-Man's Land—a fact which seems to be very much appreciated by the Japanese in the extreme east.

In this connection the recent German-Polish Pact assumes significance and indicates the possibility of an entirely novel orientation in Baltic politics. Both Germany and Poland are in need of what may be defined as room for "peasant expansion." Herr Hitler, and other exponents of Nazi ideology, like Darre and Rosenberg, have emphasised that what Nazi Germany aims at is empty territories where the German peasant can till his land, and where German communities can build up their lives as an integral part of Germany. It is an entirely different conception to the "colonial imperialism" of the Hohenzollerns, and of the modern Conservative-Nationalists like Schacht and Hugenburg. Now a successful war against Poland would not solve the German problem of "peasant expansion," for Poland itself is thickly populated, and has a growing population. But both countries have ambitions in the East which were checked in the seventeenth-eighteenth centuries by Swedish intervention, and by the rise of the Romanov Empire. They had a recent reminder of the possibilities of these ambitions when the Germans occupied the Baltic provinces during the war, and when the Poles occupied the Ukraine in 1920. The Ukrainian Nationalists, who desire separation from Russia, have very important connections with Berlin and Warsaw, and it is possible that these elements may be instrumental in formulating the basis of a common German-Polish policy in "far eastern" Europe. Any prospects of war are naturally disturbing, but it would seem obvious that the most direct manner in which to make future war inevitable in Western Europe is to ignore not only German aspirations but also German needs. And a release of German energies towards the East seems infinitely preferable to a "jam" along the Rhine and in Austria—which is the only ultimate alternative.

There is remarkably little hostile feeling against Britain in Nazi Germany, nor does there seem any tendency to direct official propaganda against Britain, in spite of the exceedingly provocative attitude adopted by sections of the Press in this country—and also by certain political groups since the Nazis came into power. There is, of course, a movement of agitation for the return of the African colonies to Germany, but the inspiration of this agitation comes largely from the now unimportant Conservative Nationalist circles. Opinions may differ as to the value of these particular colonies either to ourselves or to the Germans, but Herr Hitler himself professes contempt for "the colonial imperialism" which inspires the Nationalist groups.

Certainly a policy based on "export capitalism"—and this is the policy which demands colonies—is contrary to the economic theory of "the autarchic State," and it may be safely said that the Nazis—at any rate in the present phase—do not desire to re-enter the African field. The whole emphasis of their propaganda is on the restoration of peasant life as the basis of the Autarchic State, and on the need for further lands geographically adjacent to Germany where the German peasant communities can spread themselves and develop that German corporate life in which the Nazis see the beginning and end of all things. If such a policy brings them into conflict with powers and with interests which are not British interests, it is scarcely the business of Britain to go crusading to maintain the immunity of the most corrupting tyranny which has ever soiled the history of the human race.

Social Democracy in Decay
by John Beckett

AN analysis of the by-election results since the last General Election shows that the Labour Party has increased its average poll over that of 1929 by nearly 15 per cent. In 1929 it secured 289 seats and, with five independent Members supporting it, had a lobby strength of 294. Thirteen more victories would have given it power. On the 1929 figures, a rate of increase in the poll equal to that of the by-elections would suffice to provide the party with a clear Parliamentary majority. In the absence of any great sweep towards Fascism in its first electoral contest, one may conclusively infer that there is no other factor which can obviate such an order of events. The regular swing of the pendulum will take place and the two sides of the House will change over like football teams at half-time.

Nothing would be more amusing, were it not tragic, than to study the various opinions expressed by our "National Leaders" and Press as to the probable course when Parliament is controlled by Labour. They run from visions of Britain on the all-red route, with Sir Stafford as the driver, to the gentle comforts of Mr. Greenwood and Dr. Dalton, who paint us a picture of Britain unchanged, except for prosperity, with a Front Bench of incredibly 'gentlemanly' super-men increasing the rent-roll of Mayfair as steadily as they smooth the slums from the fair face of our country.

High tragedy, red ruin and beneficent efficiency are all predicted in turn. It is amazing that none of the prophets have taken the trouble to examine carefully the principles of Social Democracy on which the Labour Party is based, and the fate of these principles (or lack of principles) in every country in which they have been tried. This study, assisted by a survey of Labour's past history and an impartial examination of the character and records of its leaders, inevitably points to conclusions less dramatic but much more terrifying than any of those we have already considered.

It is my purpose to submit that Labour Government means neither revolution nor evolution. It means spineless government by nonentities without any guiding principles; it means drifting without direction in a welter of glib insincerities; it means inarticulate alarm amid economic insecurity and financial panic increased by nervous and inexperienced ministers.

Without benefit to the underdog, Labour may be relied upon to bark at and to alarm the top dog. The result will be no sudden catastrophe which can be readily dealt with, but a sapping of the vitality of the nation and the acceleration of decay to such a speed that it may be impossible to call a halt. The theory of Social Democracy, indeed, is epitomized in the Labour Party's own official apologia for 1933; We may have been ineffective; but we have been on the right track all the time."

In face of the altered economic conditions brought about by the enormous advance in productive power due to modern machinery and science, the three basic ideas of Fascism, Communism, and Social Democracy, have fought for supremacy in the mind of the civilised world ever since 1918.

At first glance Social Democracy is the most attractive. Communism demands impossible turmoil and sacrifice to obtain highly controversial results. Fascism makes a great call to the higher, self-abnegatory side of human beings. The average man is lazy and self-indulgent. He does not want to work and accept discipline; above all he does not want to have to think and to make sacrifices for the benefit of the race. Social Democracy promises pleasure without pain, idealism without effort, prosperity and justice without planning. No more effective form of dope for the masses could be invented, and it is hardly to be wondered at that in Russia, Italy and Germany, where the full force of the blizzard caused by the War was felt, these nations turned to the Social Democrats for salvation.

Space does not allow a prolonged examination, with quotations, of the failure of Social Democracy in these countries. It not only failed to effect the peaceful transformation from predatory capitalism to socialism, as it had promised, but it failed to provide the slightest check upon the robber, with whom in Germany at any rate, it formed a fast and firm alliance. In all three countries the workers found themselves far worse off than they had been before Social Democracy gained power, and in all three countries the lesson proved sufficient for them to turn their backs upon such forms of democracy and to endeavour to regain their prestige and efficiency under a national leadership. Russia, the less advanced country, adopted a now rapidly disappearing form of Communism, whilst Italy and Germany, with a higher standard of civilisation, turned to Fascism for salvation.

A very cursory examination of Social-Democratic theory is sufficient to show that what happened in these three countries was inevitable and must occur wherever its policy is tried.

The Social Democrat is the rationaliser of demagogy, while his party is invariably caucus-ridden, its high places filled with men who may have nothing to recommend them but the power of facile speech. Its highest offices are open to the demagogue and to him alone. Just as its principles are vague and those of its opponents are definite, so its leaders lack the fanaticism of the Communist or the sternness of the Fascist. Obtain power by vote—not power to do things, but power to take office. Promise the rich and poor alike that you will be their friend. Abolish the slums and dine with the slum-owner. Increase wages, but give titles to the bad employer. Nationalise the banks but obey the banker. Defeat international capital with a kiss of welcome. Cut down armaments while interfering in every other country's business. These are a few of the more suitable slogans for Labour candidates. It is not surprising that in a world of grim reality this mixture of opportunism, idealism and sheer weakness of character has collapsed whenever responsibility has been laid upon it.

An examination of the history of the Labour Party shows how accurately these tendencies are fulfilled in practice; and, allowing for the more advanced stage of decay in the continental countries quoted, nothing is more striking than to compare their recent history with our own experiences. Social and economic difficulties have led to a widespread recognition of the need for change in the structure of the nation. The apparently easy path of Social Democracy has been tried; chaos and corruption have followed; and leadership, mistakenly called dictatorship, has had to be invoked.

A study of our Labour Party shows exactly the same tendencies as the Social-Democratic parties already mentioned. Can its most optimistic supporter really maintain that in the whole of the party's beliefs and policy there are two consistent notes? Even if we had not the record of their previous periods of office to prove it, the speeches of their leaders and the columns of the *Daily Herald* contain every possible inconsistency. The Socialist League and the most sedate Trade-Union leader are united in their desire for electoral victory, but it is impossible to find one single point of unity in their plans for government once victory has been won. Attend any Labour meeting where there is more than one speaker, and if the orators get beyond high-flown aspirations to practical policy the most striking differences will at once appear.

The first really large Parliamentary Labour Party was returned in 1922. Never, even in the "odds-and-ends Parliament" of 1906 has such a queer collection of eccentricities arrived at Westminster. No better description could be given of them than that supplied by Scanlon in his *Decline and Fall of the Labour Party*: —

"Politics, however, like adversity, make strange bedfellows, but it is safe to say that at no time had the worst forms of adversity succeeded in bringing together such strange, diverse types as found themselves jammed side by side in our Labour bed in the Parliament of 1922 . . . everybody with a grievance joined the Labour Party in the belief that it existed solely to right individual wrongs; and when any rich person joined the Party, he or she at once felt that they ought to be adopted for Parliament so that the grievance could be attended to properly. . . I remember Mr. Egerton Wake, the Labour National Organizer, whose job it was to get candidates placed, saying that the Party's greatest affliction was an overdose of disgruntled generals.

Altogether some queer specimens found their way into the Labour Party . . . each had a fixed idea: some concentrated on worn-out horses, some on oppressed minorities, provided the minorities were not too near. There were generals who had been overlooked in the war and wanted the whole system of promotion altered. Others (not generals) were willing to give their time and energy to seeing that the Sabbath Day was kept holy; others could look with equanimity on the harsh conditions meted out to the unemployed, but would willingly have wrecked the Party if it had proposed to add one single workman's club to the list. There were others who believed that group meetings for daily intercession with God would solve the poverty problem, and there were others with no decided views about anything.

In 1906 when some of the Labour M.P.s intimated to the world the great questions to which they hoped to devote their Parliamentary lives, Mr. Bernard Shaw apologised to the universe for ever having been associated with them. There is no record of what he said in 1922."

Less than a year later this motley assembly became the official government of the country. After a few months of office, it was summarily dismissed by the country. Five years of Mr. Baldwin prepared the national mind for any alternative, and in 1929 a Labour Government, only a few short of a majority and almost always with an actual physical majority within the precincts of the House, ruled with discomfort and ignominy for two-and-a-half years until the crisis of 1931 brought about their temporary electoral extinction.

In Russia Kerensky counselled caution right up to the moment when he fled before an indignant and disappointed nation, which had turned to the Bolsheviks for the leadership he had never had the courage to show. In Italy the Social Democrats occupied the factories, and, having no plans for running them, meekly allowed themselves to be shepherded out and destroyed by the Fascists, who gave the Italians plans instead of speeches and action instead of intrigue. In Germany the Socialists had all the power in their hands in 1919, but ran to the *Junkers* in terror for assistance; for twelve years cringed behind the Weimar Constitution; and in 1933, with scarcely a bleat of protest, made way for Hitler and the disciplined leadership of the Storm Troops.

It is not surprising that we find an English ex-socialist M.P. writing that Social Democracy depends for its existence on never attaining power. This article began with a warning that the Labour Party must, if by-election figures mean anything, obtain office again at the next election. The reader may well ask how, in view of the foregoing facts, it is possible for millions of electors to vote Labour again. The answer lies in the specious excuse given from every Labour platform: — "We never had a majority."

Amazing as it may appear, the great bulk of the electorate, seems to believe quite genuinely that if in 1929 another twenty trade-union leaders or middle-class *intelligentsia* had been returned, the Labour Government would have been successful in carrying out the many and varied Utopian promises it had made during its election campaign. How the absence of a majority explains to the workers the introduction and forcing through the House of Commons,—often against some Liberal and Conservative votes,—of definitely anti-working-class legislation such as the Anomalies Act and the Coal Mines Act, I do not pretend to understand. How the preaching of class hatred and the rallying of the masses to smash capitalism should turn to rampant snobbery and crawling subservience to the City of London because there are 294 M.P.s instead of 307 is a mystery that is never explained.

Whatever else is wrong with the Labour Party, it has gone far to solve the problem of facing awkward questions. It has discovered that the best way is to turn its back upon them. Explanation gives way to denunciation; exposition is made by fulmination; and failure to redeem promises made in the past seems to be more than covered in the eyes of the electorate by an extra generosity in making promises for the future.

The chief proof that Labour cannot govern is to be found, not in its failure, contemptible as that has been in the past, but in the psychology of its leadership and the gullibility of its rank and file. The extraordinary leniency always shown in Britain to those who are popularly supposed to have worked their way up to high places probably accounts for the strange manner in which those in a position to know the truth let the unctuous claims of the Labour leaders to unusual standards of righteousness pass unchallenged.

Mr. MacDonald as leader of the National Government is today following exactly the same policy as when he was the much-revered and loved leader of a Labour Government. The only difference is that that policy is more successful because he is surrounded by capable men instead of inefficient ones. Yet we see Labour leaders who were proud to follow him before 1931 now reviling and denouncing him for exactly the same methods which previously, when he employed them they denounced other people for objecting to. So low is the standard of honesty that Labour M.P.s past and present who used to hang round his door in the hope of getting a chance to open it and say "Good Morning" now blame all the crimes of the past upon MacDonald, Thomas and Snowden. In one breath they claim to be a democratic party; in the next they say that in a Parliamentary group nearly 300 strong three men were responsible for what they now denounce as villainous conduct.

A general instance of this dishonest propaganda may be found in the statement made invariably from Labour platforms that they are the only party which publishes a balance-sheet, and their denunciation of the older parties for corruption in selling honours and concealing secret sources of income. Many of the members undoubtedly believe these statements when they make them. On the other hand many must be aware that for a number of years large private subscriptions have been received by the leaders, and used at their discretion—subscriptions which have never been accounted for in any statement ever issued. The Labour Party has always denounced the empty pomp of titles, but an examination of the Honours Lists while it was in office does not suggest any alteration in the traditional manner of compiling these lists. The larger part of the Labour leadership is consciously hypocritical in these matters, the rank and file so unbelievably gullible that it is difficult not to argue that they deserve the leadership they have.

What is to be the end of democracy? Beginning by studying the history of Social Democracy elsewhere, our examination of the Labour Party in Britain must lead us to believe that just as it shows every characteristic of the continental movements, so must its progress inevitably develop along the same lines. It may well be that this is anything but a cheering thought. Unless the nation comes to its senses within a very short time and is given a virile and practical alternative, the negative virtues of a finance-ridden Conservative Party are bound to present us with a Labour majority at Westminster. The Tories are bound to keep a Labour government in office for at least twelve months. The electorate would not realise how bad Labour was, and forget how bad Conservatism had been, under that time.

It becomes therefore of primary importance that Fascism should present that alternative without further delay. The tragic history of other countries should not be allowed to work itself out here. They turned to constructive planning and authoritative leadership as a last resource when brought by unconstructive reaction and timid socialism to the brink of disaster.

A Labour Government pledged to improve the condition of the masses will find, on attaining office, that the cupboard is bare. The days are past when, out of a superfluity, a few millions could be found to buy the workers off. Embittered by the total failure of the Labour Government to assist them, and inflamed by the reckless nature of their propaganda, the workers will turn to riots and Communism as the way out. Alarmed by the wild speeches made for the attainment of office, the investing class will draw in their horns with disastrous results to our economic position. Social Democracy will be faced with its historic problem: —How to satisfy its supporters without attacking its opponents. There is no solution in the Socialist creed. In less than three years we shall be facing a real crisis which will make that of 1931 look a very petty affair indeed.

Is it possible to believe that Democracy, as we know it at present, will survive this steady drift into disaster? Fascism must strive to convince the nation of its plans now, and not when disaster is upon us.

Labour cannot govern, and if the Corporate State is delayed till Social Democracy has reaped its harvest of chaos, the salvation of the nation will still lie in the fact that men's minds have been prepared and the Blackshirt movement consolidated.

Fascism and War
by Major-General J. F. C. Fuller

THE outlook of Fascism upon war is a common-sense one, for the Fascist is a realist. To him it is useless slopping the problem of war over with words and anathemas, as so frequently is done by those who successfully succeeded in avoiding the last one, because emotionalism is the antithesis of realism. He is open to examine the problem as a physician examines a patient, but he refuses to be diverted by "glory" on the one side or by "horror" on the other.

If the problem is solvable it will be solved scientifically, that is by seeking truth, maintaining an impartial mind and working in an orderly way. Hysteria will certainly not solve it.

Having studied war historically and psychologically, the Fascist comes to the conclusion that in certain circumstances wars are necessary and that in others they are not. Therefore he decides that circumstances are the prime factor, that it is these which create wars, and that, consequently, war itself is not a disease, but instead the climax of a diseased state of peacefulness. It is not the microbe, it is the fever caused by the microbe. Without this fever the patient might easily die of internal poisoning, yet if his temperature rises above a certain point he certainly will collapse; in any case he is likely to be physically debilitated when his sickness is at an end. It is not the fever which should be blamed, but its cause. The Fascist, therefore, says: "I will tackle this problem causally, and until its cause or causes are eliminated I will keep in hand a stock of surgical instruments and drugs, my navies, armies and air fleets, because I see no reason to put my trust in faith cures and other quackery. Consequently I will have nothing to do with pacifist witchcraft which puts its trust in incantations, spells and pacts." It is for this reason that he refuses to be drawn off the scent of his truth-seeking by disarmament and suchlike red herrings, for weapons in themselves cannot possibly create wars any more than forceps and scalpels in themselves can create diseases.

"Therefore," says the Fascist, "let us examine peace, for in the discontents of peace will be discovered the causes of war, and until they are eliminated I do not intend to throw my surgical instruments away. In fact, the more hysterical the advocates of peace become, the more certain am I that war will return, therefore I shall see that my instruments and drugs are the best procurable."

Then the Fascist turns to the age in which we live, for it is out of this age that the next war will emerge, and having studied it impartially, he comes to the conclusion that there are today two major causes of war, namely: over-population and fiscal-economic anarchy. It is these which give rise to military causes—the necessity to conquer, to terrorise and to establish unattackable frontiers.

The first of these two major causes he looks at in this wise: However deplorable and annoying it may be, it is a fact that a starving man prefers by stealing food to break the law than to die of hunger. In every civilised and uncivilised country it is agreed that a man has the right to defend his life; then why should this man kill himself through hunger when he can preserve his life by theft? Consequently, when a country becomes over-populated, two courses face it: it can commit suicide in a civil war or occupy a neighbouring territory, which means war unless it is inhabited by pact-intoxicated pacifists. These are facts which cannot be contradicted. With Japan over-populated, it is fatuous for the League to object to Japanese expansion. A far wiser course would be yearly to ship over to that country a few thousand tons of contraceptives.

The same problem faces us in India: White Paper or no White Paper, if Indians go on breeding at the present rate, unless expansion becomes possible, before this century is out India must blow up. In 1921 her population was 320 million and in 1931, 350 million. At this rate of increase it will be about 700 millions in the year 2001, and unless Marie Stopes gets busy or every stalk of corn grows two ears, a cataclysm is foredoomed. This is a fact that no pen and ink or pious words can efface; consequently the Fascist works on facts—he is a realist.

Turning to the second of the two major causes, the Fascist is at once confronted by what is proclaimed to be "economic nationalism", which by so many is supposed to be inhabited by the devil of strike. Never spell-bound by words or names, on examining it he discovers that what is really meant, but what under liberal democracy it is a heresy to whisper, is anarchic trading: Go as you please, do as you can, cheat, bribe, scramble and the Devil take the hindermost. Markets and foreign loans bulk large in this bloodless cut-purse war. Briefly I will examine them in turn.

As today all nations are producing more than under the existing financial system they can purchase, world production exceeds world demand. Markets become, therefore, causes of strife and areas for dumping discontents as well as goods. As, obviously, it is impossible for every country to sell more than it can buy, private interests involve their respective governments and governments rattle their swords in order to frighten each other—their rattlings being the insults of the daily press. Greed engenders envy, envy passion and hatred, then comes some incident which detonates pent-up emotionalism and there is war. Much the same thing happens in the struggle for raw materials.

An even more powerful cause is the struggle between the great central banks for financial control. If goods cannot be paid for by goods the debtor is compelled to accept a loan and forthwith enters into financial servitude. As one writer says of international financiers: "More than any other force let loose in the chaos of the modern world, they have led to war." Once in their grip there are but two ways of getting out of it: repudiation or fighting. As the first means bankruptcy and dishonour, the second is normally resorted to.

Thus it happens that because of the greed and emotionalism which are inherent in mass-democracies, weapons are not looked upon as surgical instruments, but as the strait-jackets of national and international discontents. By them are internal revolutions constrained and hostile neighbours terrorised, not in order to sustain justice, but to maintain greed. Again, it is but one step from a tariff wall to a fortified frontier, and if an existing frontier is weak there is every incentive to seek another which is stronger. In former days strong defensive frontiers were sought in order to secure national existence, now they are sought to secure international usury.

On July 11, 1933, Mr. Chamberlain said in the House of Commons: "We, ourselves, still remain of the opinion which we have held all along, and this is that the chief troubles from which the world is suffering today are international in their origin, and that they can only be solved by international action and agreement." As regards their origin he is right, but as Satan has a peculiar dislike to casting out Satan, the Fascist is more than dubious regarding his cure. This is why he does not believe in disarmament treaties, peace pacts and international police forces which are talked inside out and then outside in by the members of the League of Nations or its supporters.

The League does not stand for peace, it stands for the status quo: it stands for a myth, inertia, and not for a reality-change. The world moves and we must move with it; there can be no halting without rotting, and rottenness begets war, for it putrefies civilisation. For example, examine the problem of Austria, at present the centre of European rottenness: In 1918-19 a great empire was reduced to a small state with an immense capital; that is from the position of a millionaire to a pauper who has still to pay for his house—Vienna—a millionaire's rental. In 1931, Germany suggested a Customs Union, and France feeling that she was about to be torpedoed at once determined to torpedo this Union by means of that never-failing weapon of destruction, the Council of the League. Essentially an economic question, it was referred for decision to the Permanent Court of International Justice and stretched upon the political rack, the winches being operated among others by Salvador, Cuba, Colombia and China —then in a state of open anarchy. Had Cuba or Salvador voted the other way, the Union would have become an accomplished fact; as neither did so it was disallowed.

Is this sane or insane? Is this the way to integrate the world and to establish perpetual peace? It would have been sane and more honest had the League proclaimed: "Austria is an impossible country, she is the pauper of Europe, and if she is not to be allowed this Union, we must keep her and pay her a dole of millions of pounds every year." Even then what right would have been the League's to suppose that the Austrians—a proud people—wanted to live in an alms-house; for all they wanted was self-determination and they still want it but are unable to gain it, for they are compelled to live not under a government of their own choosing, but under a corrupt despotism. In fact Austria is prevented from working out her rightful destiny by imposing upon her a surreptitious international police force—the international of money which has no need to buy foreign mercenaries; for it can always hire home-bred ones. It is this kind of force, the denationalised cut-throat whose sole incentive is money, which the League of Nations Union, the New Commonwealth Movement and decaying Capitalism seek to impose upon the world. Could they do so, sooner or later the result would be a cataclysmic revolution ending in world-wide Bolshevism. Is this then their ultimate object?

Yet in spite of this flagrant political roguery, what the Fascist most of all objects to is the insidious moral attack which is launched under cover of a smoke cloud of pious platitudes and hysterical hypocrisy, against all that is virile and spiritual in mankind. Honour, virtue and belief in anything nobler than mere living are to be subjected to international legal control. But is peace or the maintenance of peace at any price the end of life? Is there nothing in this world dearer than life? Are men solely animals? With James Martineau the Fascist believes that:

"The reverence for human life is carried to an immoral idolatry when it is held more sacred than justice and right, and when the spectacle of blood becomes more horrible than the sight of desolating tyrannies and triumphant hypocrisies . . . nothing can be weaker or more suicidal than for men who are citizens of a commonwealth to announce that, for their part, they mean to hold life in higher esteem than justice. And if the day comes when nations are content to submit every dispute, whatever be its origin, to the decision of a court, it may be not that the world has grown better, but that men have become meaner and baser because there is no longer anything that they hold dearer than life."

To live, is the urge of Nature; but to live righteously—that is, in accordance with our deepest convictions—is surely the foundations of all morality and religion. Can a man who believes that he is reflecting the will of God submit his faith for judgment to a police court? "Live Dangerously" would therefore appear to be a nobler and a more righteous motto of life than "Safety First", which when applied to the heart of man can accomplish no other end than that of breeding a race of despiritualised eunuchs.

Thus it comes about that in the philosophy of Fascism life is looked upon as a means to an end and not as the end itself. The individual is mortal, but the State, not only the mass of individuals, but what is noble, inspired and inspiring in their history, in two words—national spirituality, is immortal and infinitely greater. It is for this that each individual must live, not merely in order to maintain it but to sustain it with his or her life, thoughts and actions. It is a struggle towards what shall be done and not merely a marking time on what has been accomplished. If in this spirit there is still something of the activity of the wild boar, the heavens be praised there is as yet nothing of the inertia of the farmyard pig.

Because of this dynamism, this essential virility, Fascism stands for peace, nevertheless it does not fear war, for all it fears is inert living. Therefore on peace and war the creed of the Fascist reads as follows:

The legitimate object of war is a more perfect peace; because war is a surgical instrument.

The legitimate object of peace is a more perfect man; because peace is a creative instrument.

And the legitimate object of man is a more perfect world; because man is a divine instrument.

How does he convert this creed into action, for without activity there can be no rebirth? This problem I will now enquire into.

The history of strife may be divided under two great headings—internal revolutions and external foreign wars; the first fertilising the second and the second the first. I will now examine them in turn.

What the Fascist says is this: International discontent is but the sum of innumerable national discontents. If the world be compared to a house, then, because its bricks and mortar are rotten, its foundations are always sinking and its walls caving in. Therefore the first problem in establishing a creative world peace is for each nation to set its own house in order; for as long as the nations are in a state of internal rottenness, directly a crisis becomes imminent their respective politicians will attempt to maintain their authority by turning discontent outwards, that is away from home and towards foreign affairs. This is the oldest and surest road to war.

An excellent example of this is after-war France. Her system of government is utterly corrupt, so what do her politicians do? To distract popular attention they vociferously proclaim that France is in danger and hypnotise the people on the word "Security". Were it possible to secure France against every form of attack, would the French politicians be grateful? No, they would be terrified, for they would realise that as the people would then have nothing to fear from a foreign war, they would turn their attention towards internal reform and revolution. "Security" is in actual fact not a shield held towards Germany, but in place the bullet-proof carapace under which the Staviskys crawl.

Though in nearly every country the cause of discontent is economic in origin, its expression, as it must be, is moral. Poverty not only creates want but a feeling of injustice. That in an age of potential plenty there should still be actual and excessive poverty appears criminal, and when a government is looked upon as a gathering of gangsters, the suffering and thinking man comes to believe in his right to overthrow it. This is the fundamental cause of all social revolutions. To be denied a just share in production because of an out-of-date system of distribution is nothing short of robbery. If a burglar enters your house and threatens your life, you have the right to protect it even at the expense of his own. The desperate man looks at political assassination from a similar angle, and when once he realises that it is the financier who is using the politician as a stalking-horse between him and what he considers to be his rightful share of wealth, we may expect the first slump which has ever occurred in the history of bankers.

The Fascist says: Why solve this problem of financial anarchy by social anarchy? Why not instead solve it by economic reorganisation? Poverty and, consequently, revolution are created by a maldistribution of wealth, by a rotten system of finance, by wage cuts, rising prices and a general lowering of the standard of living; why not then organise the national industries so that they can control themselves, express themselves and reform themselves? This is not Socialism, in which the State controls labour, for the control of industry suggested here is by those who create and maintain labour. It is in fact the purest form of co-operative democracy, which political democracies have never attempted to realise. This control the Fascist intends to establish by means of the Corporate State. Industries will be divided into self-governing groups each electing an industrial corporation composed of employers, workers and consumers. In such an organisation class warfare, strikes and lock-outs can find no place. Instead of fighting for increased wages, the object will be to raise the standard of living as science and industry increase the powers of production. What does this mean? That exploitation will be replaced by organisation and a new body social will be created.

Prosperity having been established, the next step is to breathe the spirit of a new life into the economic dust. As man is partly physical, partly moral and partly intellectual, so is a society of men partly economic, partly cultural and partly political. It follows, therefore, that, as in man himself, the economic factors should be grouped into organs and limbs; so also should the cultural be left almost entirely to individuals and the political should possess authority over the whole. By which I mean, that the main activities of politics will consist in regulating the relationships between individuals and between groups and in directing those organs and limbs, the national services, which they alone can control.

From this we may deduce the following: That the private lives of individuals will be as free as possible; that the prosperity of groups of workers will depend upon organisation according to functions, and that the government of the whole will be carried out by people of high intelligence, knowledge and experience. In other words: the cultural life is individual, the economic is collective, and the political is directive and authoritarian. When these three groups of activities—self-expression, group-expression and national expression work together, the highest economy of cultural economic and political life will result. This economy is true freedom and freedom from discontent is the foundation of national peace.

I will now turn to the second half of the war problem, that is from national revolutions to foreign wars, and here again we find that real peace must be established on an economic basis.

What is that basis today? The anarchy of gold, the keystone in the existing international and national monetary systems. In order to gain gold or to establish gold currencies, nations must have active "favourable" trade balances. Those who succeed in doing so can either extract gold from nations with "unfavourable" balances or compel them to borrow the difference in the shape of a loan. As one writer on this question says: "Instead of trading for goods and services to their mutual advantage, the nations are compelled to fight tooth and claw for 'favourable' balances—i.e., gold—under penalty of finding themselves in the degrading and miserable position of being in pawn to their successful competitors." This is the direct road to war, because, as I have already pointed out, except for repudiation only war can abolish this servitude.

Obviously, the solution of this problem lies in abandoning gold as the measurement of wealth and of basing currency on real wealth, not on one commodity which can be cornered, but on all commodities with a market value. Then exports will have to be paid for by imports or they will become presents to the nation receiving them. As the above writer says: State-subsidised exports will then become purposeless. Tariffs, in so far as they exclude imports will to that extent preclude exports. Exchanges will be immutably fixed, eliminating the speculator, and the fear of the money-lender will be removed.

I cannot here enter into the detail of how the existing financial anarchy should be liquidated; but it is obvious that in democratic governments, depending for their power on the interests and prejudices of gold-standard finance, the solution can be no other than a catastrophe. Look at the machinery existing in this country which would be called upon to carry out so intricate a reform. The Prime Minister must refer the problem to the Cabinet and the Cabinet to the Parliamentary Party, and should a Labour Government be in power, then the

Parliamentary Party must refer it to the Trades Union Congress and the Labour Party Conference, whilst behind all these assemblies vested interests are pulling the strings.

Under a Fascist Government, once the experts have examined the question, the Prime Minister will say "yes" or "no". If "yes" then the measure will become law. And should other nations be interested, which can hardly fail to be the case if they are under Fascist direction, the machinery of decision being the same a speedy agreement becomes possible.

Agreed, for sake of argument, that this fundamental cause of war is eliminated, we are left with what may be called the biological cause, namely, over-population which no economic readjustment can directly influence; for it stands outside the control of government.

In countries where a high standard of living exists, this problem is solved automatically by a decline in the birth-rate. But in countries where a low standard prevails, that is in countries where industrial civilisation is not fully developed, for many years an increase in the birth-rate may be expected. Turning to world statistics we find that whilst in Western Europe increase in population is declining, in Eastern it is not, whilst in Russia and vast tracts of Asia there is room for hundreds of millions of more people. Should Asia become industrialised on the lines now being established in Russia, there can be little doubt that these hundreds of millions will be born and that a time will come when over-population will force an expansion westwards. What does this mean? Nothing less than an intercontinental war between Asia and Europe. To prepare for this war European nations must cease their intestinal quarrels and unite, and unite they never will so long as economic and financial discontents separate them. If Eastern European nations cannot within their frontiers find room for their increasing populations, then of the choice between two evils the lesser is, that their expansion should be eastwards and not westwards. Not only will such an expansion run along the line of least population-resistance, but it will be towards and not away from the greatest war-threat which is ever likely to threaten Western civilisation.

From this brief excursion into future possibilities we see, and I think conclusively, that the war problem cannot be solved by peace pacts and wordy conventions. It is a real and active problem, part of which can be solved by organisation, and part can be guarded against only by a united and militarily powerful Europe.

As it is manifestly impossible, even when Fascism gains power in this country, for it single-handed to control the destinies of Europe, the most vital military problem which faces us is the security and defence of our Empire. Here we are on our own ground and within certain well-defined limits can build as we like. This means leadership and action.

Because in a civilised country the material basis of all military power is economic wealth, the first problem in Imperial security is the development of the Empire. It may be said, however, that as the Dominions are to-day autonomous self-governing nations, it is impossible for any Home Government, Fascist or other, to carry out this task. If compulsion is envisaged, then the Fascist full-heartedly agrees. But to him compulsion it quite unnecessary, for being a realist he believes that as development will depend upon co-operation, in its turn co-operation must be founded upon self-interest.

It is no use whatever talking of blood brotherhood and of traditional bonds, because these are accepted facts and nobody doubts their binding power; besides they stand outside the material sphere and so do not enter the economic question. What is of real use is, to suggest that a self-contained Empire not only means a more prosperous Empire but a securer Empire, because, in the comity of nations, it will form so powerful an instrument of peace, that it will virtually prohibit war. To a self-contained Empire, wars, other than those originating from over-population, which are outside political control, are injurious. Consequently it is to the advantage of the Empire that world peace be maintained. Therefore it is to its advantage that all its parts co-operate economically. This may mean a loss of foreign investments; but in a short time this loss will be fully compensated for by ever-increasing prosperity.

To safeguard this prosperity brings us directly to the problem of defence. Where does power to defend lie? First in the British Navy, because for many years to come the Dominions will not be in a position to build and maintain powerful war fleets. Secondly, in the Air Force and the Army.

As regards the third of these defensive instruments, as modern, that is mechanised, armies are the kind we require, the same problem of cost will present itself to the Dominions as confronts them in the construction of modern fleets. But as regards the second, the Air Force, quite another story unfolds itself, for the Dominions, covering vast spaces of land, are the natural breeding grounds of civil aircraft, and civil aircraft are the foundations of military air power.

Therefore the problem resolves itself as follows: Great Britain must first of all be responsible for her home air defence, and then imperially responsible for all sea communications and for the maintenance of a small yet powerful mechanised Army which in war will operate on the lines of an imperial fire-brigade. In their turn the Dominions must be responsible for their own air defence, and consequently establish strong and efficient air forces.

Granted such forces, then the problem resolves itself into one of co-operation, and in its solution there are two main factors, namely: the establishment of a network of defended landing-grounds similar in purpose to our existing network of defended coaling-stations, and the creation of an Imperial Air Council which can advise the nations of the Empire on air defence and air power development.

Though, if our Empire is to endure, this is our most vital problem, our most immediate is to reorganise and rearm our Fighting Services. Ever since the conclusion of the War a succession of knock-kneed Governments has reduced them to a state of impotence. Our two-power naval standard has been abandoned and today we are dangerously short of cruisers, destroyers and Submarines. As regards this last-mentioned weapon we are now at the mercy of France. Our Army has been reduced in size and efficiency, and though lack of horse-flesh has forced us in part to motorise, a superabundance of archaic brains has maintained in it such a useless mass of infantry that it is no more than an extravagantly expensive police force. Meanwhile the Royal Air Force has sunk from first to sixth place among the air forces of the world.

The Fascist will have none of this. He is not concerned with power standards and emotional limitations. He is a realist and he says: "If I happen to live, as I do and have to, in a gold-rush mining-camp, I intend to carry a gun on my hip."

His views are as follows:

We have scores of thousands of miles of sea routes to protect, and in order to defend them against not all but the most probable attacks we require a Navy in every way adequate for this purpose.

We have a nineteenth century Army; instead we should have a twentieth century one. Not an Army weighed out in tons of human flesh, but measured in terms of mechanical striking power: few men and more machines, because this is a machine age and not a muscle age.

We want and will have an Air Force which can defend us by being so powerful that any enemy within effective range will think many times before attacking us.

Lastly, we want a strategical Ministry of Defence which can plot and plan for the three Services as if they were one combined service. That is, we want a defence autocracy in peace because we know that in war nothing but an autocracy will or can direct strategy in a single-minded way.

Should other nations proclaim that this our insurance against war and in war our assurance of victory are militaristic, then let them do so. Though we do not hanker after an armament race, we do not intend next time we are attacked to find ourselves in such a position that we shall be compelled to race away from the armaments of our enemy. We prefer to face the facts openly and squarely in place of blindly blinking at them.

I think that I have now covered the more important problems which face us concerning war and its preparation, and have made it clear that the difference between the outlook of the Fascist and most other people is: that whilst they consider war inevitable or preventable in any set of circumstances, according to peace conditions he considers war necessary or unnecessary. In fact this difference is identical to that which separates the alchemist from the man of science.

War is a reality and must be treated as such. It is understandable that after the last war the people turned towards idealism, if only for a change of atmosphere. It is also understandable that all Governments which float upon popular opinion are by their very nature compelled to throw oil upon troubled waters. These are facts which cannot be contradicted; yet this does not mean that they are facts which cannot be changed. Though the Fascist does not want war, because war is a measure of peace discontentedness, and, therefore, a measurement of governmental failure, he does not rush to the other extreme and put his trust in political hocus-pocus and legerdemain. Further still, he does not believe that this is a warlike age, and he is of opinion that this belief is proved by the fact that governments never cease talking about war. How is this? Because there are only two great categories of problems in the national life: one is internal and the other is external —home affairs and foreign affairs. If you do not want the people to examine the first, focus their attention on the second. This trick, common to every conjurer, is the mainspring of democratic politics.

He believes that the problem of war is a scientific one and not an emotional one: discover its causes, isolate the virus and cultivate an anti-toxin in place of jabber and jaw. As at present and it would seem that for some time to come nothing outside a universally high standard of living will eliminate wars springing from over-population, the Fascist considers that armed forces will be required and that, consequently, efficient ones will prove more serviceable and economical than obsolete ones. Though a human being is influenced by traditions, and virile traditions are of the utmost value in war, weapons obviously cannot be. Therefore, the Fascist does not mix sentiments with cannon-balls.

Though a united Europe is a great ideal and one the Fascist welcomes and believes to be possible under Fascist control, because all governments will then deal with each other through an organised system, the supreme fact today is that the only real league of nations in the world is the British Empire. Here, then, is our true starting point on the road towards a creative peace. A starting point which approximately covers a quarter of the globe and embraces a quarter of its inhabitants. Peace is in our hands if we would but grasp it in a realistic way. Are we, as a nation, after centuries of toil, now going to fall out of the line of march and become a rabble of stragglers? The Fascist answers "No"; hence his watchword is "Forwards".

Forward In Fascism
by Oswald Mosley

FASCIST Propaganda is established as an integral part of our National life. Two years of work and sacrifice brought as their reward the recognition of this Movement by the people as a patriotic, revolutionary, and inherently British power.

The British worker has at last been enabled to identify his natural love of country with his righteous and necessary desire to fundamental improvement in his conditions.

The Imperialist who had formerly given no thought to the misery and want which oppressed millions of his own people has been enabled to understand that for unemployment and poverty there can be neither excuse nor extenuation in this modern scientific age.

The third year of our Movement's life has seen unprecedented victories in propaganda; but its greatest achievement has been the creation of the scientific and thoroughly reliable organization without which no propaganda can produce results of abiding value.

The organic structure of the Movement as a whole now comprises nearly 500 District Formations in process of being organized according to Parliamentary area, and all correlated and unified by organization which rests on Blackshirt activity. The construction of this entirely trustworthy machine is indeed the more remarkable because it has not absorbed so much of the Movement's energy as to impair propaganda. On the contrary, it has contributed immensely to the success of two of the greatest propaganda operations in modern British history. The now famous "Mind Britain's Business" campaign roused the opposition of the people to a senseless war in a measure which is being more fully appreciated from day to day, as the politicians recede from the fantastic and bombastic attitude which they adopted when, unaware of our propaganda power, they first contemplated the use of military and naval force in a dispute which cannot concern us.

The second great operation will be remembered in the motto

"Fascism Next Time". Throughout the recent election campaign, our Movement held meetings as numerous as any of the old Parties could organize. Our meetings were generally full to capacity, theirs were often all but empty. Our meetings were, almost without exception, peaceful and orderly; theirs were very frequently characterized by scenes of hooliganism and violence which would be permitted at no Fascist meeting. In the event, we have maintained free speech; they have sought to deny it and lost it themselves.

At our meetings large numbers of recruits were enrolled in the midst of the electoral struggle. That we should be heard with interest we believed; that we should not be silenced by the oriental sub-men we knew; but that masses of people should join our ranks precisely at a time when we refused to nominate candidates is the highest tribute that could be paid to the wisdom of abstaining from election contest until such time as we could attack the enemy with the highly technical machinery which is necessary, throughout the length of his battered and divided front.

Thus, as the year 1935 closes, we can reflect upon equal success in propaganda and in organization. If we can never be happy until our task is complete, we can all be proud of every hour's work that we have done, every little sacrifice that we have made for the cause which is to save our people by unifying all that is noble in Nationalism with all that is serviceable in Socialism.

In retrospect, it must moreover be acknowledged that our resistance to the Jewish assault has been as triumphant as it proved to be needful. Because the Jews would not suffer a British Movement to work, think, and feel for Britain alone, because they would have plunged us into catastrophic strife with a great people whose Leader has saved Europe from Communism, they have found themselves hurled back upon a steadily declining defensive, as they evoked in Britain an anti-Semitic sentiment for which they have themselves alone to blame. We may proudly reflect that unless our Movement had possessed the courage to challenge the menace of Jewish International Finance and Jewish Bolshevism, it would not only have failed to justify the confidence of the people: it would have evaded the crucial test, from the fires of which it has emerged as a thing of tempered steel.

We rejoice in trials of this sort, for they alone can secure that our membership shall be steadfast, true, and willing to sacrifice in superb manifestation of that high human quality evoked by Fascist struggle "the power to endure".

In the year which is to come, all efforts must be redoubled and every record of success must be broken. Now we have engaged ourselves to fight the next election; and this engagement will be fulfilled by the immense work of forming in several hundred constituencies electoral organizations superior to those of the old Parties. The task is hard; but our active membership considerably exceeds that of any of the old Parties.

A three weeks' tour, concluded just before Christmas, has revealed both a personnel and spirit which no other force in Britain can emulate. Officers from each district gathered for Area conferences every evening and on many afternoons. They were worthy representatives of the characteristic British manhood which they lead in their respective localities. Women officers too represented the ever-growing strength of our Movement of true British womanhood. Local problems of organization and policy were examined with a close attention to detail impossible in the brief, vague and jejune annual conferences of the old Parties. National plans for the coming year were fully and frankly discussed and throughout the length and breadth of the land were received with an encouraging universality of enthusiasm. Above all, that close personal contact and relationship was maintained even in the present great growth of the Movement which so vividly characterized the early days of Fascist brotherhood.

A New Year of Fascist strength lies before us. The Movement which has been bold enough to laugh to scorn the concerted force of Jewish International Finance and the propaganda resources which it commands; the Movement which has successfully defied "Vested power, Red Front, and Massed Ranks of Reaction", can be content with the defensive no longer. Having overcome the mighty obstacles placed in our way, we have now to work for our own victory. The extent and rapidity of this conquest must depend on the unremitting and purposeful efforts of every member.

Strength Through Joy
by Dr. Robert Ley

THE National Socialist *Strength Through Joy* organization was called into being at the command of our Leader, Adolf Hitler. He sent for me one day and said : "I want the German worker to have sufficient recreation and holidays, so that the nerves of the nation shall be sound; for it is impossible to achieve anything, even with statesmanship of the greatest genius, if the nerves of the nation are destroyed." It became my duty to carry out this command of the Leader's, and in November, 1933, *Strength Through Joy* came into existence. Many, even amongst my most intimate collaborators, did not understand what I was aiming at, nor yet what the intention of the Leader was. Many thought it was to provide a means of throwing dust in the eyes of the worker and diverting his legitimate desire for social justice. Others again saw in it a new field of activity for the creation of new offices. Only a very few recognized at that time the stupendous undertaking which today pulses through the whole of Germany and already stretches out into the world far beyond the boundaries of our own country. It seems like a miracle when one reflects how an idea laughed at by many, despised by others, insulted and covered with abuse by opponents, and viewed even by our closest friends only with anxiety and misgiving, has in the short space of little more than two years won the hearts of the people and been carried into practice by the people themselves.

As a description of the object we have in view, the name is absolutely right: National Socialist Community *Strength Through Joy*. One must carefully consider the significance of each individual word: National Socialist Community. The community is its foundation, and here once again is a clear expression of the fact that the community alone is able and competent to be the purveyor of joy. In this, once again we National Socialists see clearly that culture and art are bound up with the community of nation and race, and cannot have an isolated existence in a vacuum. *Strength Through Joy* I was advised to call it "After Work". But I have never been in favour of imitation, preferring always to see whether it were not possible to create something oneself.

The "Dopolavoro" of young Italy can certainly show great results; it is undoubtedly a great achievement. But it does not coincide precisely with the object which we have in view. It is a neutral expression which does not convey our desire nor what the Leader commanded. The Leader said, "I want to have a strong nation: see that the tempo of work, which rationalization and the whole trend of events have in any case made pointless, is counterbalanced by the recreation and holidays which these men get; and see that the nerves of the people are not ruined." The command of the Leader was to give the nation strength, and at the same time he showed how this strength was to be obtained: by recreation, by holidays, through joy.

Strength Through Joy is perhaps the shortest and most concise expression of the whole object of National Socialism. It is the embodiment of a life-outlook which National Socialism has given to Germany; it expresses that positive attitude towards life which throbs in us, and which replaces the denial of life which dominated our nation in a past century. For that which we saw in the past in every walk of life, that which characterized all of our vanished parties, was the denial of life!

We National Socialists do not wish to think of life as a journey through an earthly vale of tears, as a constant preparation for a better Beyond. We want to make life—and particularly the lives of our poorest fellow-Germans—as beautiful and bright as we possibly can. We believe that this life of ours is worthy to be lived; and we believe that our Lord God did not create the multiplicity of our life in order to abandon it all again to eternal destruction and annihilation. All who believe that by their life and works they have a holy mission to fulfil in this world, all who are filled with this belief, are in their own heart of hearts National Socialists.

Therefore we want strength for the struggle. Our life is not filled with the riches of paradise; for us the principal thing is the struggle. Life is struggle, and struggle is living. We know no terminus where some in eternal idleness wait upon their own pleasure and the others are perpetually damned. In all eternity we know only struggle as the expression of our belief and of our life. And for this struggle we seek to give our people a constant supply of new strength. Work is indeed only another expression for struggle. Every one of our compatriots, be he worker or peasant, artist, scholar, or soldier, is at each moment in the midst of this struggle for the existence of his people and of himself. And since this struggle consumes nerves, substance, man needs the means for this struggle, and therefore also replenishment of these means and renewal of his strength. Consequently recreation and holidays are for us an inward necessity.

Some time ago I was asked by a great foreign student of social economy: "What is your attitude to the question of holidays? Will you in Germany settle the amount of holidays by law, and at the same time regulate the rate of payment by law?" I replied : " We will not merely tolerate the general introduction of holidays, but we will make them legally compulsory, because this is one to our demands." "But excuse me," he said, "in every country the employers fight against their employees, and yet you in Germany maintain that even the employers will gradually come to demand these holidays?" "Yes, the time cannot be far off when the keenest champions of holidays and recreation will be not the workers but the employers."

National Socialism is the victory of reason over unreason, and it is only reasonable that an exhausted and run-down man should recreate himself, so that he may be able to perform his future work so much the better. This means that holidays become a demand of healthy, reasonable common-sense. We do not demand holidays out of pity, but in recognition of the fact that they will still further increase the productive power of our people. The employer of labour has no advantage in having a tired and exhausted man working for him; such a man simply uses up energy, whilst the machines go on running, consume power, cost money, and wear out. The man, too, ceases to be productive, so that the employer has a double loss: he not only pays wages for a diminished productivity, but he also pays for the energy and power of the unexploited machine. On the other hand, if the man is fresh the employer easily recovers the difference made by the holidays for which he has paid. And the employer will see that his balance will become no debit one, but will show, on the contrary, an improvement on the credit side; he will see that he, as well as the worker, stands to gain.

It is indeed characteristic of National Socialism that it does nothing to the advantage of one side only. If we were to do anything which would help only the worker and at the same time damage the employer, that would be no advantage to the nation as a whole; a thing is good for the individual if it is good for the German people as a whole, and it is good for the German people that men should have recreation and holidays. It has often been our experience, and it is so still today, to hear a man say: "I would like to have eight days off; give me my money; but I don't want to go away for recreation, I will stop at home. No, that is wrong; that would be throwing money away; for at home a man cannot find recreation. The very idea of the thing is that he shall for once in a while be dragged out of his attic, where he constantly sees only distress and want, and sent for a sea trip, or into the mountains, or to the Rhine, and learn to forget the work-a-day world for eight days. What the Marxists preach is not enough: "We want holidays"; something must be done with the holidays—that is *Strength Through Joy*.

At the end of the first year I was able to say that *Strength Through Joy* has conquered Germany with a rush. Today our achievements are so great that foreign countries, too, are paying attention to them. Quite irrespective of whether they are for or against Germany, everybody abroad is watching with interest our young organization, which has made possible something which hitherto had been considered impossible, a dream for many years of every Socialist in the world. We hope to lead the world to think of the New Germany in a way different from that which a malicious Press would often have us believe.

The *Diario da Manha,* for instance, gives as an example of the growing favourableness of world-opinion; in a number dated October 12th, 1935, we read the following concerning a *Strength Through Joy* sea-voyage: "That is the revolution which Germany, with the firm and disciplined will of its people grouped around Adolf Hitler, is preparing to carry out. What will be its effects and final results? It is still too early to be able to estimate them; but one thing is certain, which is that the German spirit is working at the creation of new life-concepts and the solution of the most unsettled problems of our time." The Norwegian paper, *Karmoy Posten,* of September 27th, 1935, publishes an interesting discussion about the value of the *Strength Through Joy* journeys between a Norwegian and a Mr. *Rabinowitz.* The Norwegian writes concerning sea-voyages: ". . . with reference to the sketches which you give us of how horrible life on board must be during such a tour, with little room and cramped in every way, I should like to point out that I have personally taken part in one of them, and know that this is nonsense. . . You have certainly never been on board a *Strength Through Joy* steamer . . . One must not throw overboard all sense of justice . . . Any democratic country you like might well be proud of the *Strength Through Joy* organization."

I could extend the list of similar friendly Press utterances from abroad indefinitely; but one thing is clear from the judgements formed by all those who have taken a serious interest in our organization, which is that the idea of *Strength Through Joy* is establishing itself on the strength of its achievements unchallenged in other countries also.

We were therefore right in undertaking journeys into other countries. We will go forward on the way we have begun, and in March of this year we shall travel with our *Strength Through Joy* fleet over the Atlantic to Lisbon and Madeira. Further than that, from 1936 onwards every Spring and Autumn we shall make trips to the South. The experiences which we had during our first Atlantic crossings to Portugal were so favourable that we have resolved upon the above-mentioned development of these voyages. No one can represent the new Germany better than the German worker who travels with *Strength Through Joy*.

Apart from this, we shall carry out this year a series of great special projects. When one considers where the five millions of *Strength Through Joy* holiday-makers of 1934 and 1935 actually travelled to, one discovers that of these five millions more than three millions went to the frontier districts of our country. There they have constructed a living wall of German Socialism. The population of the border lands was visited by brother Germans from all parts of Germany. And the great comradeship, which is precisely what distinguishes *Strength Through Joy* journeys from private journeys, gave to these brothers on the border a new spiritual support. We shall continue this methodical work and considerably extend it. In order to attain this goal, we have initiated a great drive, and intend to reduce the already low *Strength Through Joy* prices by a further 30 per cent. When this was proposed, many experts shook their heads and believed that this could never be accomplished. Now, after a short period of preparation, I am able to say that in this very year the cheaper rates will be available for 350,000 holiday-makers, and this without requiring those who provide the accommodation to depart from the approved tariffs.

This means that for average distances the German worker can go away for a whole week's holiday at a cost of from 12 to 15 or 16 marks, including fares, full board and lodging, and collective activities of every kind. This will enable us to include new sections of the workers, who, on account of their economic condition, have hitherto been unable to participate in a *Strength Through Joy* trip. These new masses will be the best holiday-makers, because they will be the happiest and the most satisfied. We shall take them into beautiful border-lands, which at the same time stand most in need of the care which National Socialism can give them.

In all activities of the *Strength Through Joy* movement which stretch beyond the confines of our Fatherland, we are mindful of our German brothers abroad. We want to make them into a living bridge linking us with other countries, and our holiday-makers shall be messengers of friendship to enable other countries to see Germany as it really is. And so we shall bring to Germany our brothers resident abroad and their children, who otherwise would never be able to think of visiting Germany. We shall make use of our *Strength Through Joy* fleet in the Winter and intermediate season, and will carry out these journeys at very cheap rates. In all these undertakings we offer no competition with any industrial institutions whatever, for the individuals who are to take part in these journeys will be very carefully selected by us. If a man has money enough to afford an ordinary passage to Germany, let him travel in the ordinary way. We are providing the above-mentioned cheap facilities for a visit to Germany only for those who are not in such a fortunate position.

To conclude my remarks concerning travel and holidays, I should like to touch upon one little anxiety which is current in some quarters. On the whole, everybody is enthusiastic about the *Strength Through Joy* expeditions, our hosts as well as the holiday-makers. All are full of praise for the institution which does indeed, as has been proved, exert in many ways a very beneficent influence. There is just one criticism that can be heard occasionally: it is said that a great part of the holiday-makers consists of people who could even without us go away for their holidays. But this objection is unjustified. My collaborators have investigated the composition of a large number of trains. This was easily possible, since each participant is dealt with by means of a special detailed questionnaire. The result of the investigation of all holiday trains from four districts was as follows: no less than exactly 50% of the passengers were workers engaged in industry. The remainder was composed of small employees, independent tradesmen, people of private means, members of liberal professions, etc. I can also give figures concerning the income of the *Strength Through Joy* holiday-makers. The investigation of these same trains showed that one third of all the holiday-makers had incomes of less than 100 Marks per month. Another third earned monthly between 100 and 150 Marks. The incomes of the remainder were higher, but were on the average between 150 and 250 Marks per month. Only 6% earned more than 250 Marks. In this category we find principally married couples with numerous families, who, in consequence of the heavy charges upon them, have the right to take part in *Strength Through Joy* journeys.

We must reach the point—and everything up to the present indicates that we shall reach it—when a journey from Berlin to Rügen with transport there and back and an eight days' holiday by the sea, is available from 12 Marks. The ultimate goal is as follows: according to the present level of the population of Germany, we must be able to send every year 14 millions of working men and women on recreational journeys of from 12 to 14 days. The existing facilities for transport and accommodation are totally inadequate to cope with this problem. Today they have already reached the limit of the possible. When we prophesied this two years ago, we were laughed at.

We shall, therefore, without delay set about the construction of new accommodation facilities and new ships. In the next three years the German Labour Front will erect buildings to the value of 100 millions of Marks. These will include a sea-bath on the island of Rügen, with 20,000 beds and all appointments for recreation. The plans and models for this unique enterprise have already been made. We owe them to a generous-spirited command of our Leader, Adolf Hitler. Furthermore, we shall build two ships to accommodate 1,500 persons each, without mass-dormitories, all cabins to be for two or four persons, each cabin provided with a port-hole, and the whole ship provided with a deck of unparalleled capacity. In addition to the two ships, *Der Deutsche* and *Sierra Cordoba,* which we already have, we shall, this Spring, buy four more ships of similar size. Apart from these projects, the number of beds in the country recreational homes which the Labour Front already owns will be increased to 30,000. When in three years' time the whole thing is finished, we shall be able to provide accommodation for 1.2 millions of human beings in our own recreational resorts. Of course, the claims of the private hotel and catering trade will always receive privileged treatment. So we shall work tenaciously to attain the final goal, until the last working German is able to satisfy his legitimate claim to recreation and holidays in full measure.

Amongst the different sections of the National Socialist Community *Strength Through Joy* organizations, sport occupies a specially important position. This office has the fine, but infinitely arduous responsibility, of turning the German worker's free evening spent in cheerful physical culture, into a source of strength as well as recreation. Today, after two years of work, we are able to ascertain with satisfaction that the result has far surpassed our expectations. More than three millions have followed 8,500 courses in the different categories of sport (swimming, gymnastics, light athletics, skiing, etc.) which we arranged. Medical centres for sporting, matters and special courses for those suffering from physical defects are serving to set up even the last of our compatriots. Our sailing expeditions on the high seas have always been booked to capacity, and many applications had to be rejected. In this direction, too, we will extend our work, and in particular carry out the journeys with a greater radius of action than in the past year. During this winter, at the moment of writing, instructional courses in skiing are being held in the loveliest winter-sport districts of Germany; 35,000 will take part in these. There are available in connexion with these courses 30,000 *Strength Through Joy* skiing outfits, consisting of skis with straps, boots, and stocks at 35 Marks. This figure may seem high, and yet last year 18,000 outfits were sold in the ordinary retail trade. 42,000 *Strength Through Joy* holidaymakers followed with enthusiasm the Olympic Games in Garmisch-Partenkirchen, being brought to the venue by our *Strength Through Joy* trains.

For countless Germans this meant the fulfilment of a long cherished and seemingly unrealizable dream; for in Germany today sport is no longer a matter of record-breaking by the select few or economically more fortunate individuals, but it has become a national hobby. There is already a shortage of suitable practice grounds, and the influx to the *Strength Through Joy* sport courses is steadily maintained. The third year will, according to past experience, again show a balance which will prove that in Germany it is not only championship sport which is cultivated, but more particular, the popular training of the body. We will not rest until even the 50 and 60 year old consider sport or physical training as a daily necessity.

The newly-formed department in "Strength Through Joy," for Schooling and Popular Education, began its practical work only a short time ago. But in the few months of its existence it has already rendered valuable service to the German nation by thousands of lantern lectures, by means of libraries which possess hundreds of thousands of books, and by carrying out visits and conducted tours of every sort.

Until the year when the National Socialist Party came into power, millions of German men and women had never seen a theatre from the inside. Not only did it seem to them quite natural not to go to the theatre, but they had also, as a result of the Marxist influence to which they had been exposed, such an inferiority complex that it even seemed to them out of keeping with their social condition to go. Here, too, fundamental change has been made. The cultural possessions of the nation shall no longer be the privilege of the owning classes. One figure chosen at random throws a striking light on the very considerable significance, from the point of view of cultural policy, of the work which has been done in "Greater Berlin" alone: from December 1st, 1934, to November 30th, 1935, *Strength Through Joy* has taken more than one and a half millions of working men of Berlin to the theatre. Striking as this figure is, we appreciate its true worth considerably more when we recollect that this represents men and women who either never, or practically never, went to a theatre. These people, therefore, represent additional patronage for the theatre. The reasons why they never visited a theatre before were principally economic. A worker or employee with a monthly income of 100 to 200 Marks was simply not in a position to pay the normal theatre prices for himself and his wife.

As a result of our generous measures the patronage of the great masses has been won for the theatre and the concert hall—the masses who knew these institutions only by hearsay, and viewed them with complete indifference. This is a fact which must not be ignored, and which has, of course, a favourable repercussion on the private theatres which are not visited by *Strength Through Joy*.

The investigations which we carried out at the beginning of 1934 in the Siemens Works, concerning visits to theatres, confirmed these observations. One or two figures easily prove this: 87.6% of the men and 81.3% of the women who were asked had never seen an opera; 63.8% of the men and 74.2% of the women who were asked had never visited a theatre. Since these questions were put to everybody employed in the Siemens concern, without respect of persons or position, from the director to the supplementary hand, it may be justly asserted that those members of the works' staff who had already witnessed theatrical or operatic productions were to be found amongst the economically better situated groups of employees.

Recent observations in the different factories show the happy result that the manual workers are especially well represented in the activities organized by *Strength Through Joy*. A work of cultural education is being performed, of which the effects will be seen later on.

In Berlin alone, seven theatres cater either exclusively or preponderantly for *Strength Through Joy*; whilst the average number of patrons throughout the Reich lies between 60% and 70% of the number of seats available, the theatrical productions of *Strength Through Joy* are fortunately always sold out long ahead. Patronage of this quality can scarcely ever have been equalled by German private theatres.

The "Master Concerts", which were newly introduced a year ago, and the "Musical Hours", which we visit similarly enjoy great popularity. Our great concerts, which are conducted by the most famous German conductors, are generally sold out long before the beginning. Famous orchestras which have taken part in the concerts include amongst others the Berlin Philharmonic Orchestra, the local orchestra from the Berlin region *(das Landesorchester Gau Berlin)*, and the orchestra of the German Opera House. The Ninth Symphony of Beethoven has twice been performed to a full house.

In the museums the worker has hitherto seen a definitely bourgeois institution, which he on principle did not visit. Since it was difficult for us also to get the worker inside a museum, we arranged many thousands of conducted parties. But in addition to this we brought art into the factory by means of exhibitions of works, which were carried out on a large scale and with still greater success throughout the whole Reich. Contact with the manual workers of Germany, moreover, offers the artist strong inspiration for artistic creation consonant with the times.

Within a few years, every one of the larger factories will have arrangements for a permanent exhibition. Every year millions of Germans will be able to hail the work of German artists. What we have brought about, then, is that the German artist has gone where the working masses of the nation flow together, that is, to the work-yard and factory; and that for his trouble and for the artistic treasures which he brings to the manual worker the artist is richly rewarded by the stimulation which his artistic creation receives from contact with the manual worker and with machine-rooms.

Altogether, our 66,000 *Strength Through Joy* functions were attended by 25 million people. With our film vans we have visited the lonely villages and the odd corners of Germany hidden away in the forest and uncultivated land, to give our brothers there, for once in a way, a lively change and relaxation from the burden and weariness of the day.

But our activities extend still further. In thousands and thousands of factories during many years grime has become lodged in nooks and crannies, and nobody ever thought of making the work-place beautiful. People had become so used to dirty, close, muggy working quarters that they were accepted as a matter of course.

In this, with fresh courage and energy, the *Beauty in Work* department took a hand. A fresh wind blew through all the factories and swept the dirt and the dust off the windows and out of every nook and cranny of the yards and the factories. Well over 200 million Marks were spent by managers, very often with the help of the works' staff themselves, in rendering work, at the instigation of the *Beauty in Work* department, fit for human beings. Where before old junk and rubbish were lying about, there are today little gardens, plots of green, tidy courts, sports grounds, bright airy work-rooms, swimming baths, lavatories and washrooms. Work-places which it is a pleasure to see have been created in the last two years. Up to the present roughly 17,000 factories have been dealt with. Along with innumerable improvements of greater or lesser importance the following were constructed: 4,314 canteens and common-rooms for the works' staff; 1,580 ornamental grounds; 276 sports grounds; and 93 swimming-baths.

This work which is today being carried out by *Strength Through Joy* in the factories automatically reacts upon the home of the German worker. For a man who is accustomed to a beautiful and clean place to work in will only feel comfortable in a beautiful and clean home.

The construction of works' groups in factories is very rapidly advancing. The idea is to weld the members of the N.S.D.A.P. and its branch-organizations within the factory together with the best workers between 18 and 25 into a solid, unbreakable block, in order even in times of crisis, in union with the "cell" and "block" leaders, to keep alive the idea of the community. Furthermore, these works' groups should form new customs in the factory, and should inspire functions such as inspections and community evenings.

Concerning the organization of *Strength Through Joy*, the following figures may be given: the National Socialist Community *Strength Through Joy* is divided into 32 regions, 771 districts, and 15,051 local groups with an equal number of local wardens. Added to these are the works wardens, whose job lies inside the factory, totalling 57,000. All these 75,000 collaborators give their services free to *Strength Through Joy*.

Strength Through Joy employs only 2,547 salaried officials.

This mighty undertaking, which in the first two years required to be subsidized by the German Labour Front, will, we hope, be independent this year. This is perhaps the most remarkable and the most interesting fact, especially when one considers that the amount of money mobilized and put in circulation by *Strength Through Joy* is more than a million Reichmarks, whilst the Italian Dopolavoro has not even approximately reached this level, and the American Leisure-time and evening organization requires very considerable subsidization; whereas from all Marxist efforts, which—whether in the old Germany or in Bolshevist Russia or in the industrial countries of the West—have everywhere totally failed. National Socialism is on the right road.

The German Winter Relief Work
by Max Hunger

THE Winter Relief Work, inaugurated by the National Socialist Party, and taken up with high spirit by the whole nation, has become a recognized institution of the Third Reich and a blessing to many millions of needy, enfeebled and sick men, women and children.

While the State through direct action does everything to combat unemployment and to overcome distress by providing work on a comprehensive scale, it has not had sufficient time yet to find work for every able-bodied man and woman willing to work, although it has accomplished the almost incredible miracle in the face of world-wide trade difficulties of reducing the number of unemployed within three years from 7 million to less than 2 million. But, like every family, it will always have its poor within its fold.

Social legislation and Public Assistance have done, and are doing, a great deal to alleviate want, but these institutions cannot abolish want altogether.

It is to help all those whose means of subsistence are just below the border line that the Winter Relief Work was set up. Winter Relief Work is not to supplant Public Assistance, its main object is to supplement it.

When National Socialism assumed power on 30th January, 1933, it found the State, as Dr. Goebbels described it: "a field of ruins", a political chaos, with empty coffers and every fifth man in receipt of the dole.

It required stout hearts and an iron will to master an almost hopeless situation which former governments had in vain tried to mend. The way these gigantic problems were handled has already become a matter of history, but it will be remembered for all time as an amazing example of bold and constructive statesmanship.

The nucleus of the great National Socialist Welfare Association was already formed in the spring of 1932, but its real action did not set in until the party had come into power. The first official function of the association was held on May 6th, 1933, when, in presence of the Führer, Chief Commissioner Hilgenfeldt, who had been placed at the head of the organization, made known the order of the Führer sanctioning the Association as an official body within the party for the Reich, authorized to deal with all questions relating to public welfare and relief.

The Association was called to action for the first time on the Führer's birthday on April 20th, when it was entrusted with the distribution of food parcels to the unemployed, and on May 1st, when it made the first street collection for the holiday-fund for children.

In the summer of the same year the Association received executive powers for the organization of the Winter Relief which had been planned by the Führer, and it began at once with the organizational preparations for the great task. On September 13th the Führer opened the campaign, declaring that no-one in Germany should suffer hunger or cold during the winter, and Dr. Goebbels, in his send-off, said that this Winter Relief Work should be carried through with the cleanest and most decent methods imaginable, and that in sympathy with the poor the whole nation should have on the first Sunday of every month a "one-dish stew" and offer the differences of the cost of the ordinary dinner to the relief of the needy. The date for the Winter Relief Work to begin was fixed for October 1st, and on September 16th the Chief Commissioner Hilgenfeldt went with a staff of 36 helpers to offices which had been placed at his disposal in the building of the Reichstag.

In a speech delivered on December 11th, 1935, Hilgenfeldt describes some of the difficulties he had to contend with in the organization of the work he had been entrusted with. From the outset it was clear that the success of the undertaking depended on the building up of efficient machinery for collection and distribution and on getting the whole nation to take an active part in it. Therefore, the lukewarm and the indifferent had to be roused to a higher sense of citizenship and the selfish to a new altruism; it had to be brought home to every German that true fellowship was based on self-sacrifice and mutual succour. The Führer, in opening the Winter Relief Work, declared: "This great action against hunger and cold, must be initiated under the motto: The international solidarity of the proletariat has been smashed by us. In its place we shall erect the living national unity of the German people."

Hilgenfeldt recognized from the first that the organization, to be effective, had to be elastic in its application to necessities and adaptable to the varying conditions of actual want it was intended to relieve.

"No-one is to suffer hunger and cold!" This was the injunction of the Führer laid upon his trusted followers.

How was it to be done? There were about 17 million people who had to be cared for: nearly one-third of the whole population of Germany. Indeed, a formidable task! However, Chief Commissioner Hilgenfeldt knew that in the first place he could rely on the devoted collaboration of about 30,000 local sections of the party, but he knew also that they could not function satisfactorily unless minute plans, embracing every contingency, had been laid down beforehand.

For this reason he called in the help of experts of finance, industry, and transport, and in the potato, flour and coal trades; he also made use of existing charitable institutions from the Church Missions, the German Red Cross, the Technical Emergency Corps right down to the small band of enthusiastic workers, called the "Adventists". It was a general mobilization of all the forces trained and experienced in public assistance work and of those ready and willing to help as honorary workers, irrespective of party and social standing.

Every local branch of the party throughout the country collected and held the names of all persons in need of supplementary relief. As the work increased a special section of the National Socialist Welfare Association was affiliated to every local branch where men and women of all classes worked together with one will for one common object.

In organizing relief the special needs of the different areas had to be studied and provided for. As the habits of life were different in the different districts, even in the food line, and as the distressed areas coincided chiefly with the densely populated industrial centres, the Association had to make arrangements to meet all these special requirements. These difficulties are best illustrated by a concrete case: the population of the Rhenish-Westphalian province for instance is accustomed to consuming a yellow variety of potatoes; the same applied to Essen and Hamburg; consequently all white and red sorts of potatoes had to be sent to other parts of Germany where they were fancied, especially Baden.

The collection and distribution of potatoes placed an exceptional strain on the resources of the organization owing to the unequal local requirements of the population. To Bavaria for instance, which in regard to potatoes is self-sufficient, hardly any deliveries were made, whereas for the district of Essen a supplementary quantity of 1.45 million cwt., was needed and for Saxony 0.92 million cwt. Amongst other towns and districts requiring additional supplies were Berlin, Central Germany, the Rhenish-Westphalian industrial areas, Baden, and parts of Wurttemberg. During the campaign of 1933/34 approximately 60,000 railway truckloads of potatoes were collected and distributed. Of this quantity Berlin alone received daily from 700-800 truckloads. The monthly potato ration distributed equalled about 30lb. per head of the whole population. But, as only about one-third of the population was in receipt of additional relief, the ration per head of the actually assisted amounted to about 100lb. per month. Similar conditions prevailed with regard to the requirements and distribution of fuel.

In some districts chiefly wood is burned, in others turf or coal or lignite briquettes. Naturally, ovens and stoves are specially adapted to the fuel used. Therefore, care had to be taken that each locality was supplied with the requisite fuel in sufficient quantity. The quantity of fuel allowed for each household was computed to suffice for the heating of one room for the whole of the winter. Families with 3 or 4 children were allotted sufficient coal to heat 2 rooms all through the winter.

For the transport of all fuel needed in 1933/34, about 140,000 railway trucks were required, the quantity of coal representing about 16% of the total quantity of fuel used in Germany. The quantity of coal supplied during the winter to one family with 2 children represents approximately 9 cwt., while each household in the mining districts, where coal is burned more extravagantly, received approximately 22 cwt. during the same period.

The distribution of coal is effected by the local coal dealers. Those persons entitled to relief receive warrants for the delivery of 1 cwt. each. The warrants are handed to the coal dealer who then delivers the coal against payment of a small charge for porterage. Recipients, who are unable to pay, receive the coal delivered free of charge.

It will convey perhaps a better idea of the magnitude of the coal supply, if it is explained that it would take 3 months' work of the miners of the Saar basin to get the quantity of coal needed for the purpose of the Winter Relief Work.

Winter Relief includes also the supply of shoes and clothing. The lengths of material used for clothing would make up a total length of quite 5,000 miles.

In addition to potatoes also other articles of food are distributed: rice, flour, cocoa, milk, fats, meat, fish, and other comestibles. There are also free meals provided, and at Christmas time Christmas trees for the young. In 1933/34, 300,000 Christmas trees were distributed in Berlin alone.

For the gathering-in of the gifts necessary for the purchase of all these huge supplies, various ways have been adopted: street collections in which even the highest state functionaries take part as collectors, benefit performances, social functions, street lotteries, monthly "one-dish-stew" collections, gifts of pound parcels of food, public subscriptions, special levies on income, private collections, street sales of badges, etc., etc.

The thoroughness of the organization is best illustrated by the method in which the "one-dish-stew" collections are carried through in Berlin.

The town of Berlin consists of about 125,000 houses; of each house a list of inhabitants is prepared, and in each house each family or independent lodger is called upon and the money collected. The contribution, according to the means of the contributor, is entered by him in the list, which, within a few hours, is returned to the local branch together with the sum collected. In Berlin alone there are on an average 140,000 voluntary helpers engaged in the Winter Relief Work.

It should also be mentioned that the making of the badges and favours, which are sold in the streets on special occasions, provided work and bread for many unemployed in the distressed industrial areas. In the winter of 1933/34, for instance, orders to the amount of 4 million marks were placed with manufacturers in the Bavarian Forest, Thuringia and Saxony, and even East Prussia with its amber industry was not forgotten. For 1934/35 the value of these orders was increased to 5 million marks.

The relief is dealt out to all eligible persons, irrespective of race or nationality.

In 1933/34, for instance, 69,336 aliens were assisted, of whom 29,108 were Jews. In Berlin alone 13,818 Jews and 8,054 aliens were being looked after by the Winter Relief Work. The total sums in money and money's worth collected for the Winter Relief Work were:

in	1933/34	Mks.	357,136,040.71
in	1934/35		367,425,484.89
in	1935/36		370,000,000.00

The number of assisted was as follows:

in	1933/34	16,617,681
in	1934/35	13,866,571
in	1935/36	12,923,247

Special mention should be made of the unparalleled assistance given by the farmers to the Winter Relief Work. A few figures will illustrate it: In 1933/34, for example, Pommerania supplied 841,477 cwt. of potatoes.

in Kurmark	1,600,000 cwt.
in Saxony	447,000 cwt.

All the goods for the Winter Relief Work were carried by the State Railways free of charge. In the campaign 1933/34 the contribution of the State Railways in this connexion amounted to 14,672,957 Mks., while the total weight of the transports amounted to 59,025,995 cwt.

The number of honorary helpers engaged in the Winter Relief Work reached on an average 1½ million every year, while in the administration of this organization the following numbers of officials, clerks, etc., were employed:

in	1933/34	4,116
in	1934/35	5,398
in	1935/36	about the same number

The entire cost of the administration is just below 1% of the total receipts.

The Führer and Reichskanzler Adolf Hitler, on receiving on 27th May last, Chief Commissioner Hilgenfeldt in company with his principal workers, expressed his high appreciation for the work done by the organization, and when he concluded by saying that "the Winter Relief Work is a unique historical feat of social work", he only voiced the sentiment of every true German with regard to this great national effort of mutual good will and personal sacrifice.

www.ingramcontent.com/pod-product-compliance
Lightning Source LLC
Chambersburg PA
CBHW070909270326
41927CB00011B/2497
9781913176075